GUERILLA WEB STRATEGIES

GUERILLA WEB STRATEGIES

Vince Gelormine

CORIOLIS GROUP BOOKS

PUBLISHER	KEITH WEISKAMP
PROJECT EDITOR	DENISE CONSTANTINE
COPY EDITOR	LAURIE SMITH
COVER DESIGN	ANTHONY STOCK
INTERIOR DESIGN	MICHELLE STROUP
LAYOUT PRODUCTION	NICOLE BIRNEY AND MICHELLE STROUP
PROOFREADER	GWEN HENSON
INDEXER	SAT-KARTAR KHALSA

Special thanks to The PostMaster and Cool Site of the Day for supplying cover screen shots.

The Coriolis Group, Inc.
7339 E. Acoma Drive, Suite 7
Scottsdale, AZ 85260
Phone: (602) 483-0192
Fax: (602) 483-0193
Web address: http://www.coriolis.com

ISBN 1-883577-80-2 : $24.99

Printed in the United States of America

10 9 8 7 6 5 4 3 2 1

Contents

CHAPTER 3   HOW TO FIND ALMOST ANYTHING ON THE INTERNET   53

CHAPTER 7 "HOT" AND "COOL" LINKS SITES, WHAT'S NEW PAGES, AND MORE   187

CHAPTER 8   META-INDEXES:
INFORMATION ABOUT INFORMATION   211

CHAPTER 9   PROMOTE 'TIL YOU DROP
WITH CYBERMALLS   225

CHAPTER 10   BEYOND THE WEB: PROMOTING YOUR SITE WITH USENET NEWSGROUPS, INTERNET MAILING LISTS, EMAIL, FTP, AND GOPHER   239

CHAPTER 11   THE CONSUMER ONLINE SERVICES   267

CHAPTER 12   "GUERRILLA PR"— ANNOUNCING YOUR WEB SITE WITH PRESS RELEASES   293

ANATOMY OF A PRESS RELEASE   295

CHAPTER 13   OFFLINE WEB SITE PROMOTION   311

CHAPTER 14   THIRD PARTY WEB SITE PROMOTION SERVICES   325

CHAPTER 15   HOW TO KEEP 'EM COMING BACK   339

How My Web Site Gets Respect and How Yours Can Too

BY Rodney Dangerfield

My first exposure to the Internet was in January 1995. I saw a world of entertainment at my fingertips and wanted to contribute a few more laughs for folks who were browsing their brains out on the Web. So my site, **www.rodney.com**, was born. The first thing I did was to go through my material and find a great deal of humor that would fit on my site. I looked for photos of different things I wanted people to see (like the letter I just received from Roddy McDowall and The Academy of Motion Picture Arts and Sciences rejecting me for membership). This content attracts users to my site; Chapter 2 has a lot of information to help you do the same.

I enjoy the freedom the Internet and Web allows—to put up whatever you desire for the world to see. I could finally say what I wanted with no reporters to misquote or censor me or take things out of context. Control was mine. I could share my projects or vent a little steam. But the best thing was, I could talk to my fans and they could talk back through the fast and powerful communication tool of email. And talk back they did. I gained a rapport with fans who can only be found on the Net.

I offered some contests to users of my site, like what I should say to The Academy. I was bombarded with thousands of letters speaking derogatorily of The Academy's decision and when The Academy found out about them, I was finally invited to join. Because the Web was instrumental in getting me recognized, I thought I would throw it back out to my fans, asking them if I should join and once again received an overwhelming response blasting the Acadamy. I took their advice and didn't join! I'm glad people like to participate, not just observe. Be sure to leverage the interactive nature of the Web, it might generate ongoing traffic to your site and help you solve your problems too.

The most challenging element of having one's own Web site quickly surfaced, however. How do you get folks to hit you? And once they do visit your Web site, how do you get them to keep hitting you? The first thing I did was promote my site by submitting http://www.rodney.com (my URL) to various search engines and hot lists. This book shows you the whys, hows, and wheres to do this in Chapters 5 and 7 respectively. Soon I received national press coverage for being the first entertainer to have his own personally owned Web site. *USA Today*, the *New York Times*, *Entertainment Weekly*, *Wired*, and countless other publications featured stories about Rodney's venture into cyberspace. CNN even televised a tour of the site! You don't have to be famous like me to get some press coverage, though. Chapter 12 shows you the ropes to getting your own PR.

Recently, *Websight Magazine* named me as one of the Top 100 Most Influential People on the Web. Ahh, respect at last!

The most popular page on the site is my Joke of the Day (which changes daily). I even offer an audio clip which tells the joke in my own voice. I envisioned people sitting at their computers listening to my joke and getting a little laugh break during their busy day. This worked. Over a million hits are currently received each month. In addition to this, rodney.com offers a virtual autographed picture, movie clips, contests, and online ordering of my set of classic comedy videos and latest album *La Contessa*. Many of these features and the contests give people a reason to come back to the site over and over again. Once you get 'em to visit, you'll want to get 'em to return. As you'll see in Chapter 15, that's an important thing!

My site also links over to my wife's Web site (Jungle Roses at http://www.jungleroses.com) and her site links back to mine. You can do the same with Web sites of your friends and business associates. You can never get enough promotion and links to your site.

I tell you, it's not easy out there on the Net! Getting respect for your Web site requires hard work and vigilance, but with some of the things you'll read in these pages, your job will be a lot easier.

Rodney Dangerfield
April 1996

PS: I never had any luck with computers. I bought an Apple, it had a worm in it!

Preface

Making Your Internet Marketing Pay Off

You wouldn't walk into a crowded hotel meeting room, put your business card on a table, and walk out expecting to have reached your audience, would you? No, you wouldn't. Yet that's pretty much what you're doing whenever you practice "Internet Presence."

Internet Presence, simply stated, is when you put an electronic "billboard" on the Internet, either by installing your own World Wide Web server, or by renting space on someone else's server. By placing your billboard on the Internet, it becomes accessible to everyone on the Net. (The exact number of Internet users is still somewhat speculative. I've seen estimates as large as 30 million. In any case, it's a very large number.)

Internet Presence Is Not Enough

Sure, when you practice Internet Presence, you make your information accessible. But does that mean that everybody will see it? More importantly, will the most likely buyers of your product see it? Probably not. It takes more than Internet Presence to succeed in Internet marketing. Just like in the real world, you need to target the precise audience that you expect to buy your product.

Putting your information on the Internet is the easy part. It's a straight forward technical issue. The real tough part is getting to the right audience, and getting them to visit your site. (Remember, there are rules of netiquette in the electronic world. If you break the rules, you'll get flamed--or worse.)

Finding your audience via Internet is similar to finding it via print, radio, television, or other method. When you choose your print media, for instance, you select the types of publications that your prospect is most likely to read, then put forth your most compelling case, hopefully in a portion of the magazine that is keyed to your audience. You even pay extra for preferred positions in the magazine, such as inside the front cover or adjacent to related editorial.

Attracting Your Most Qualified Audience

In the real world and on the Internet, getting to the right audience implies that you know where your audience can be found. There are hundreds of thousands of domains on the Internet, and your audience might be lurking in any of those locations. Of course, you also have many print choices, too. But your print choices are summarized by printed publications such as Standard Rate and Data Service (SRDS), and the circulation numbers of many printed publications are audited by independent companies.

On the Internet, there's no such luck—at this writing only a few Web publishers are actually having their sites audited in any accurate manner. There are a handful of servers that attract large audiences who want to find pointers to other locations. But those servers are crowded; and your message can easily be lost. There are also timing issues, since most of the information on those servers turns over frequently.

So your game plan for Internet marketing must include a large component aimed at finding your qualified market and drawing your prospects to your site. It's not easy. It takes patience and vigilance. When you submit pointer information to some of the heavily used sites, it may take weeks to get the pointer you want. I know people who have waited as long as 90 days to get their announcements printed in the Mosaic What's New page, although the time has shrunk dramatically, and should now only take you a few weeks. Certainly you should take advantage of the obvious opportunities like What's New and the major search engines such as WebCrawler, LinkStar, Excite, OpenText, and Yahoo. But you should also seek out the less obvious places like other Web servers that attract audiences similar to the one you seek, as well as newsgroups.

On the Net, some of the pointers that you can control the best are placements within online publications like GNN and Stellar Business. These and other publications allow you to place your own advertisement within the publications, so you determine the content. They're targeted at certain markets, so you'll be able to purchase "advertising space" within the appropriate section of the publication to appeal to your audience. The publications also pre-release editorial calendars for interested parties. Whenever related articles are published, you gain the added benefit of being easily available to your target reader as soon as he or she has finished reading the article.

Don't feel that you need to stay on the Internet. Find ways to place your pointers on proprietary online services such as CompuServe, America Online, and Prodigy. These services deliver a large Web audience. And by all means, include your Universal Resource Locator (URL)—a.k.a. your Web address—in your print advertising, press releases, product literature, and trade show booths. The more people you can point to your Web address, the better it will serve you.

These activities are easier said than done. That's where *Guerilla Web Strategies* comes in. Vince elaborates on many of the topics that can spell the difference between Internet marketing success and failure; and he shares with you methods that you can use to make your Internet marketing pay off. He starts with the basics such as ensuring that your site is well designed, and proceeds through the more advanced issues like promoting your Web site on and off the Net.

As I said earlier, Internet marketing requires vigilance. First, new servers are being added daily, so you need to find those that are targeted at your audience. Second, the Internet community is expanding so rapidly that you need to consistently update your announcements to reach new users, even through the same entry points. Expect to spend hours every week to find complementary and competing servers on the Net. Add sufficient hours to hold email discussions with the Webmasters and email list managers.

The goal is to attract individuals and organizations who can buy or recommend your product, and to use the Internet to target your audience much like you use other media, not to attract every Tom, Dick, and Mary on the Internet. Those of us who have been involved in Internet marketing to date have had to learn the hard way. Thanks to Vince and this book, you'll be able to learn how to promote your site before you start—to increase your odds of success.

David R. Radin
Pittsburgh, Pennsylvania
March 1996

David Radin is president of Marketing Masters/Stellar Business Online and chairman of the marketing conference at DCI's Internet Expo, the world's largest Internet, World Wide Web, and email conference and exposition.

If You Build It, They Might Not Come!

Chapter 1 Topics

The Internet Marketing Process

The Importance of a Simple Web Address

Ways to Promote Your Web Site

Did you know that the number one reason commercial Web sites fail to reach their owners' expectations is the lack of adequate promotion? Building a World Wide Web site and placing it online doesn't "automagically" generate traffic. Unfortunately, the vast majority of organizations with a Web site are using this "Field of Dreams" marketing approach.

In the "old days" of Internet marketing (1994), the aforementioned approach worked OK. There were a lot fewer Web sites online. There were far fewer ways to find them as well. Several search engines and directories were used (today there are dozens of major ones and over a hundred smaller ones), as well as cybermalls, Usenet newsgroups, and Internet mailing lists (these are still used today, of course).

Since there was less for the Web surfer to see, there was a greater chance of each site actually being visited. Today, the growth of new sites is nothing short of amazing. Hundreds, if not thousands, of new sites go online each *day* worldwide. The noise level makes it very difficult for these new sites to stand out in the crowd. The fact is, the ratio of new Web sites to new Internet (Web) users is getting greater as each day passes. This means that new Internet users will have more places to go, which is great for them but bad for the organization that has just put its Web site online.

The Web Anxiety Factor

Imagine we finally get those 500 TV channels we've been promised. The Information SuperHighway arrives. There always seems to be one person in each household who controls the clicker (TV remote control). With 500 channels to choose from, the person with the clicker is likely to develop Carpal Tunnel Syndrome with all the clicking that's going to be taking place! There will be more choices and, presumably, so much neat stuff to see that each channel will have to do more to keep the clicker controller's attention.

Well, the Web is today's equivalent of tomorrow's 500 channels. Jim Lobel, a principal in CyberAd, Inc., a high-end Internet Presence Provider (IPP) in Ft. Lauderdale, Florida, has stated that the Web/Internet is really the "sum of all human knowledge." There's so much out there that you'll never be able to see or learn it all.

Web anxiety is an emerging affliction that is the result of all these new and exciting Web sites that go up every day. If you have ever been on a long road

trip with children, you'll probably relate to the following analogy. While en route to your destination, a point is reached when the kids start saying "are we there yet?" or "when are we going to arrive?" This tends to be repeated every half hour or so until arrival. Then, after you arrive, there's a point when they start saying "when are we leaving?" Sometimes, that point is very soon after arriving! This often has a distressing effect on the adults who feel it was only a couple of minutes ago that the kids were complaining about not arriving soon enough.

Web surfers can be quite impatient as well. As soon as they get to your Web site, many are probably already thinking about moving on to the next one. And when they get to the next one, they are thinking about going to another one, and so on. The trick is to stop this *site hopping* while the visitor is at your site. Chapter 2 will focus on tips to create an interesting Web site and how to catch surfers in your Web. Chapter 15 will concentrate on how to keep users coming back—which is probably as big a challenge as attracting them to your site! The chapters in between will concentrate on techniques and strategies for making people aware of your Web presence and for enticing them to visit.

The Internet Marketing Process

The Internet marketing process is essentially composed of five steps:

1. Obtaining a domain name (optional)
2. Creating your Web site
3. Placing your Web site on a server
4. Promoting that Web site
5. Ongoing maintenance, updating, and getting people to return

There are a number of good books on Internet marketing that cover this process in more detail (with the exception of step 4, which I feel is important enough to warrant an entire book). Here are some of the ones I recommend (I authored the last one):

How to Grow Your Business on the Internet, 2nd Edition Vince Emery, Coriolis Group Books, (800) 410-0192, ISBN 1-883577-29-2, 1995.

The Internet Business Guide, 2nd Edition, Dave Taylor and Rosalind Resnick, SAMS, (800) 428-5331, ISBN 1-57521-004-5, 1995.

The Internet Marketing BlackBook, Vince Gelormine, published by Legion Publishing Corp., (954) 978-3444, ISBN 0-9643834-0-3, 1995.

I discuss steps 2, 4, and 5 later in this book. For the sake of completeness, I'll briefly review steps 1 and 3 right now.

Obtaining a domain name

The InterNIC (NIC = Network Information Center) is the clearinghouse for domain name registrations. If you are unclear what a domain name is, it's a unique identifier such as **mcdonalds.com** or **whitehouse.gov** or **ohio-state.edu** that organizations use for part of their Internet address. Domain names were created for the convenience of Internet users. Each domain name translates to an IP (Internet Protocol) numerical address. For example, the domain name **phantom.com** corresponds to **198.67.3.4**. You can use either address to reach Phantom Access Technology's computer.

Not only are domain names easier to remember than numerical IP addresses, they can act as a mini-advertisement for your company as well. If the name of your business is CompanyX, every time your domain name (companyx.com) is advertised as part of an email or Web address, it creates additional awareness and name recognition. A great example of this is 1-800-FLOWERS. This phone number is also the name of the company and is easier to remember than 1-800-356-9377. Its domain name is **800flowers.com**. I think you now understand why registering a domain name for your organization is important.

The InterNIC charges $50 per year for maintenance of your domain name (it used to be free). To register your name, you need to submit a form (available via anonymous FTP from **rs.internic.net** in the **templates** directory with the filename **domain-templates.txt**), preferably by email. Your Internet provider will usually do this for you. All you need to do is give them your contact and billing information, the domain name, and an email address. Your provider will also need to add its server IP address information. Some providers charge up to $100 or so to register a domain name. Additionally, the InterNIC will subsequently send you a bill for $100 to cover the first two years of domain name maintenance. Just like 800 telephone numbers, you can take your domain name with you from one Internet provider to another or from an Internet provider to your own server.

Be aware that there are still some legal issues concerning domain names, such as who has the right to what name (various legal disputes have arisen when one party registers a name that is trademarked by another). Domain names have traditionally been registered on a first-come, first-served basis. The name you want may already be taken, in which case you can request that the registered entity give or sell it to you, or you can choose a different name that is available. You can check the availability of a domain name by calling the InterNIC at (703) 742-4777 from 7:00 a.m. to 7:00 p.m. (EST) Monday through Friday or by visiting its Web site at **http://www.internic.net** and choosing **registration services** (and then searching the "whois" database).

Placing your Web site on a server

Your Web site is nothing more than a group of computer files. These files can contain text (HTML), graphics (GIF and JPEG), sound (AU and WAV), and video (MOV and MPEG). Additional file formats can be used other than those I listed in parentheses. These files need to be placed onto a computer that is directly connected to the Internet. That computer has Web-server software that handles all requests for Web pages from clients (Web-browser software). When a request for a Web page is received, the files associated with that page are transmitted over the Internet via HTTP (HyperText Transport Protocol) to the client software, which interprets that information and displays it on the screen for you to see.

You can create your own Web pages or hire a consultant or IPP (Internet Presence Provider) to do them for you. If you want a first-class professional site, the right IPP or consultant will likely do a better job than if you have to learn HTML and do it yourself. If you want a rather plain, run-of-the-mill site, doing it yourself is the more cost-effective option. Anyone can create a Web page. In less than one hour, I have taught people to create a bare-bones Web page. It's not very good, but it's a page. The next chapter will provide you with Web page/site style guidelines and resources for creating your own site.

Once your Web pages have been written, you have four options for where to place your Web site:

1. Rent space in a cybermall

2. Rent space on a server, but your storefront is a *stand-alone* store rather than part of a cybermall

3. Hire a company to set up a Web server and have *it* house and maintain it for you (The server can be moved to your location later if you wish.)

4. Set up your own Web server, and *you* house and maintain it

The least expensive routes are options 1 and 2. Pricing can range from $20 a month to several hundred dollars per month. The most expensive routes are options 3 and 4. Pricing ranges from several thousand dollars to tens of thousands to set up (hardware and software costs), and monthly fees range from several hundred dollars to three thousand, depending on what type of bandwidth (dedicated leased line) you request. Option 3 avoids the immediate need of hiring and training your own *Webmaster*, thus freeing you to concentrate on the content and promotion of your site rather than on keeping it running 24 hours a day.

When you rent space, be careful to understand how you are being charged. Some providers charge a flat monthly fee, some require a six-month or year contract, some charge by the *hit*, and some charge a monthly fee for disk space and additional money for a certain number of hits. The problem with being charged on a per-hit basis is that you never know what your bill is going to be at the end of the month. In fact, you're penalized for your success.

One of the major goals of this book is to help you generate visitors (hits) to your Web site. To be charged more for more hits is counter to what you're trying to accomplish. The reason some providers charge extra for more hits is that visitors to your site take up bandwidth—that is, some of the volume of the data "pipe" that your information flows through. When that pipe gets saturated, people wait longer to receive your information. If you make people wait too long, they'll get frustrated and move on to another site. Basically, charging extra for hits is a way most Web space providers protect themselves. After all, if ten different Web sites are paying the same amount and sharing one server, and one of those sites receives more hits than all the others combined and slows down data transfer for everyone, that's not very fair. But still, I recommend hooking up with a provider that does not charge extra for hits. Now that your site is up and running, the next step is to make people aware that it exists.

URLs—Simple Is Better

The act of promoting your Web site centers around one single piece of information: the site's URL (Uniform Resource Locator, pronounced "earl"), which is commonly known as *your Web address*. Web addresses begin with **http://** and contain something like **www.mybiz.com** and will sometimes end with additional words and slashes. The act of advertising that URL and providing *hyperlinks* to it is called *Web site promotion*.

The longer and more confusing your Web address is, the more challenging certain segments of your promotion will be. For example, picture driving down the Interstate at 65 miles an hour. You pass a billboard that advertises XYZ Company's Web site, whose URL is:

```
http://www.providername.com/xyzco/index.html
```

You quickly yell to your significant other, "Honey, quick! Write this down: htt....oh, nevermind!" This Web address example is typical of those that don't have their own *domain name*. It uses the name of the Web server provider, which in this case is called **providername.com**. The additional words designate the directory path **xyzco** that the file **index.html** is located in. The entire address was just too long to grasp and remember while passing by at 65 mph. A better URL for XYZ Company would be

```
http://www.xyzcompany.com
```

This is not only easier to see and remember as you speed past a billboard where it may be displayed, it is also easier to tell people over the phone and for people to type in when they want to look you up on the Net. If you don't have a concise URL, talk to your Web space provider about simplifying it. They often call it a *top-level URL* or a *virtual host name*. Please note that many providers charge extra to have this type of address. The more typical address is something like

```
http://www.xyzcompany.com/xyzcompany/
```

or

```
http://www.xyzcompany.com/xyzproductname/
```

That last word is simply a subdirectory in which the files of the Web site are placed. Most people select a word that is descriptive of their product or service if their domain name is descriptive of their company name or initials. Some clients choose a domain name that is descriptive of their product or service, and use their company name or part thereof as the last word. Here are some examples:

```
http://www.roasters.com/kennyrogers/     Kenny Rogers Roasters Restaurants

http://www.cyberlawyer.com/advice/       The CyberLawyer Office

http://www.cyberhealth2000.com/video/    CyberHealth 2000

http://www.legion.com/books/             Legion Publishing
```

If you are running your own Web server, odds are you already have a URL that's similar to the shorter one.

Smart, Very Smart

Let me give you an example: I recently saw a TV commercial for Magnavox, a manufacturer of TVs and other consumer electronics products. I applaud them for including their Web site address in their TV commercials. They were one of the first companies to do so. Probably one reason they did it is because having a site on the Web fits in nicely with their "smart, very smart" ad campaigns. I'll expand upon this logic in the next chapter. Having an Internet presence and advertising it with their TV ads makes them look like a *techno-*

savvy organization, which they are. Anyway, the point is that their Web address was displayed at the end of the commercial for about one second, if that. Hardly enough time to really grasp it, at least for those people new to the Web. I, on the other hand, have an intimate knowledge of the Web and know that most Web URLs begin with **http://www.** and end with a period followed by a three character extension, for example, **.com** for a commercial organization, which Magnavox is. Common extensions are

- *.com* for commercial organizations
- *.net* for network
- *.edu* for educational institution
- *.org* for nonprofit or some other type of organization
- *.gov* for a governmental site
- *.mil* for military

When I got that brief glimpse of Magnavox's Web address, the only word I needed to remember was Magnavox, which I already knew. The Web address they displayed on the screen was:

`http://www.magnavox.com`

It was easy to identify and subsequently remember. The next time someone fires up his or her Web browser, this URL is no problem to recall, and type in, to visit Magnavox's Web site. My only complaint is that they should try to keep the address up another second so that more people can make a note of it. Toyota is another example of this (**http://www.toyota.com**), and more national advertisers are including their URLs in their TV spots each day. If you can't remember the address, you can still find the Web site. Chapter 3 is dedicated to showing you how to find things on the Internet—which will provide you with better insight into how to *be found* on the Net (a major purpose of this book).

Scratching the Surface or Digging Deep?

Once you have settled on an appropriate Web address, your next step is to advertise that address. If you have a Web site, you may be listed already in a few of the Internet directories (also called *search engines* or *yellow-page sites*) such as Yahoo, WebCrawler, and Lycos. If that's the sum of your Web site promotion effort, you've only scratched the surface.

Did you know that there are dozens of places that allow Internet users to search by keyword for Web sites like yours? My research has shown that less than 10 percent of all commercial Web sites are listed in more than a dozen directories, and even fewer promote their sites in other ways.

Getting listed in as many of the search engines as possible is the least you should do—although I believe it is a crucial step. These sites have online forms that allow you to add your site's URL and, in many cases, enter a description of your site along with relevant keywords, so that Internet users can find you. But that's the thing—users have to be looking for something to find you, which users aren't always doing on the Web. In a later chapter, I go into much greater detail about how you can get listed in the many search engines and directories out there *the right way.*

You'll also want to perform what my colleague David Radin, president of Marketing Masters, calls "marketing by stumbling around." That is, Internet users just stumbling around the Net should be able to find you as well. There are a lot of people lost in cyberspace these days. About 15 percent of all people who fill out an online form to enter a contest on my first book's Web site check "stumbled upon it while browsing around" as the method they used to get to my site.

Many people browsing the Web check out places that are related to a subject they are interested in. There are sites out there called *meta-indexes* (Chapter 8) that have gathered a fairly comprehensive list of Web sites that pertain to a certain subject. The people who create these Web pages have done lots of work in finding Web sites that center around a certain topic. They are always looking for more sites to add to their list. When you find a meta-index that's related to your Web site, ask them to add you to their list. Most Internet directories and meta-indexes will list your site for free.

In addition to meta-indexes, certain Web sites can benefit from being listed in cybermalls—those online shopping centers that rent space to a variety of tenants. The bad news is that cybermalls will typically charge you a fee to be listed in their directory (in the form of a hyperlink). The good news is that there are some decent malls (defined as those that attract a respectable amount of traffic) that charge as little as $50 to $200 per year if you have your Web site located elsewhere.

In addition to the Internet directories, meta-indexes, and cybermalls, you should also promote your Web address in the following:

- Appropriate usenet newsgroups (announcement only and subject oriented)
- Appropriate Internet mailing lists (announcement only and subject oriented)
- Sponsorship banners on popular Web sites (GNN, LinkStar, Yahoo, etc.)
- Your traditional marketing materials (business cards, letterhead, fax cover sheet, and so on)
- Your traditional advertising (newspaper ads, TV, even billboards)

As you can see, there's more to Internet marketing than just slapping some Web pages onto the Internet. The key to generating traffic to your site is UBIQUITY. Be everywhere that makes sense.

If you promote it, they will know you exist, and hopefully they will come.

Successful Web Site Ingredients

Chapter 2 Topics

Resources for Creating Web Pages

How to Choose an Internet Presence Provider

Web Site Design Tips: Planning Your Web Site

Web Site Design Tips: Graphics Considerations

Web Site Design Tips: Features of a Good Site

What makes a Web site successful? Well, that depends on how you define successful, of course. Let's put promotion aside for now, since no matter how well promoted your Web site is, if it stinks, you probably won't be successful. I refer to successful (in the context of this chapter) as a site that is interesting, attractive, easy to navigate, useful, professional, and interactive. I don't want to give you the impression that you need all kinds of whiz-bang, neato stuff on your Web site in order for it to be successful. There are many well-thought-out, attractive Web sites that are nothing more than online brochures that do a good job of generating leads or sales. However, adding content, resources, interactivity, and various "goodies" will certainly strengthen your existing site. Many companies, though, ultimately judge their success on actual *sales*, not leads or *hits*, and I do the same.

A 1995 study conducted by ActivMedia, Inc. entitled *Who's Succeeding on the Internet and How?* found that only 22 percent of Internet marketers considered their sites financially rewarding at the time of the survey. Another 40 percent of respondents felt that their sites would be financially rewarding within the next one to two years. There were a number of reasons why some sites weren't meeting expectations. A primary reason was the lack of online promotion.

We all know that in order to have a market, you need to have sellers *and* buyers. We know we've got plenty of sellers on the Net—the question is, how many of those millions of users are actually online buyers? There's been much grumbling about how much Internet users browse online storefronts but don't buy anything. Some feel that the lack of a widespread secure payment system has held things up. Others feel that the medium/market needs to mature a little more. One thing is certain: more people are buying more things online than ever before.

If success equals sales for your site, here's one thing I've learned about the Web: **Price is key**.

A survey I read recently found that 82 percent of shoppers (traditional, not online) use price as a key criteria for buying. A separate survey conducted by Arthur Anderson found that 49 percent (of the 1,013 people they asked) would not want to pay *any* more money for extra service (like faster shipping). Personally, I only offered one way to ship my first book within the United States: Priority Mail by the U.S. Postal Service. The cost with handling is

$4.50. Eventually I offered book rate shipping for $2.50 and had about half the people choose that option. In my case, I've seen that people either want it fast, or they want it cheap. If they can get both, that's all the better.

Many Internet vendors don't offer discounts. Why would customers buy a product from you online that they can get for the same price around the corner? That's a question you need your Web site to answer for your prospective customers if you don't offer a discount. It may be that you offer something unique. That's good. Niche market companies are doing well on the Internet specifically because people can't find their products around the corner. If you're a service-oriented business, the price issue usually doesn't come up right away, so your site needs to be designed to generate leads.

Lead generation is one of the primary strengths of the Internet from a business standpoint. I created a Web site for *Success Magazine's* 1996 Entrepreneurial Leadership Conference. Rather than take all the information from their print brochure and place it online with a registration form, I felt that using the Net as a lead-generator made a lot more sense. Why? Because on average, people return to less than 10 percent of all Web sites they visit and most people don't make an $895 purchasing decision on the spot. The Success site's strategy was to whet the users' appetites with the benefits of attending the conference and with the attractiveness of the session speakers and titles. This induced many visitors to click on the option to obtain a free brochure via postal mail. Rather than taking a direct sales approach, we took a relationship marketing approach. If you've been in sales, you probably know that on average, it takes 5–7 contacts before someone buys from you. Customers buy from people whom they know, like, and trust. By sending interested attendees a print brochure, we've already established three contacts:

1. Prospects see conference mentioned in an announcement, Usenet message, directory, or search engine result and subsequently click on the entry or types in the URL.

2. They connect to the Web site, look around, and request that a brochure be *snail mailed* to them. Snail mail is Internet slang for postal mail.

3. They receive the brochure within a week by mail.

Additional contacts can then be the following:

4. Prospects receive an email message (no postage or telephone costs!) asking if they received the brochure in the mail.

5. A telemarketing campaign for the conference is conducted, and among those who are called are prospects who entered their telephone number online.

6. A "last chance" follow-up letter or postcard is snail mailed.

There you have it. If they don't register for the conference by the sixth contact, they probably won't. But one thing is for sure, they certainly know about the conference and weren't given a chance to forget about it! If nothing else, maybe they will tell their friends and colleagues, who may attend.

So, online success may also be defined by how many leads are generated. The problem is that generic leads are fairly meaningless. The important thing is that you have generated *qualified and interested* leads. The Net is well-suited for this. As you may already be aware, the Internet is more of a series of *micromarkets* rather than a mass market. Each Usenet newsgroup and Internet mailing list consists of a micromarket. These markets can be targeted and, if approached correctly, can be the source of solid leads and sales. We'll revisit promoting via Usenet and Internet mailing lists later in this book.

I recall a *Wall Street Journal* article's headline to be something like "The Web is the Junk Mail of the Internet." If you have been surfing the Web for any length of time, you'll probably agree. The Web is like a giant flea market seen through mishmashes of text and grainy pictures. The quality of the majority of Web sites is abysmal. Many sites are crammed with text, stale information, huge graphics, awkward page flow, and confusing layout.

This chapter tries to help you avoid being grouped into the previous description. I discuss good Web page/site design, provide tips on how to choose an Internet Presence Provider, critique and share examples of good and bad sites, and provide additional HTML/Web site design resources. If you already have a site, you learn ways to make it more appealing. If you don't have a site, you get a good idea of the types of things you may want to consider when designing your site. This chapter is not an HTML primer however. There are a number of good resources that will help you learn HTML or create Web pages with HTML authoring software. When appropriate, I mention some of the HTML *tags* necessary to accomplish a certain desired effect. If you've never heard of the term, HTML tag, it refers to the text inside angle brackets. An example would be <B> and </B> which is the opening and closing (designated by the slash) tags for bolding text. The word(s) you want bolded would be inserted in-between the two tags. The following is a selected list of resources I feel is worthwhile.

HTML Books

How to Create Cool Web Pages with HTML, Dave Taylor, IDG Books Worldwide, 1995, ISBN 1-56884-454-9, $19.99, (800) 434-3422 or (415) 655-3000, http://www.idgbooks.com.
Covers the basics, an easy read with three chapters on promoting your site.

HTML Publishing on the Internet, Brent Heslop & Larry Budnick, Ventana Press, 1995, ISBN 1-56604-229-1, $49.95, (919) 942-0220, http://www.vmedia.com.
One of the best I've seen. It's one of the few books that's actually worth its $49.95 price. A CD-ROM is included with lots of HTML resources and graphics manipulation software.

Teach Yourself More Web Publishing with HTML in a Week, Laura Lemay, SamsNet Publishing, 1995, ISBN 1-57521-005-3, $29.99, (800) 716-0044 or (317) 361-5400, http://www.mcp.com/samsnet/.
This book is the sequel to the best-selling Teach Yourself Web Publishing with HTML in a Week. *If you've read the first book and want more detailed information for advanced issues in HTML and Web site development, or even if you didn't read the first book but want to find out more than just the basics, this 500-page book contains the answers, along with many examples.*

HTML Online Guides

A Beginner's Guide to HTML by NCSA
http://www.ncsa.uiuc.edu/General/Internet/WWW/HTMLPrimer.html

Composing Good HTML by James "Eric" Tilton
http://www.cs.cmu.edu/~tilt/cgh/

Web Communication's Comprehensive Guide to Publishing on the Web
http://www.webcom.com/html/

HTML Authoring Software

HotDog and **HotDog Pro** from Sausage Software
http://www.sausage.com

HTML Assistant from Brooklyn North Software Works
http://fox.nstn.ca/~harawitz/index.html

Incontext Spider from InContext Corporation
http://www.incontext.com

Ken Nesbitt's WebEdit from Nesbitt Software
http://www.nesbitt.com

WebAuthor from Quarterdeck
http://www.qdeck.com/qdeck

HotMetal from Soft Quad
http://www.sq.com

How to Choose an Internet Presence Provider (IPP)

My previous firm went from being the only company providing Internet presence (Web sites) for businesses in south Florida to one of 50—all in the course of a year and a half. We started by creating *Gopher storefronts* (Gopher storefronts are text pages arranged in a hierarchical menu structure) and when the Web emerged, we migrated to creating Web sites. As time went on, we started running up against an increasing number of competitors. After winning contracts sought by competitors (and losing contracts), I've learned what people look for in an IPP. I'm no longer in the Internet Presence business. Therefore, I can provide you with an unbiased opinion of what you should look for in an IPP. If you decide to do your Web site in-house, you may still consider hiring an industry pro as a consultant to guide you. Odds are, your site will be better, and you'll save time and money in the long run. Table 2.1 shows which choice companies that spend more than $500,000 in advertising each year made when deciding to create their Web presence.

One of the problems with handling Web site projects internally is that it is nearly impossible to accurately budget them. In WebTrack's survey, none of the companies who did the project in-house were able to give an estimate of the total cost. Outsourcing allows you to gain a much better idea of how much you actually spend on your site.

Table 2.1 Percentage Breakdown of Web Site Designers
(Source: WebTrack's InterAd Monthly)

Choice	Percentage
In-house designer	55%
External firms	33
Combination	12

What follows are some of the things that I think you should do when looking for an IPP.

Ask about their experience

I recommend that you do business with an IPP that has been in business for no less than a year. Don't allow the newer companies to learn on your dime.

Check out their Web site

See what they've done for themselves and their client companies. I remember going to pitch a prospect, and after the meeting, they said they had talked to several other IPPs, but we were the first ones to actually *show them* some of our sites. This made a significant impression. We entered the meeting, and after an hour or so, we set up a computer projector and hooked it up to a laptop. We had dozens of sites stored on the hard drive. There was no doubt that we had experience. You'll get a better quality Web site from a company that has created at least a dozen medium-sized sites (12+ pages). You'll probably want to keep away from any IPP whose client sites look similar to or the same as each other. The noise level is ever-increasing on the Net. Why would you want to look like everyone else?

Scrutinize the quality of their sites

Unless you want your site to fail, don't hire a low-level Web site creator who'll do it for cheap. I saw many competitors spring up who created small, plain, boring sites. The price was right, but those sites really didn't benefit the client much. But you don't always get what you pay for. Unfortunately, there is no shortage of IPPs out there that charge exorbitant fees for passing work.

Now, you may say that you wouldn't know Web site quality if it hit you in the face! But after reading this chapter, as well as trusting your instinct and eye when looking at various Web sites, you'll be able to discern a poor site from a good one.

When reviewing the customer sites of a prospective IPP, make notes about various things that catch your eye or that you are curious about. Then ask the IPP why they did certain things. Some IPPs do have a wide mix of clients, some of which require just a basic site, while others require something more elaborate. Be sure to inquire about the cost of the sites you review.

Keep an eye out for misspellings, dead links, and other signs of a lack of attention to detail. A good Web site is nearly flawless and without silly errors.

Ask yourself, "Do the IPP's client sites sell me?"

Keep away from those IPPs that just slap together what the client gives them. A good IPP does more than type up words inside angle brackets (otherwise known as HTML). A knack for marketing is also required. We made changes or additions to what was provided in nearly every site I was involved in. If the sites of your prospective IPP don't sell you (assuming that's the purpose of the site), how is the site going to sell anyone else? By the same token, what makes you think that the site they do for you is going to be any different?

Does the IPP sell a physical product of its own on the Net?

I don't mean their Web site that sells their creation services. Nearly every IPP has one of those; they don't mean *diddly*. My ability to help my clients succeed on the Net increased significantly after I started selling my first book online. The more successful I was (and the more mistakes I made), the more I learned that I could use to help my clients. They ultimately benefited.

I've done some informal surveys and found that fewer than 1 in 15 IPPs actually has sold a physical product (remember, not a service!) on the Internet. Even fewer have had any measure of success. I'm not saying an IPP without practical experience can't do a good job, but it is another consideration, especially if your site is geared toward the selling of product. If you are selling a service, perhaps an IPP that has successfully marketed a service (but not Web site creation services!) online would be the right one for you.

The previous tips should keep you safe from the sharks. The big secret out there is how easy HTML is to learn. That's why very few presence providers conduct seminars on HTML. They want to do the work themselves. Ask for references, and then call them. Find out whether the site was completed on time, whether there were any "forgotten-about" add-on fees. Be as selective when looking for an IPP as you would be if the firm was going to build your house or office. After all, your Web site is more than just an advertisement— it's another business location or branch that needs to be taken seriously if you want it to yield results.

Web Site Design Tips

It's interesting to see what ingredients go into the Web sites of various companies. Table 2.2 gives you an idea of what some organizations that WebTrack surveyed included in their sites. I averaged the percentages from several months of their polls and added a few features from polls of my own.

If you are planning to do your site in-house, the following tips will keep you from falling into the many traps that plague new Web sites. Please note that these are my opinion. There are no hard and fast rules, but I feel that by abiding by these tips you will have a much more attractive and useful site.

Table 2.2 Web Site Design Features
(Source: WebTrack's InterAd Monthly)

Included in Web Site	Percent
Feedback Mechanism	25%
FAQs	24
Contest Competition	24
Outlet Locator	21
Press Releases	21
Downloadable Files	17
What's New Section	16
Audio Content	16
Survey of Visitors	14
List of Links	14
Video Content	11
Employment Opportunities	5
Registration	4
Interactive Chat Lines	3
Interactive Bulletin Board	3

Remember, though, that if you don't have good content, no matter how nice you make the site look, people aren't going to bother. Having something useful, interesting, and important to say goes a long way on the Web. If you plan on hiring an IPP, share with the Web designers some of the things you feel apply to you.

Check out other Web sites to get ideas

Obviously, one of the easiest ways to get ideas for some of the elements of your Web site or to upgrade your existing pages is to surf other sites. These may be those of competitors, sites that just caught your eye, sites that are popular, or those that have been nominated as a "cool site." (Check out Chapter 7 for a list of cool sites pages.)

Look at how they arranged their information, the colors and patterns used for backgrounds (if any), the types of features the site offers (contests, order forms, FAQs (Frequently Asked Question lists), etc.), whether image maps (graphics that have various clickable areas that link to other pages) were used, various interactive features, and so on. While you're doing this, I recommend that you also take note of any features you did not like, such as typographical errors, color clashes, cheesy graphics, dead links, etc. Sometimes knowing what you don't like helps you determine what you do like.

Use the information gleaned from others to better your site. Be careful, most sites have a copyright notice on their pages, and copyright laws still apply in cyberspace.

Thoroughly plan your Web site

The structure of your Web site's information is important to how the overall site will look. Your Web site begins with the home page (level 1), and from that page, one or more links to additional pages (level 2) are placed. On each level 2 page, there may be additional links leading to a third level, and so on. Figure 2.1 shows a typical site plan for a Web site. The site contains four legs (main branches off of the home page).

While writing this book, I read an article in the newspaper about a Web site that the NRC (Nuclear Regulatory Commission) created. It was dubbed one of the first *virtual hearing rooms* on the Net. The site is used to help the NRC write rules. Part of the rule-writing process is to hold public hearings. They expect

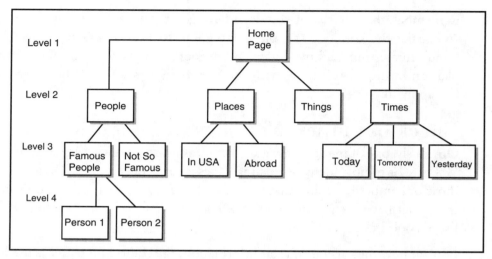

Figure 2.1 A site plan for a fictitious Web site.

that in the future, Internet users will be able to interact with the site and be part of a virtual hearing. The virtual hearings will not replace public ones but will augment them.

My point is, a spokesperson for the Union of Concerned Scientists, a watchdog group, was quoted as saying that the site wasn't structured for the average person to use as easily. One issue was the complexity of the content.

The moral of this story is that while you are planning your site (or restructuring it), make sure that it is not only easy to use, but also that you don't have to be a Ph.D. to understand the information inside Unless it's geared solely toward Ph.D.s, of course.

You'll also want to decide what image you want your site to portray. That is, do you want to be viewed as conservative or aggressive, bland or flashy, serious or fun, etc.? The tone of your text and the design of your graphics will convey your intended image. Therefore, in order to create a site that is consistent with your intended image, you will want to clearly define that image and proceed from there.

Make it easy to get to your information (3-4 levels max)

Smaller Web sites don't have more than a few levels of information. Larger ones may have many levels. Try to structure your site to eliminate unnecessary extra levels. Levels are often created to segment information according to the different topics or themes within a site (called *chunking* in Web site development lingo). If your site is more than four or five levels deep, you may want to see if combining Web pages or grouping them differently will help eliminate unneeded levels and streamline the site. The last thing you want is for people to get lost within the bowels of your site, and never find the good stuff.

Provide a hypertext index or table of contents to your site

Following up on the previous tip, if your site is many levels deep, create a textual hypertext index. This index will contain one link/description for every Web page. Use Unordered Lists (<UL>) or the <BLOCKQUOTE> tag to indent each level. Figure 2.2 is a good example of how First Virtual, a company specializing in electronic commerce, structured its textual index. The figure shows only one of several screens that contains the entire index. As you can see, the page is devoid of graphics except for small bullets that are quick to download. People wanting to go to a certain page on the fourth level (such as "About the InfoHaus") would simply click on that page description and thereby

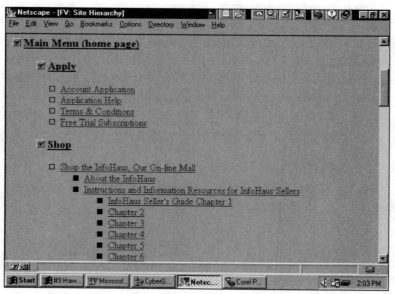

Figure 2.2 First Virtual's textual Web site index (http://www.fv.com/help/
hierarchy.html).

avoid downloading two levels of additional Web pages that they aren't interested in. Your index or site table of contents should be accessible from the home page as well as from any other Web page by placing it on a navigational bar (explained in the next tip). A table of contents can be less detailed than a full index. Figure 2.3 shows how First Virtual uses a graphical approach.

Avoid creating dead-end Web pages—add a navigational bar

A dead-end Web page is a page that provides you with nowhere to go when you reach the bottom of it (except to scroll back up, of course).

A navigational bar is a series of links to key Web pages within your site. Navigational bars can consist of a graphical image map (Figure 2.4), a series of graphical buttons or icons (Figure 2.5), or a series of text descriptions (Figure 2.6). They can be placed at the top of each Web page as in Figure 2.4 or at the bottom (which is more common) as in Figures 2.5 and 2.6. One benefit of placing the navigational bar at the top of each page is that people wanting to move within your site don't need to scroll down to

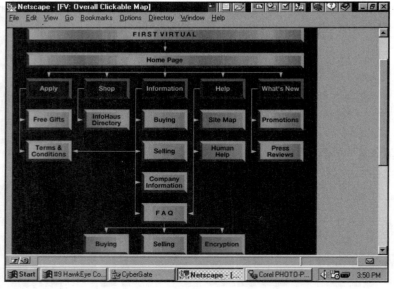

Figure 2.3 First Virtual's graphical site contents page (http://www.fv.com/help/overall_map.html).

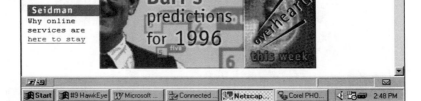

Figure 2.4   clnet's image map navigational bar is located at the top of its pages (http://www.cnet.com).

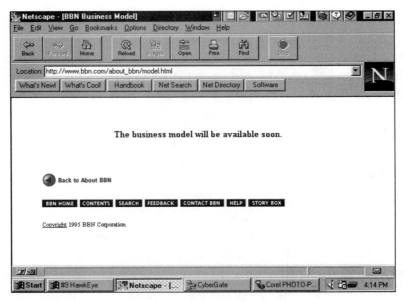

Figure 2.5   BBN Planet's navigational bar consists of seven graphical buttons (http://www.bbnplanet.com).

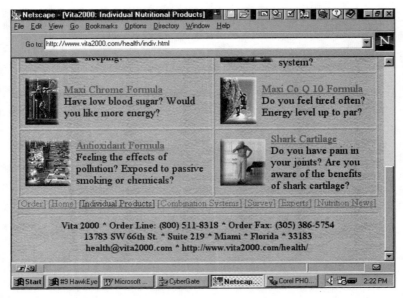

Figure 2.6   Vita2000's textual navigational bar is shown near the bottom (http://
www.vita2000.com/health/).

the bottom of the page to navigate. Top-based navigational bars pop up immediately upon loading each Web page, and links can be activated without waiting for the rest of a page to be displayed. This is desirable for sites whose users are expected to return. The down side is that if you scroll down to the bottom of a page, you have to scroll back up to navigate. That's why most Web sites that use top-based navigational bars have short Web pages.

Capture the casual browser's attention right away

The average Web user scrolls down on just 25 percent of all pages browsed. Remember the *Web anxiety* phenomenon I mentioned in the first chapter. If you don't get 'em quickly, you may lose 'em! If your Web page is more than one screen, give people a reason to see more. I take more of a Zen approach to Web page design. Less is more. A single screen Web page guarantees that users will see the entire page. They may not read it, but they'll see it—and hopefully interact with it. Try to avoid creating pages that seem to go on and on forever.

Don't overwhelm users with too much information too fast

Look at the paragraph in Figure 2.7. This is an example of a text-intensive page (which is fine), but it has way too many hyperlinks in one paragraph. Personally, I'm a bit overwhelmed with choices when I view that type of Web page. Rather than just choose an option, I feel like running away to another site that's simpler and less intimidating! (Sounds wimpy doesn't it?)

Keep your home page clean and neat

Your home page is probably the most consequential page of your site. In most cases, it is the first page users will be exposed to. Try to fit it into one screen if possible. The shorter the better, in most cases. Figures 2.8 through 2.11 are good examples of clean Web pages.

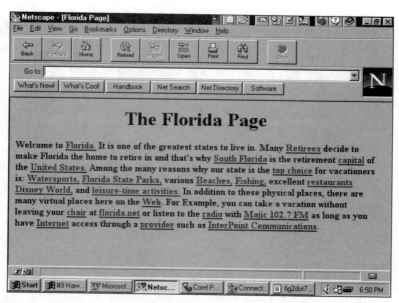

Figure 2.7   What NOT to do: A Web page with a bazillion hyperlinks!

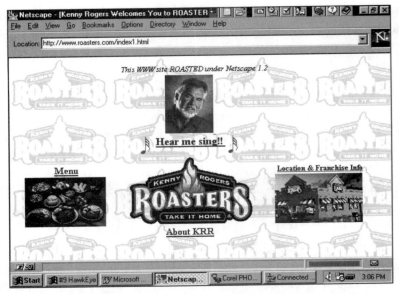

Figure 2.8　Kenny Rogers Roasters Restaurant's site offers four choices, no overwhelm here (http://www.roasters.com).

Figure 2.9　Video Production System's home page is clean and neat but a bit overwhelming (http://www.vps.com).

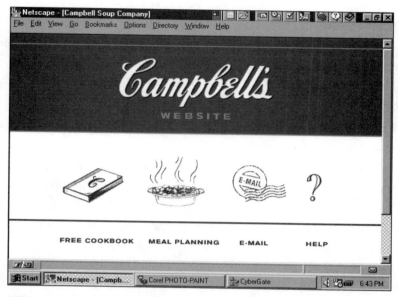

Figure 2.10   Like its soups, Campbell's home page is simple and good (http://www.campbellsoups.com).

Figure 2.11   The Marketing Music site's home page (http://www.magicnet.net/rz/web_music/).

Keep your graphic files below 50 K

For the time being, the majority of Internet users have 14.4 Kbps modems or slower. Yes, computers with 28.8 Kbps modems are rapidly gaining, as well as people who are looking into ISDN connections. But for now, you have three options when it comes to the size of graphics within your site:

1. Keep all your graphics below 50 K. This way people won't be waiting too long for them to appear.

2. Use thumbnails, and link them to expanded, larger files. If users want to see more detail, they can click on the smaller thumbnail file.

3. Provide large graphics in one leg of your site and smaller ones in another leg. Use a home page that gives the user the option of which type of site they want to see—a site with large graphic files or a site that is trimmed down and uses smaller graphics. This option requires that you double the number of Web pages for your site. One leg is the high-graphics version, the other is the low-graphics version. An example of this technique is shown in Figure 2.12, where T-Square Express, a south Florida-based chain of digital color copy centers, wanted to show off its graphics but also wanted to provide an option for people to bypass those heavy graphics.

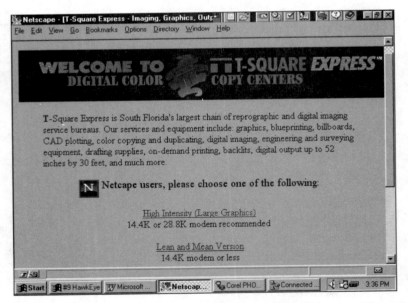

Figure 2.12 T-Square Express gives its users the option of big graphics or reduced graphics (http://www.t-square.com/output/).

I'm no graphic artist, but I do know a few tricks to reduce the file size of your images:

- Save images at 72 dpi. Make sure the resolution of each image is 72 dpi since that's the resolution of most computer screens. Graphic artists who are used to doing work for print have trouble with this because they are used to much higher resolutions. Let whoever is doing your graphics know that the images are to be displayed on computer screens only and should be designed as such.

- Trim the fat. Have you ever bought a steak with lots of fat around it? You take a knife and trim around the edges excising unneeded fat (you leave a little because it adds to the flavor). You should do the same for your graphic images. Extra pixels situated around the important part of the image should be removed by *cropping*. In most cases you leave a little bit around the edges for contrast.

- Reduce the number of bits per pixel. This really translates to reducing the number of colors within your image. Most images for the Web look good at 256 colors (8-bit), but in some cases you can get away with using 16 colors (4-bit). This substantially reduces the file size but also reduces the attractiveness of the image in most cases. Black-and-white images can be reduced to 2-bit images. You can save images with 65,536 colors (16-bit, common on Macintosh computers) and even 16.7 million colors (24-bit), but your file size will be substantially larger than a 256 color image.

Limit the number of in-line graphics on a page

An "in-line" graphic is one that's part of a Web page that also contains text. When clicked upon, some thumbnails display just the graphic while others display another HTML page that contains the larger graphic. The latter case would be an in-line graphic, as would the page that contained one or more thumbnails.

A Web page that contains ten 5 K graphics, (which totals 50 K) takes longer to download than a page that contains one 50 K graphic. The reason for this is that for each graphic, your Web browser must open an HTTP connection to the server to retrieve it. So, for ten 5 K graphics, ten HTTP connections must be made. It takes time to make each connection. In the case of the single 50 K graphic, only one HTTP connection is made. In either situation, after the HTTP connection is made, a file is downloaded. It's simply faster to download one file than to download 10. Another way to look at this is it takes longer to make ten 5-minute telephone calls than one 50-minute call because of the added time to dial and wait for the phone to be answered.

Warn users about large graphic, audio, and video files

There's nothing worse than clicking on a link and not knowing how long it's going to take to download the image, audio file, or video clip. I never know if I should abort, let it go on for a few more seconds because maybe then it will be done, or go to lunch. Figure 2.13 illustrates typical comparative sizes of multimedia files.

If you use thumbnail graphics that expand out to more than 50 K, it's a good idea to add some text that says how large the file is. Audio and video files should *always* be labeled with their file size. This way, users know whether they should hang around for a minute or go eat lunch and come back when the file is done downloading. My point is that with all the effort to get people to visit your Web site, the last thing you want to do is frustrate them to the point of leaving.

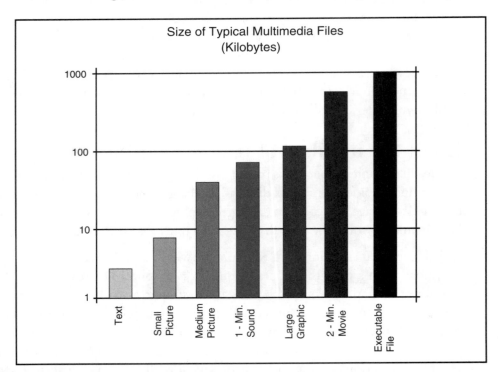

Figure 2.13　Typical comparative sizes of text, graphic, sound, and video multimedia files.

Don't forget about the text users!

While we're on the subject of the use of graphics, let's discuss the non-use of them. There are still a lot of people who use the Internet with *shell* accounts. These are text-based, command-line interfaces whereby standard communications software is used to access a Unix-based computer. Before Mosaic (the first graphical Web browser), this was the only way to access the Net. Now, with point-and-click interfaces available, many people don't realize how it was done in the "old days" (1993 or so). Many university students and most users in countries like Columbia are limited to text-based Internet access (although this is quickly changing). If they want to surf the Web, they typically use Lynx, a text-based Web interface.

Basically, you don't want to rely too heavily on your graphics. Many people turn off the graphics capability of their browser software to save time while surfing around. For these people, your informational content will be a critical factor for success. The actual text (called *copy*), needs to tell your message as well. Make sure that if there is no text description of your graphics on the page, you use the <ALT> tag to explain it. For example, the HTML for displaying a graphic on the screen is

```
<IMG SRC="graphic.gif">
```

But if someone accesses the page with Lynx, they'll just see [IMAGE] where the graphic would be. This doesn't say much about the picture does it? A better way is

```
<IMG SRC="graphic.gif" ALT="[Picture of Person Surfing]">
```

In this case, we'll assume the graphic is a picture of someone surfing. Therefore, when someone using Lynx accesses the page, they see

```
[Picture of Person Surfing]   instead of    [IMAGE]
```

Which is more descriptive?

If you use image maps in your Web pages, be sure that there are also textual links to the information on the page, as in Figure 2.14. Otherwise, all the Lynx user will see is

```
[ISMAP]
```

Figure 2.14　Exotic Garden's image map also offers text links (http://www.exoticgardens.com).

There won't be any way to get into your site without some text hyperlinks to the other Web pages. If you don't have any clue as to what I'm talking about, you'll just want to bookmark this page (and any others that discuss HTML stuff) and show it to the person who creates your Web site. Don't assume the person or company that creates your Web site knows these things. Some do, and some do not—and some do forget to implement these important things.

There are some Web sites who have the gall to say that if you're using a Lynx (remember, text-based) Web browser, they don't want you viewing or don't care what their pages look like to you. A good example of this is IMAGEX, whose page can be found at **http://www.image-x.com/index_v20.html**. Not only do they recommend the Web browser (Netscape of course), they also recommend how wide your browser screen should be opened to. The Captain Morgan spiced rum Web site does this also, but with an "X marks the spot" on the left and right side. Y-100, a south Florida radio station, dedicates an entire page of its site to how you should view and navigate around it (see Figure 2.15).

Aside from making sure text describes graphics, you also want to make sure the text you use in your pages makes sense. One of the biggest mistakes organizations make is to use their traditional print material verbatim for the Web. In most cases, you need to repurpose the copy for the Web. Sometimes,

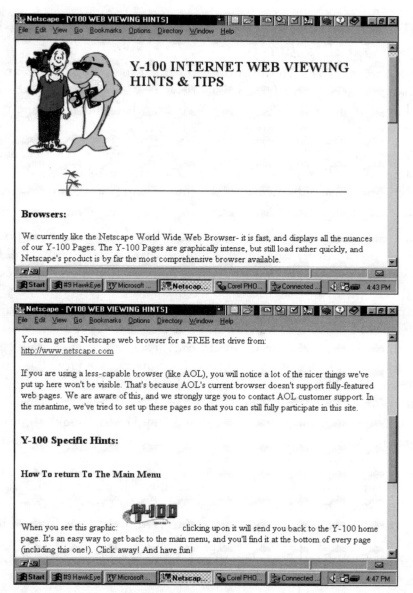

Figure 2.15 South Florida's Y-100 radio station's site viewing tips page (http://www.florida.net/y100).

it's just a minor adjustment, sometimes it requires an entire rewrite. If you're not sure, there are people (few and far between unfortunately) who specialize in writing Web-site-friendly copy. One of those people is David Citron (dcitron@gate.net).

Create online forms that are easy to fill out and visually crisp

Forms are used by Web site visitors to request more information about your product or service, for feedback about your Web site, or to place an order online. The order form is to your Web site what your telephone is to your business. It's the communications interface. It's crucial.

When your Web site first goes online or when you make a change to any online forms pages, please, *test it!* I don't know how many times I've encountered forms that didn't work. Make sure it works; as common-sense as this sounds, I cannot stress this enough.

Now that your form works, ask for as little information as possible. A psychological survey I heard about found that nearly everyone will fill out a form (paper based) that asks 5 questions or fewer. About one-third less people will fill out a form that asks between 6 and 10 questions. Less than 50 percent of those who would have filled out a 5-question-or-less form will fill out an 11- to 15-question form. And less than 10 percent will fill out anything that's more than 15 questions. Since you have essentially unlimited space on a Web page, it's easy to get caught up in asking for all kinds of extra information like demographics, purchasing habits, etc. There's nothing wrong with doing that. In fact, I do it on the site that sells my first book. But it's not on the order form. It's on a "Win a Copy of the Book" contest page—separate from the order form. Besides, some Web browsers cannot handle forms that are too long.

Once you've tested your form and streamlined it, make sure it's visually appealing. Some forms I've seen on the Web can be very intimidating to a new Internet user. Figure 2.16 provides a good example of a bad form while Figure 2.17 provides a good example of a great form. Which one would you rather fill out? Remember, the easier it is to order your product, *the easier it is to order your product!*

One last thing about order forms. If you accept credit card numbers via the Web, be sure to provide your customers the option of being contacted for their credit card information. Simply provide an option worded, "Contact me for credit card information" in the pull-down menu or radio-button option on your page. About 15 percent of all people who order via my Web site choose this option. Interestingly enough, about 65 percent type their credit card numbers in right there on the Web order form! I don't run a secure server

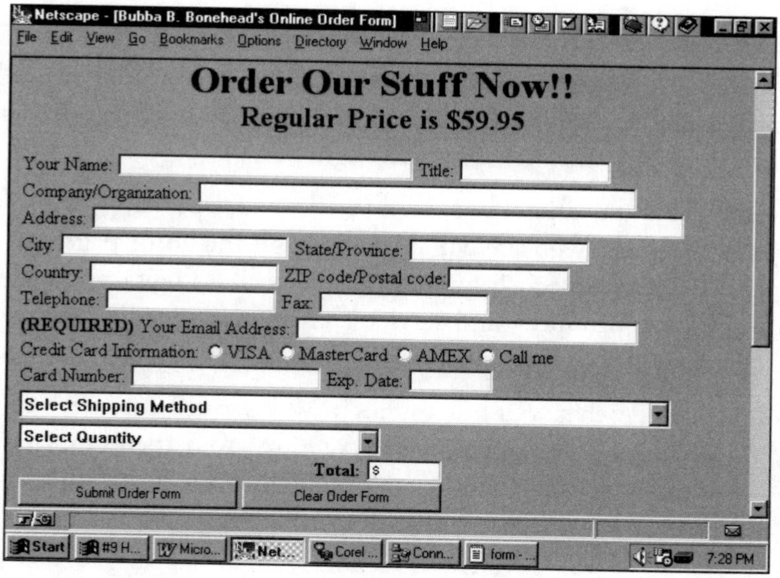

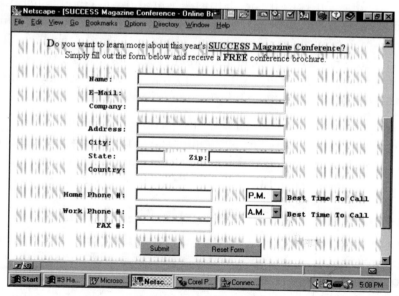

Figure 2.16   An example of what NOT to do in an online order form!

Figure 2.17   Clean but not mean: Success Magazine's Conference Brochure request online form.

either. This is the way most Internet vendors operate, and although there are some risks involved from a security standpoint, so far there hasn't been much actual crime.

Create "brand name" recognition

It's a good idea to place your name and logo on *all* your Web pages. Digital Equipment Corp. has more than 8,000 Web pages! On the upper left-hand corner of *every single one* of them is the Digital logo.

Why do this, you may ask? If you need to ask, you're probably assuming that people who visit your Web site will do so through the home page only. That's not always the case, especially with a company like Digital, that has many different divisions, products, and services. The larger your site, the more you should anticipate multiple points of entry into it.

For example, let's say that your interest lies in Web server hardware, and you ask a friend for Web pages of server hardware vendors. Your friend may give you a URL that goes directly to Digital's Web server hardware section rather than to its home page. This is actually preferable to you, because now you won't have to wade through several levels and pages of information before getting to what you want. If Digital didn't have its logo on that page, you wouldn't necessarily know who the vendor is if your friend didn't tell you and you couldn't tell from the domain name within the URL (another reason why you should have your own domain name). Some organizations list various sections of their Web site with the various Internet directories, in addition to their home page. When someone clicks on the hyperlink, they go directly to that particular section. This is another reason to have identifying information on every page.

It's also important for many organizations to apply their brand identity consistently from traditional advertising to online advertising. If your company has spent a lot of money paying an ad agency for a corporate identity or advertising campaign, you may want your Web site to mirror or augment that theme.

Consider adding a "What's New" page

When someone first visits your site, everything they see is new. If the user returns (unfortunately, for most Web sites this is a big IF—see Chapter 15 for more on this), he or she will probably want to know if there is anything new that has been added or changed within your site. Don't make him or her wander aimlessly around trying to find out because he or she will just up and leave. Add a link or button to a page that contains the latest changes and additions to your Web site. Be sure to label the link or button with the date that the What's New page was last changed. This way your users will know if anything has changed since their last visit.

Make sure people can find you again

One piece of identifying information you may also want to add to your Web pages (or at a minimum, to your home page), besides your organization or site name is the URL for the site. This is left out of 99 percent of all Web pages. Have you ever printed out a Web page? I do it all the time. If I want to go back to that page or make photocopies to give to friends or as a handout at one of my seminars, I need to handwrite the URL on it so the people will know how to visit it. This isn't necessary if the URL is on the page (or at a minimum, the home page URL). The newer versions of Netscape Navigator include the URL of the Web page when you print, but most other Web browsers don't. (They eventually will; it's a great idea.) If you want to make sure people know how to find your site again after they print one of its pages, place your URL at the bottom in what's called a Web page *footer*. Figure 2.18 shows a good example of this.

Provide your contact information

One thing I can't stand in a Web site is the absence of a phone number! I like to obtain more information via phone. There are a lot of Web sites that force you to hunt around for a contact information page. Add a link to a page that contains

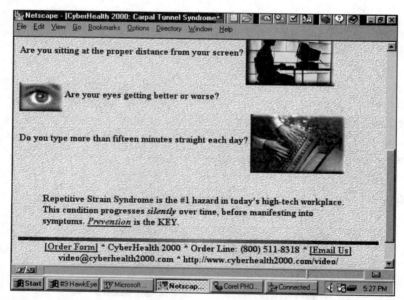

Figure 2.18 Notice the URL of the site listed in the footer of CyberHealth 2000's home page.

all the ways you would like people to contact you. I personally don't buy from any Web vendor that does not display its phone number. In my opinion, companies lose some credibility when they withhold their contact information.

When appropriate, use interlaced and/or transparent graphics (GIFS)

An interlaced graphic is one that appears very quickly on your Web browser but is really blurry at first. Kind of like a venetian blind effect. In total, there are four sweeps made, each causing the image to become clearer and clearer, with the fourth bringing the graphic into its final clarity. I feel that the larger a graphic is, the more reason to make it interlaced. This way, viewers can at least see something on their screens while the picture is being downloaded, and they can start to look at the rest of the Web page. Noninterlaced graphics download one line at a time. Most Web browsers display them one line at a time as well, while some wait until the entire picture is downloaded before displaying it. Interlacing is accomplished when you save a graphic image, and not with any magical HTML tag. Some graphics manipulation programs (such as LView Pro) allow you to save images in "GIF89a Interlaced" format. If you haven't noticed interlacing on Web pages, go out and surf a bit. You'll see that the more professional-looking sites (and some less professional) use interlaced images.

Some images look much better when they are transparent. This is particularly true of images that are nonrectangular. All graphics are saved as a rectangle (or a square, which is a special case of a rectangle). That is, if you create a blue circle with a program like Corel Draw, you cannot save it as a circle. It will be saved as a blue circle with white (if that was the background color for the page you drew the circle on) surrounding it. An example of a transparent graphic is shown in Figure 2.19. The image on the left is transparent, while the one on the right is not. In many cases, making a graphic transparent looks more attractive. People like attractive Web pages.

Figure 2.19 Transparent GIF on left and nontransparent GIF on right.

You can make your graphics both transparent and interlaced, but for some reason they don't always appear correctly on a Web browser. Unfortunately, you'll have to try it and check for any problems.

Smooth out jaggedy text placed on images

I know graphics may not be your forte, so just pass this information on to the person doing your Web page graphics. When you place text on graphics in certain programs, the edges of the image can end up looking like steps on a stair ("jaggies"). It makes your text look computer generated (which it was, but you don't necessarily want it to look that way!). You can smooth out those steps by choosing the *anti-aliasing* option within your image editor or graphics program. The program actually adds intermediate colored pixels between the steps. This gives the appearance of a smoother edge.

Always use height and width tags for graphic images

Few Web browsers recognize these tags but the tags are *backward compatible* and will be ignored by browsers that don't recognize them. Basically, when you download a graphic image with a Web browser such as Netscape, the browser needs to download the entire graphic (or the first pass if it's interlaced) before any text can be displayed. This is detrimental to the Internet users since they have to wait for the graphic to be received before they can read through your page. What happens behind the scenes is that the browser needs to determine exactly what size the graphic is before figuring out where the text is going to be displayed. It's a matter of planning out the screen real estate.

When you tell the Web browser the dimensions of the graphic, it can immediately display the text on the screen since it reserves the space for the graphic. As the graphic is downloading to fill that space, text can be read. The height and width of a graphic can be easily determined with any image editor software. Just load in the graphic and there should be an option somewhere that either tells you the size in pixels or allows you to resize the image, which will tell you what the original size is. To save time, have the person who creates the graphics for your site make a note of the size of each image (in pixels) along with the associated file name.

Once you have the sizes of your graphics, just use that information in your HTML document. Here's how it would look if you had a graphic that was 468 pixels wide and 60 pixels thick (the size of a typical banner advertisement):

```
<IMG SRC="banner.gif" HEIGHT=60 WIDTH=468 ALT="Company X's Banner Ad">
```

You can also size the graphic with the height and width tags. I could have chosen to make the graphic appear larger or smaller than it really is, simply by changing the height and width numbers in the HTML. I don't recommend this for either case. If the graphic file is smaller than how you want it to appear on the screen, it may distort. If the graphic is larger, it will take longer to download than it would if you physically resized the graphic and saved it.

Keep graphics within the default Web browser width

Most people have their screens configured for 640×480 pixels. Subtracting out some of the area used by the Web browser, the width available for viewing is about 470 pixels. If you create any large graphics, be sure the width is 470 pixels or less; otherwise it will "fall off" the screen a little bit. Users will be forced to use the horizontal scroll bar to see the rest of the image.

Design image maps objectively

If you've surfed the Web, you have probably seen an *image map*. It is a single graphic that has multiple hot links to different Web pages. Image maps are often used to display a hot linked map of the world or a country. All too often, sites contain image maps that do not give the user any idea as to what is clickable and what's not. Be sure to define which areas within the map are clickable. Also, an image map should fit within the standard viewing area within a Web browser. Don't make people scroll around to see the entire image.

Be careful when using backgrounds

Be sure to test that new snazzy background you created for your Web page. Many times a background looks fine on a screen that is configured for 256 colors but makes it very difficult to read text on a screen configured for just 16 colors. The fastest way to scare users away is to use a background that overwhelms the page's text. Three tips to backgrounds are:

- Keep them small in size. The optimum size is 96 by 96 pixels square, but certain effects require that you use a nonsquare image. Keep the total size below 10 K if possible.

- Create unique backgrounds. Why look like anyone else?

- Use good contrast. Keep the background light in color so that users can read the text (if it's dark) or use a dark background for light text.

Keep the display time of your pages to <u>60</u> seconds or less

This is just a rule of thumb. Like people, the Internet has its good days and its bad days. Sometimes the Net runs a bit slow, sometimes, nice and quick. Time the download time of your pages on an "average" day. If it takes too long, you can reduce the size of all your graphics, or use a trick. This trick works with Netscape (remember, 65 to 75 percent of people who visit will be able to take advantage of this).

There is an HTML tag called <LOWSRC>. Let's jump right into the HTML, and use the previous banner.gif example:

```
<IMG SRC="banner.gif" LOWSRC="banner.jpg" HEIGHT=60 WIDTH=468 ALT="Company
  X's Banner Ad">
```

Notice <u>LOWSRC</u>="banner.jpg". JPEG (Joint Photographic Experts Group) is another graphics format. All Web browsers display in-line (within an HTML page) GIF images, but only some display JPEGs as in-lines. As an aside, to be safe, only use GIF images unless you offer a *Netscape Enhanced* set of pages, in which case JPEG images can be used.

One of the differences between GIF and JPEG is that GIF files are about three times larger (in K) than JPEGS (when the images are saved as 256 color images). Therefore, if you use a JPEG image for one of your Web pages, it will download in a third of the time that a GIF would. So, why not always use JPEGs? Well, the in-line graphic situation mentioned in the previous paragraph is one reason, and the other is that JPEGs are, on average, of a poorer quality than GIF images. JPEGs tend to be grainier and sometimes fuzzier. The bottom line is that you gain speed but lose quality.

One way to speed up the download time of your graphics by using JPEGs (yet still maintain the quality) is by using the <LOWSRC> tag. When you download a Web page that uses <LOWSRC> tags and JPEG images with Netscape, the JPEGs are displayed first, and while you are scrolling through the page, reading text, etc. the higher quality yet slower GIF images replace the JPEGs. You are in no way adversely affected while this is happening. Basically, it's a trick to speed up the download time of your Web pages. People using less capable Web browsers will just see the GIF images, and the download time would be as long as if you didn't use the <LOWSRC> tag. To save time, your graphic person should save each image as a GIF and a 256-color JPEG, while recording the height and width of each image.

Remember that the Web (and Internet) is international

Colors and hand signs have different meanings to different cultures. One hand sign may mean "OK" in the United States and may mean something entirely different in another country.

One of my previous clients is a florist. When the home page and the order form were initially created, they said "Local and Worldwide Delivery." We knew what local was, but people elsewhere on the planet think local is where they are located. Seeing how there is a $4.95 difference in the delivery charge for local and worldwide orders, we quickly realized the mistake and changed the word "local" to "South Florida."

The Vermont Teddy Bear Company started to receive Web orders from Germany in German. The problem was that no one at the company spoke German! They had to quickly rethink how they were going to handle international orders. Even though English is widely used on the Net, there are many people who speak and sites that use other languages. If you want all orders in English and paid in U.S. currency, be sure to say so on your order page.

Some Web sites offer several language versions to their site. Fitness & Nutrition Center offers both English and Spanish versions of its site (located at **http://www.fitnessweb.com/nutrition/**). Fitness & Nutrition Center is a wholesaler of health products and does a significant amount of export business with Spanish language countries. They didn't want to exclude that market from their Internet presence. Does part of your market speak another language? If you want your site translated into other languages but can't do it yourself, contact a company that does translating, like The Language Solution at (407) 750-7468, or visit its Web site at **http://www.language-solution.com**.

Avoid "under construction" signs

The Web, by definition is under construction! Your Web pages, by definition, are under construction! In my opinion, it's a bit redundant to have under construction signs on unfinished Web pages. I've seen some really fancy under construction pages. With all the time it took to create a slick looking under construction page, they could have finished the page that's supposed to be there in the first place!

If you have a couple of empty Web pages, just disable the hyperlinks that point to them. Don't make them *vaporlinks* (a link to a page that hasn't been completed). When the pages are ready, simply activate the hyperlink by adding the <A HREF> tag. Another option is to hide the entire line, by using the HTML comment tag. For example, if I want to add a Web page that contains statistics for my favorite football team's current season, but the season isn't over yet, I may do something like

```
<!-- [A HREF="seasonstats.html"]This Season's Statistics[/A] --!>
```

When the season is over, I can remove the <!-- and --!> from the line and change the [to < and the] to >. The page will now be active.

Some people think construction signs are fine on a Web page. This is primarily a matter of taste, but I prefer not to activate a Web site until it's complete. Some people feel that under construction signs prompt visitors to return later; others feel that when people see them, they never return. With differing views like these, I just prefer to avoid the issue entirely and not use construction signs at all.

Use <BLINK> sparingly, if at all

There is an HTML tag called <BLINK> that causes the text enclosed within the tags to flash on and off on the user's screen. Many Web surfers dislike this effect. I personally like it if it's done correctly; for example, when only a single word that is of some importance is blinking. Don't cause entire sentences or more to blink. Your users may hate you for it!

Test the URLs you link to frequently

The Web is huge, and links break from time to time even though they are "good links." Veteran Web users know to try clicking on the link again. Sometimes just trying again will work. Other times, it won't. Ever click on a link only to get an "ERROR 404" message? That's called a *dead link*. Either the Web page has moved, the server has been removed from the Net, the file referenced in the HTML <A HREF> line doesn't match the file name of the actual file on the server, or the security permissions aren't set correctly on the HTML file. Regardless of the reason, it's frustrating to the user.

If you link to Web pages outside of your own server, be sure to test them from time to time. People who visit your Web site may not realize that the bad link is to a site other than your own. This is especially true for new Internet users. They'll think it's your fault that the link doesn't work, even though it may be a problem with the remote server or the Internet itself. Obviously, this would reflect badly on your organization.

Test your Web (HTML) pages with other browser software

Different Web browsers display Web pages differently. When you request an HTML document over the Web, the HTML is transmitted using HTTP (HyperText Transport Protocol). When the file is received, it is loaded into the memory of the Web browser and interpreted. Those words inside angle brackets determine how and where graphics and text are displayed on your screen. However, each Web browser interprets the codes differently. Often, the differences are subtle. This is the case when Web pages use HTML version 2.0, which is standardized. Some Web browsers use certain proprietary or nonstandardized HTML codes (such as Netscape). The Web browsers that don't understand those codes will ignore them. Therefore, the Web page will be displayed differently.

If your Web pages aren't tested in different Web browsers, people who access them with a Web browser that didn't understand some of the HTML tags would be scratching their heads wondering why it looks so weird. There are many Web sites that state on the top of the page that they are "Netscape Enhanced" or "Optimized for Netscape Version x.x." This at least warns people who are using a different Web browser to expect some surprises in how the page is displayed. I recommend doing this as a minimum even though as of this writing about 65 to 75 percent of people who surf with a graphical Web browser use Netscape anyway.

Some people simply design their Web pages to look similar in all the major Web browsers. This is fine, too, but the pages aren't as jazzy as those who make use of the more advanced features of certain Web browsers or nonstandardized HTML versions.

The solution to the above dilemma (as shown in Figure 2.20) is to build a duplicate of your Web site and remove some of the *non-backwards-compatible* HTML tags like <TABLE>. Some *backwards-compatible* HTML tags are <CENTER> and <BODY BACKGROUND>. When Web browser software encounters these tags and doesn't understand them, the information is left justified instead of centered, and the background is ignored, respectively. The page still looks OK though. In the case of a table, however, the <TABLE> tag is ignored, and the text and graphics within the table are tossed all over the place on the page. It pretty much makes the page unreadable.

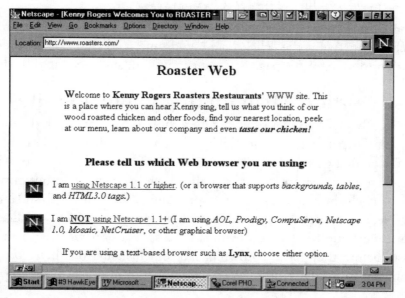

Figure 2.20 Kenny Rogers Roasters offers a Netscape and a non-Netscape version of its Web site.

Add a © copyright notice

If you are concerned about your site design and text being copied by someone else and used on their site, you'll want to provide a copyright notice somewhere within your site. Some contain a link to a separate page while others simply have a copyright line in the footer (bottom of page).

Listen to your audience

The users of your Web site are your best source for improving it. Request their feedback and, more importantly, fix any problems or errors promptly. Acknowledge all feedback quickly, and thank them for their input. This small amount of effort can go a long way on the Web.

Create meaningful hyperlinks

Have you ever seen a Web page with a sentence like the following?

"To read our new report click here."

The word "here" is meaningless in this context. A better hyperlink is:

"Would you like to read our new report?"

Notice how "new report" is underlined (which indicates it links to another Web page)? Avoid the "click here" syndrome, and find the most descriptive word or phrase for the page you want to link to, and use that as the hyperlink.

Use caution when linking to outside sites

I've seen many Web sites provide a hyperlink to Netscape with the intention of helping Internet users who don't use it to download it. This is great for Netscape that gets tons of visitors to its site. The problem with providing this service to your visitors is that once they leave your site, the "out of site, out of mind" cliché holds true. If you say something like, "This Web site is enhanced for Netscape, click here to download it," people who click will end up at Netscape's site. If they do download the software, it will be 15 minutes (at least) before they have it downloaded and installed on their computer. By then, do you really think they will remember to return to your site?

Let's be honest here. My goal for those who visit my book Web site is to get them to my order form page. That way, they have the opportunity to order my book. That's the purpose of my Web page—to sell books. If your goal is to sell something, you want to urge your site visitors to action in a subtle manner.

Some sites add a "take a guided tour" icon and have them click on a right arrow icon or a "next" button. Where do you think you end up? Wherever they want you to! Adding a guided tour to your site may make sense as well. The Net is a different medium, so if you are trying to sell something, you want to draw people in further and further to hear your message, without making them feel as though they're being sold.

Top-Rated Web Sites

Because of the increasing noise level on the Web, there are more and more sites that are guiding *netizens* to high-quality Web sites. You can learn a great deal from the sites listed in the following "Top Sites" lists and in the cool sites pages listed in Chapter 7.

Cool Site of the Day
http://cool.infi.net

Lycos' Top 250
http://www.lycos.com

Point Communication's Top 5% of the Web
http://www.pointcom.com

The WebCrawler Top 25
http://www.webcrawler.com/

Whole Internet Catalog Select Top 50 (GNN)
http://www-e1c.gnn.com/gnn/wic/wics/top.new.html

The World Wide Web Top 1000 (Print Book)
by Point Communications, ISBN 1-56205-577-1, New Riders Publishing, $29.99.

Conclusion

As you can see, there's more to a Web site than just slapping together some text and graphics and throwing it all up onto a Web server. I've covered a lot of style guidelines in this chapter, but I'm sure there are more good ideas that I haven't thought of here. Like I said in the first tip, check out other sites to get ideas.

Now that your Web site has been upgraded or finally put together and placed online, it's time to start thinking about promoting it!

How to Find Almost Anything on the Internet

Chapter 3 Topics

What People Look for on the Internet

All about URLs

The Basics of Net Searching

Finding Things with Search Engines and Directories

Tools to Search Multiple Engines at Once

How to Find Businesses, Products, and Services

Finding People

Reasons Why You Can't Find What You Were Looking For

When I used to talk to prospective clients about creating a Web site for them, the one question they always seemed to ask was, "How will people be able to find my Web site?" Obviously, if people can't find your site, you won't have many visitors. Attracting Web site visitors is what this book is all about. So why a chapter on finding things on the Internet? In order to know how to be found, it's advantageous to know how to find things. When I discuss how to use search engines and Internet directories effectively, you'll see how to make sure that your Web site comes up in a search, or why your site may not appear in the search results (both discussed in Chapter 5).

There's a famous quote about having all the water in the world but not a drop to drink. In this chapter, I try to help you avoid drowning in a sea of information. Some people have likened the Internet to the sum of all human knowledge. There's so much information on the Net that the problem is no longer not finding what you're looking for but finding *too much*. In addition to this challenge, another problem is that there are many different types of resources (FTP, Usenet, mailing lists, WWW, Gopher, email, and so on) and tools (directories, search engines, meta-indexes, etc.) to find information. There's still this myth that the Net is hard to navigate. If you learn how to use a few tools well and how searching works, you'll have no problem.

Certain tools are better at finding certain types of information. In this chapter, you learn what you can find on the Net, the tools to find information with, how searching works, how to formulate a winning query, and common mistakes to avoid. There are lots of resources and tools out there to aid you in your quest for knowledge. I intentionally restrict this chapter to the more powerful ones.

What do people look for on the Internet anyway? Contrary to what you may be thinking, the most popular query on the Web is not sex (it's number 2) but "blank." That is, people pushing the search button without typing anything into the query box. This doesn't mean that they are looking for nothing, but it does make for an interesting statistic. Table 3.1 shows (in no particular order) the things that users seek the most while online.

The question now becomes, what do people use to find the things listed in Table 3.1? The fact that there are a number of Internet search tools that are multipurposed to find different types of information causes a good deal of confusion among new Internet users. Table 3.2 displays some of the more popular Internet search tools and what they are used with.

Table 3.1 Types of Information People Search for on the Internet

Articles

People (email addresses)

Businesses

Products and services information

Generic information on various topics

World Wide Web pages/sites

Software

Advice

There are two models for finding information:

- The search model

- The browse model

In order to determine which model is appropriate for you, ask yourself whether you really know what you're looking for or not. If you know what you are looking for, then the browse model—that is, sifting through subject categories on Yahoo! or pouring through dozens of messages on a specific Usenet newsgroup—is probably your best bet. If you don't really know what you are looking for, but have a general idea, the search model will apply.

Most Internet research resources are free. However, more and more pay services are springing up. The question you may ask yourself is, "Do I really need to pay for information?" The answer is: "That depends on how bad you need the information and how fast." Pay services like Dialog (accessible via the Net by using the Telnet program) are great but expensive (up to $2.50/minute for

Table 3.2 Popular Internet Resources and Their Search Tools

Web resources with directories & search engines

Web resources with Web-based meta-indexes

Gopherspace (articles and general information) with Veronica or Jughead

FTPspace (software and computer files) with ARCHIE

Usenet newsgroups with DejaNews, Infoseek, Excite, etc.

Internet mailing lists with The Liszt

some databases). Infoseek Professional, a subscription-based search service available on the Web is powerful and inexpensive ($10/month plus minimal per-search fees). For the vast majority of the things you or your audience need to find on the Net, the free services will suffice.

URLs (Uniform Resource Locators)

The Internet is full of resources, but how do you identify them? With URLs, that's how. A URL is essentially the address of an Internet resource. It is a standardized term for representing any computer or file on the Internet. Think of a URL as an Internet telephone number. In order to call someone on your phone, you need to know their number, and then you dial that number. No two telephone numbers are the same. By analogy, the same applies to a URL—each is unique.

If you want to access or visit a particular URL, you simply enter it into a box within your Web browser software. Most URLs have an associated protocol, such as HTTP for HyperText Transfer Protocol (Web) and FTP for File Transfer Protocol. A URL contains no spaces and is one continuous line. One misspelling or one word with the wrong capitalization (URLs are case sensitive!) can cause an error. Table 3.3 contains some examples of URLs.

The first part of a URL, before the colon and the two forward slashes, shows the Internet access method (protocol) to be used. The characters after the two forward slashes direct the client software to where the data is located. In the case of Usenet, there are no slashes. Just enter the desired newsgroup name that you want to access.

Table 3.3 *Examples of Different Types of URLs*

http://www.cnet.com	World Wide Web site
ftp://rs.internic.net	File Transfer site
gopher://gopher.gate.net	Gopher site
telnet://phantom.com	Telnet to connect to an Internet computer
wais://nameofdocument	Wide Area Information Server
file://www.linkstar.com/linkstar/button/linkstar.gif	GIF graphics file
news:comp.infosystems.www.announce	Usenet newsgroup

Let's look at the URL for the NCSA What's New Web page:

```
http://www.ncsa.uiuc.edu/SDG/Software/Mosaic/Docs/whats-new.html
```

Notice that the transfer protocol is *http*, which tells you that this URL will bring you to a Web site. You will then see the computer and domain name, *www.ncsa.uiuc.edu* where *www* indicates a World Wide Web server, *ncsa* is the name of the computer or network server, *uiuc* is the domain name, and *edu* is the domain extension type. A series of forward slashes follows with words in between; this is the path name where the file is located within the server. The file is *whats-new.html* (an HTML text file) and is contained in the *SDG/ Software/Mosaic/Docs* directory of uiuc.edu's NCSA WWW server. Please note the UPPER and lower case letters. If you enter *SDG* as *Sdg* or *sdg*, you will receive a "404 Not Found error" which means that the directory path or file does not exist on the server.

Most Internet searches turn up URLs or colored, underlined words that take you to a particular URL (called a *hyperlink*). Now that you understand a bit about URLs and linking, it's time to venture into the world of Internet searching.

Hide and Go Seek: The Basics of Net Searching

Unfortunately, most Internet search engines require the use of advanced search logic (the user types specific characters or makes certain selections in order to receive good results from a search). I've provided a "cheat sheet" for many of the Web-based search systems located in the next section. These will allow you to make use of some of the more advanced features of the particular site without reading the pages of documentation that are available there. The following terms and explanations will help you understand the lingo of searching.

Query box

A box in which keywords and phrases are entered for a search. Additional options with check boxes or radio buttons may be associated with a query box. When you are ready to submit your query, you click on a submit button.

Hit

Not to be confused with a file access or visitor to a Web site (see next chapter), the term hit when used in searching refers to a match. If you perform a search for video AND game, and receive 38 matches, it is also commonly referred to as 38 hits.

Keyword searching

Most search engines utilize this method. You type in a few words and depending on the search utility, documents that contain any or all of those words will be returned. On the first try you usually get too few, or too many, hits.

Boolean operators

Keyword searching uses Boolean logical operators such as: AND, OR, or NOT. The problem with Boolean searching is that it is somewhat difficult to formulate a query.

Plus/minus operators

A few search engines permit these while formulating a query. Plus and minus operators mean the same as the Boolean AND and NOT operators respectively. For example, you could use

```
blue+book-project
```

or

```
blue and book not project
```

which will find documents that contain the word blue and book but not the word project.

Natural language searching

Boolean searching has been around for a long time while natural language searching is relatively new. Many commercial systems now use a *natural language search,* in which the user may type the query in plain English. The results are sorted in relevance order, which is what the search engine thinks you want. A benefit to natural language searching is that no training or experience is required. Ask the question as you would ask a person something.

For example, "How can I lower the risk of getting cancer?" The search engine will pretty much ignore words like *the* and *of* and *a* since these are relatively unimportant. In search lingo, these are called *stop words*. It will, however, utilize words like *lower, risk,* and *cancer*. These significant keywords will be ANDed together for the search. You will receive a list of documents that have all three words in them, ranked from first to last by how relevant the search engine thinks the document is. This process is called *relevance ranking* and is explained next.

Relevance ranking

When performing a search, it isn't the *number* of documents you get back that's really significant, it is the *order*. That's where relevance ranking comes in.

The relevance rating process varies from search engine to search engine. Some of the criteria a search engine may use are:

- **Frequency**—Many search engines rate the results based upon the frequency of the main words within the document. The more times *lower, risk,* and *cancer* appear in a document, the more likely it will be rated high.

- **Location**—Where the words are located within the document. If all three words are in a document title, that document will likely be rated higher than another document that contains those words only in its body. Therefore, the title of your Web pages should contain words that your users would use to find you.

- **Weight**—A search engine will pick out a word like *cancer,* which appears infrequently in documents in the database, and therefore give it a high weight. A word like *risk* may have a slightly lesser weight and a word like *the* may have almost no weight due to its commonality.

When determining the rating of a document, a search engine may multiply the number of times a word appears in the document (frequency) by the weight of the word and combine that with a location multiplying factor. The numbers that are calculated for each document can then be sorted from highest to lowest (the ranking process) after all the documents have been selected and rated. The result will, in theory, be a list of what you are looking for, with the most relevant document being listed first to the least relevant being listed last. If you list your Web site correctly with search engines (for example, using good keywords in the right place), it's more likely that your site will be listed near the top of a search results page. The higher your site is listed, the more likely the searcher will click on it and visit.

Concept-based searching

Concept searching returns what you *mean*, not just what you *type*. If you are looking for a "home in Florida," a keyword search would miss documents that contain something like "apartment in sunshine state" or "house in Ft. Lauderdale." A concept-based search would realize that sunshine state is Florida's state motto and that Ft. Lauderdale is a city in Florida. It would also realize that house and apartment are places people consider "home." Concept-based searching is quite advanced. The Excite search engine performs concept-based searches.

Stemming

Most search engines found on the Net permit *stemming* (aka *substring matching*). For example, if you are looking for information about gambling, your search results may include documents about *a gambler, gamblers, to gamble,* and *the act of gambling.* All these words have the stem of *gambl.* Stemming can be a good thing and a bad thing. If you are looking for information about sports and a document contains the phrase sporting goods, the document would appear in your search results if stemming is used. If you were looking for something in general about sports, the document that is returned in the search results related to sporting goods would be superfluous and would be unneeded by you. When you search a database that contains hundreds or thousands of documents that contain a word that is stemmed, you get back lots of hits on your search criteria. Basically, you get way too much information to choose from, with lots of it unrelated to what you are looking for.

Case matching

Most search engines treat queries using words in lower case as a case-*in*sensitive query. That is, it will return all words that have any combination of uppercase and lowercase letters. When you perform a query using words with uppercase letters, words that match the case exactly are returned. For example, a search using *Ibm* will miss documents containing *IBM,* but a search using *ibm* will return documents with *ibm, Ibm, IBM, IBm, iBM,* and *IbM.* Keep this in mind when you list your site in the various search engines (see Chapter 5).

Phrases

A *phrase* is a string of words located next to each other in sequence. Many search engines accept phrases, but they often need to be placed in double quotes ("). Some engines assume words that are separated by punctuation marks (such as dashes) are phrases. An example of a phrase search would be if you are looking for something about the *World Series* and you submitted the search as a phrase, you would get a document like:

The Atlanta Braves: 1995 *World Series* Winners!

but would not get a document like:

An analysis of the television *series* As The *World* Turns.

Notice that both document titles contain the words "world" and "series." If you performed an AND search (world AND series) or an OR search (world OR series) instead of a phrased search, you would have received both documents as matches (50 percent accurate).

Spider (aka crawler, robot, or gatherer)

A *Spider* is an automated program that indexes documents, titles, and/or a portion of each document acquired by traversing the Web. Spiders do this in one of two ways: *breadth first* (start at the top level of a Web site and follow all the top level links to other Web pages) and *depth first* (follow each link as far down as possible before following links to external pages). Lycos is a good example of a depth first crawler. Spiders typically offer less accurate search results than indexers. If you have ever heard the phrase "whatever the cat drags in," you have a good idea of how a Spider operates. Some Webmasters (people who run Web servers) don't like Spider programs because of the high load that they can put on the server while indexing.

Indexer

A type of search engine that indexes documents, titles, and/or descriptions of documents from user-supplied submissions. Probably the best known indexer is Yahoo!.

Harvester

A program that keeps indexing until it has exhausted all the sites it can find. Veronica is a good example of this. A Harvester differs from a Spider in that a Spider continuously seeks new resources and is never done.

Finding General Information, Articles, Web Sites, and More with Search Engines and Internet Directories

Search engines are the most popular way to find resources on the Internet. There are quite a few search engines on the Net, each with its own strengths and weaknesses. The more familiar you are with a particular search engine, the more productive your searching will be on it.

How Search Engines Differ

- Accuracy of search (whether they return the documents/information you asked for)

- Depth of search (whether they return all of the documents available in the database that are relevant)

- The amount of content (size of database) that is indexed

- What they index (Lycos indexes part of each document, Open Text and Infoseek index all the words in each document)

- The selection algorithm used (how they rank results)

- Types of searches available (keyword or phrase, Boolean or natural language)

- The currency of the information in the database (Infoseek is updated every 30 days or so while a link in Yahoo! may be dead for months)

- Speed of the search (most are very quick, typically within a few seconds)

- Format of the results (WebCrawler returns titles while most others return short summaries)

Armed with the information from the beginning and end of this chapter, you'll be able to make the most of the sites listed in this section. Most people end up trying them all, and then they pick just a few as their search systems of choice. In many cases, which one you use is determined by personal preference and what you are looking for. For example:

- When I'm looking for a Web site and I know part of its URL or I know the name of the Web page, I'll use a spider search engine like Lycos, WebCrawler, or Alta Vista.

- If I'm looking for a subject or topic, I'll use LinkStar or Yahoo!

- If I'm looking for a business product or service, I'll use LinkStar or the Commercial Sites Index.

- If I'm looking for a person, I'll use Four11.

For the most part, there's an approximate 60 percent to 80 percent overlap in content with most search engines because many duplicate each other's work (especially spiders).

Included with each entry is my own personal opinion/review of each search site when it comes to the content (amount and quality) and accuracy (at finding what you are looking for) of each system. For the most part, they all are about as easy or difficult to use as the next one. The ones listed here will help you find that needle in the Webstack.

Alta Vista by Digital

http://altavista.digital.com
Type: Spider/Crawler
Content Rating: ★ ★ ★ ★
Accuracy Rating: ★ $^1/_2$

Publicly unleashed on the Net in December 1995, Digital's Alta Vista search engine instantly claimed to be the largest Web index offering users access to over 8 billion words contained within more than 16 million Web pages (see Figure 3.1).

Unique features include the ability to perform a proximity search using "near" (for example, look for a word *near*, rather than adjacent to or far away from, another word) and selecting a start and end date to include or exclude documents. Using *near* returns documents if the two words are within 10 words of each other.

Cheat Sheet for Alta Vista

- Alta Vista offers simple and advanced query screens, as well as detailed help.

- Use quotation marks for phrases (for example, "bozo the clown").

- A lower case search will return capitalized words as well.

- Using capitals causes case matching and excludes words not capitalized the same way.

- It requires an asterisk for stemming: (run★ gives run, runner, running, runt, etc.).

- It accepts plus/negative (+/-) to add or delete terms in a query.

- Punctuation is treated as a space (bozo.clown = bozo clown).

Excite

http://www.excite.com
Type: Indexer
Content Rating: ★ ★ ★ $^1/_2$
Accuracy Rating: ★ ★ ★ $^1/_2$

Excite is a product of Architext Software and claims to have the largest fully indexed Web database, containing more than 1.5 million pages. The specs are as follows:

- Web Documents: Over 1.5 million full Web pages.

- Usenet: Indexes over 1 million articles from 10,000+ Usenet newsgroups.

- Classifieds: Search Usenet classified advertisements. Contains two weeks worth of ads.

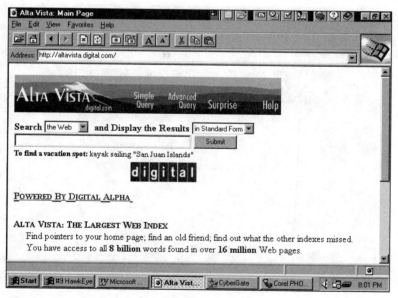

Figure 3.1 *Digital's Alta Vista Spider.*

- Reviews: Search Excite's database of more than 35,000 Web site reviews. It's essentially a guide book to the Net, helping users decide whether they should visit a particular site or not.

Cheat Sheet for Excite

- Excite doesn't use any special searching syntax. Just type in words or phrases, and Excite will do the rest (see Figure 3.2).

- If you want a word to have a higher weight to it, simply repeat the word several times in the query box, and Excite will give that word extra consideration.

- If you are searching for something that has several common spellings, just type all the variations.

- If you know what you are looking for, leave out words that aren't unique.

Infoseek Guide

http://guide.infoseek.com
Type: Indexer
Content Rating: ★ ★ ★ $^{1}/_{2}$
Accuracy Rating: ★ ★ ★ $^{1}/_{2}$

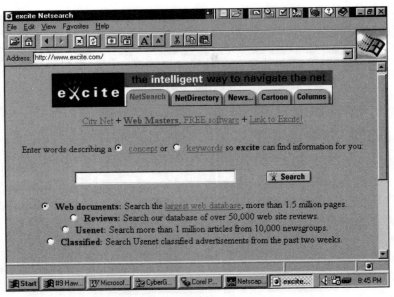

Figure 3.2 Excite uses concept-based searching.

Widely believed to be the most comprehensive search engine that indexes Web sites, newswires, Usenet, magazines and more, Infoseek claims to receive over 5 million information requests per day from over 1 million unique Internet users worldwide. It received *PC Computing's* "1995 Most Valuable Product" award for the best Internet tool.

The Infoseek Guide, shown in Figure 3.3, lets users both search and browse over 1 million Web pages, 10,000+ Usenet newsgroups (and their FAQs), Gopher and FTP sites, and various other Internet resources at no charge. Infoseek Guide is the site used by Netscape's Net Search facility, considered by many to be some of the most valuable Real Estate on the Net.

Infoseek also offers a fee-based search service called Infoseek Professional. It offers comprehensive access to public and commercial databases for $9.95 a month, which includes up to 100 queries. The service is available at **http://professional.infoseek.com,** and there is an option to sign up for a free trial with no obligation.

Cheat Sheet for Infoseek

- Infoseek utilizes natural language searching.

- It treats adjacent capitalized words as one word or name. To search for multiple names, separate them by a comma.

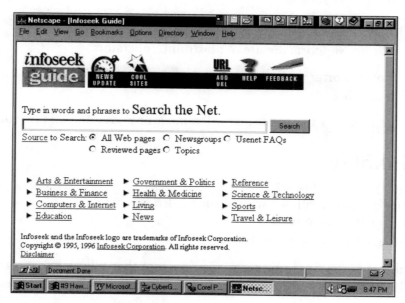

Figure 3.3 The Infoseek Guide.

- Use double quotation marks (") to identify a phrase.

- Use square brackets [ ] around words that you want to search for which occur within 100 words of each other within a document.

- Use plus and minus signs in front of words (without a space between the sign and the word) to tell Infoseek to find documents that must contain or not contain that word respectively.

- Boolean operators and wildcards are not needed.

Inktomi

http://inktomi.berkeley.edu
Type: Spider/Crawler
Content Rating: ★ ★ ★
Accuracy Rating: ★ ★

Inktomi is a name used by Plains Indians for a mythological spider. The search system is part of a project at the University of California at Berkeley and was implemented by graduate student Paul Gauthier and Professor Eric Brewer. Inktomi uses "parallel computing technology to create a scalable Web server" that results in very fast searching.

Cheat Sheet for Inktomi

- You may enter up to 10 query words.

- Inktomi supports the use of plus/minus operators.

- Words shorter than three letters and common words like *and* are ignored in searches.

- Stemming is automatic and will remove any common ending you add on.

LinkStar

http://www.linkstar.com
Type: Indexer combined with a true fielded database
Content Rating: ★ ★ ★
Accuracy Rating: ★ ★ ★ ★

LinkStar is the first Internet navigation tool that fully integrates traditional full-text keyword searching with a true fielded database. The result is an

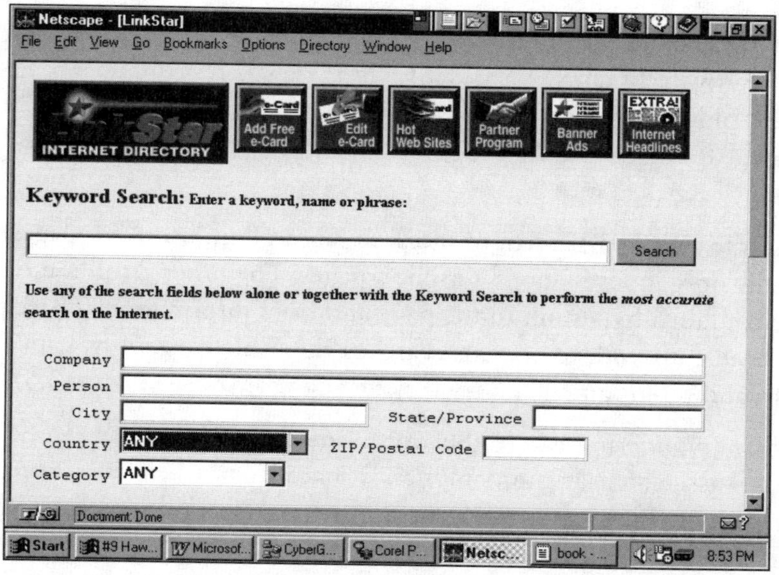

Figure 3.4 LinkStar, a "next-generation" search engine and Internet directory.

unprecedented precision in localized Internet searching (see Figure 3.4). LinkStar users can find listings down to the city and/or zip code level. It's the first directory that makes it easy to find organizations with an Internet presence that are physically located in your neighborhood.

The content of the directory is comprised of *e-Cards* (electronic business cards). These e-Cards include contact information, applicable subject categories for the Web site, and a 50-word description of the site or Internet resource.

Aside from the localized searching capability, LinkStar's unique features include email and URL address verification (which ensures an accurate and up-to-date database), the ability to email yourself the search results, and password security for user submissions.

Cheat Sheet for LinkStar

- You can search LinkStar three ways. You can perform a simple keyword search; combine it with company, name, city, state or zip code fields; or search by category.

- The system is icon driven and very easy to use.

Lycos

http://www.lycos.com
Type: Spider/Crawler
Content Rating: ★ ★ ★ ★
Accuracy Rating: ★ ★ $^1/_2$

Claims to index 91 percent of the Web (about 8 million Web pages); however, it really only indexes about a million pages. The other 7 million or so listings only contain a hyperlink to the page and brief information. These pages have not been fully indexed. Lycos searches the Web constantly, catalogs what it finds, and builds a new index every few days or so (see Figure 3.5).

If you're wondering where the word *lycos* comes from, it's Greek for spider. Lycos was created at the computer science department at Carnegie-Mellon University in Pittsburgh and went commercial after teaming up with a venture capital firm. Today, it's a public company.

Cheat Sheet for Lycos

- Lycos defaults to an OR search. You'll probably want to choose *Search Options* to fine-tune your search and change to an AND search.

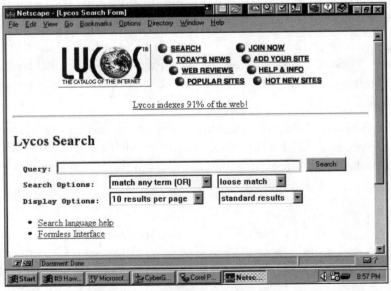

Figure 3.5 Lycos considers itself to be "The Catalog of the Internet."

- You cannot use plus (+) in your search. If you want to search for the computer language of C++, use quotes "C++."

- Lycos gives you the option of how loose or strict it is when trying to provide you with matches to your search criteria. Choose "strict" to really narrow your search.

- You may choose a more detailed list or a summary of your results to be displayed. Choose summary if you have lots of documents you want to sift through quickly.

Open Text Index

http://www.opentext.com/omw/f-omw.html
Type: Indexer
Content Rating: ★ ★ ★
Accuracy Rating: ★ ★ $\frac{1}{2}$

Open Text Corporation sells search software, and it created a site to showcase its Open Text 6 product. The Open Text Index has fully indexed over 1 million Web pages and 1 billion words.

Cheat Sheet for Open Text Index

- Three types of searches are offered: *simple, power,* and *weighted.* Power and weighted are a bit confusing for newbies. Stick with simple when possible.

- Use drop-down box to select a PHRASE, AND, or OR search.

- You can avoid stemming by adding a space to a word.

- Plurals must be specified in the simple search or you'll need to use the power search.

- There's a lot of help documentation for advanced searching available online.

WebCrawler

http://www.webcrawler.com
Type: Spider/Crawler
Content Rating: ★ ★ ★
Accuracy Rating: ★ ★

Initially developed by Brian Pinkerton as a research project at the University of Washington in Seattle, WebCrawler was later bought by America Online, which hired Pinkerton to continue its development (see Figure 3.6).

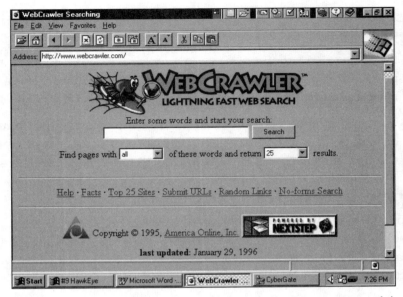

Figure 3.6   WebCrawler, another academic project gone commercial.

WebCrawler's index is roughly 130 MB, which contains information on over 250,000 different documents. This is what WebCrawler has already explored. The rest of its database (tables of all known, unvisited documents) occupies another 200 MB or so, and contains data on over 1,800,000 different documents.

Cheat Sheet for WebCrawler

- Its interface is very easy and self explanatory. Help is available, but you probably won't need it.

World Wide Web Worm

http://wwww.cs.colorado.edu/wwww/
Type: Spider/Crawler
Content Rating: ★ ★ ★
Accuracy Rating: ★ ★

Created by Oliver McBryan, the WWWW serves about 3,000,000 URLs to 2,000,000 users each month. It was voted the "Best Navigational Aid" in the *1994 Best of the Web Awards*. A search is conducted, on average, every 10 seconds, 24 hours a day.

Cheat Sheet for World Wide Web Worm

- WWWW allows you to select 1, 4, 50, 500, or 5,000 citations, which is more than any other tool (most restrict you to about 100 max.).

- Keywords are not case sensitive.

- Any non-alphanumeric characters in keywords are replaced by spaces.

- Keywords of one or two characters, and certain common three- and four-character words, are omitted from the search.

Yahoo!

http://www.yahoo.com
Type: Spider/Crawler
Content Rating: ★ ★ ★
Accuracy Rating: ★ ★ ★ $^{1}/_{2}$

Yahoo! was created by David Filo and Jerry Yang while at Stanford University in California. They started compiling lists of neat Web sites for themselves, and one day they decided to share their list with the Internet community. In a short time, it became wildly popular, which prompted them to compile even more sites and then offer others an opportunity to submit their sites to the list. It has been likened to the "table of contents to the Net" due to its detailed, hierarchical subject index with various levels of depth (see Figure 3.7). Yahoo! is privately funded by venture capital and some minority investors (e.g., Reuters) and went public in April 1996.

Content is generated from users who fill out a form (see Chapter 5 for how to add your site). Yahoo! does not accept every entry that is submitted as they use what's called an "editorial filter" whereby Yahoo! employees review each submission. They have over 110,000 listings as of this writing.

Cheat Sheet for Yahoo!

- For a more accurate search or to have better control over the results, choose *options*.

- Capitalization is ignored in searches unless you choose it in options.

- Yahoo! has the best categories of any search site I've seen. If you know what you are looking for, the categories can help you find multiple sites fitting your criteria. You can even search within a category for very accurate results.

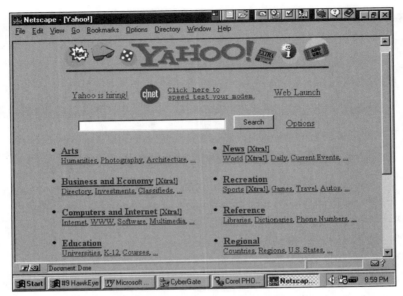

Figure 3.7 Yahoo! Probably the most well-known of all the Internet search engines and directories.

Multiple Search Submission Pages

These Web pages are a compilation of various forms-based search tools found on the Internet. The search tools have been combined to form a consistent interface and a centralized search point. These are essentially one-stop sites where you can choose among many search engines. Go to these to compare search results among different engines without having to know each site's URL.

ALL-IN-ONE Search Page

http://www.albany.net/allinone/

Created by William D. Cross, this page contains a lot of search sites. I was very impressed with how quickly new site requests are made. If you submit a new resource that isn't yet part of the ALL-IN-ONE search page, you'll get credit and a hyperlink if you so desire.

Categories, places, and things you can search include: World Wide Web, General Internet, Specialized Interest, Software, People, News/Weather, Publications/Literature, Technical Reports, Documentation, Desk Reference, and Other Interesting Searches/Services.

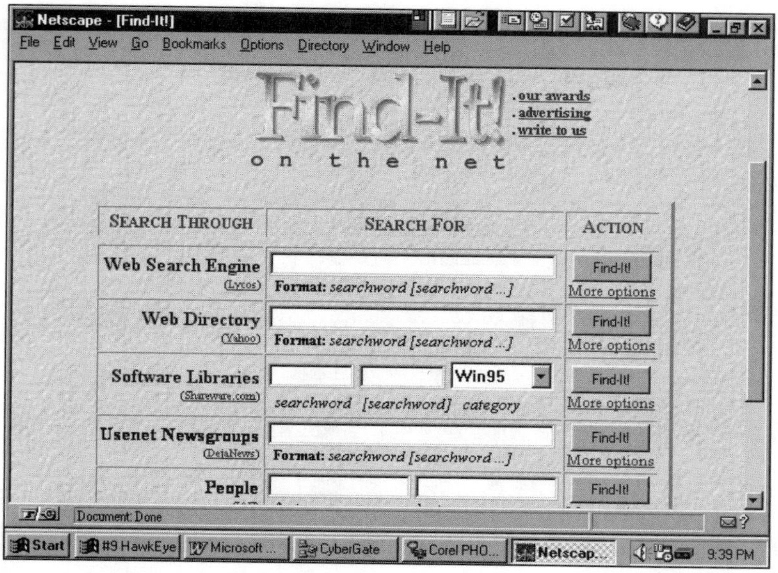

Figure 3.8   *The name says it all.*

Find-It!

http://www.itools.com

Run by Paul Sarena, the It! media site offers three separate sites in one: Find-It!, Research-It!, and Promote-It! All of these are worth visiting, especially Promote-It!, which is a great resource for helping you promote your Web site.

Internet Sleuth

http://www.intbc.com/sleuth/

The Internet Sleuth is a collection of over 900 searchable databases on the Internet on a wide variety of subjects from Agriculture to Web Search Engines (categories shown in Figure 3.9). The Sleuth was created by Sally Elliott, an information broker, who found that there were just too many searchable sites out there to keep track of effectively. The Sleuth contains more searchable databases in one place than any other Internet site and is one of the most useful sites on the Internet when it comes to looking for things.

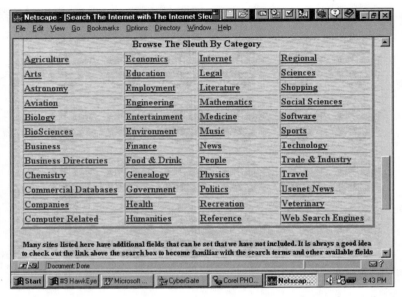

Figure 3.9 *The Internet Sleuth is essentially a meta-index of search engines.*

MetaSearch

http://metasearch.com

Another one of Scott Banister's (of Submit It! fame) creations. Permits you to separately search the Web, search for software and search through a list of Net-based dictionaries and thesauruses.

WebSearch

http://www.websearch.com

WebSearch was originally inspired by NCSA's (National Center for Supercomputing Applications at the University of Illinois) Experimental Search Engine Meta-Index. The page lists search boxes for information servers, software, people, publications, news/FAQs, and documentation. Some of the information servers available include: WebCrawler, Open Market's Commercial Sites Index, AliWeb, CUSI, Jump Station, WWW Worm, Yellow Pages, Yahoo!, EInet Galaxy, InterNic, Savvy Search, Infoseek, Starting Point, and Lycos.

Multi-Threaded Search Sites

If you don't know which of the search engines to use, try a multi-threaded search site. These let you search across multiple directories and publications simultaneously. By rummaging through many databases all at once, you should be able to find what you're looking for without clicking all over creation in the process. They typically permit you to choose which engines to search and how long you will wait for results (some queries may take minutes or even an hour!). Your search is as slow as the slowest search engine. Try the following as one-stop search shops.

Amdahl's Internet Exploration Page

http://www.amdahl.com/internet/meta-index.html

Amdahl, the computer manufacturer, sponsors this page. It is a combination multi-threaded search page and a multiple search submission page.

MetaCrawler

http://metacrawler.cs.washington.edu:8080/index.html
Created by Erik Selberg and Oren Etzioni, MetaCrawler searches eight different search engines. Results are displayed in a uniform format, and you can sort the results several different ways.

SavvySearch

http://parsons.cs.colostate.edu/~dreiling/smartform.html

SavvySearch is an experimental search system designed to query multiple search engines simultaneously and in real time (see Figure 3.10). Sites that SavvySearch queries include: Aliweb, CSTR, DejaNews, EINET Galaxy, FTPSearch95, Infoseek, Inktomi, Internet Movie Database, Lycos, NIKOS, Open Text, Pathfinder, Point Search, SIFT—Stanford Information Filtering Tool, Tribal Voice, Virtual Software Library, WebCrawler, Yahoo!, and Yellow Pages.

Finding Businesses, Products, and Services

You can find businesses through the typical search engines like Yahoo and Lycos, but your search will often return a lot more than just businesses. This

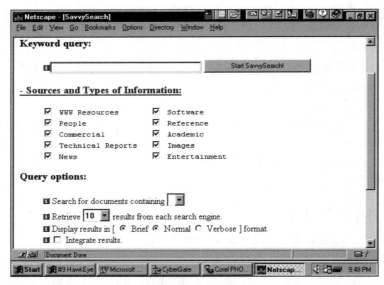

Figure 3.10 *SavvySearch is great for the unsavvy searcher!*

extra noise makes it difficult to find what you are looking for. The following sites are some of the most popular when it comes to looking specifically for businesses, products, and services.

555-1212.com

http://www.555-1212.com

Based on the popular telephone information number, this site is great if you are looking for businesses within a specific area code.

BizWeb

http://www.bizweb.com

Lists a couple of thousand companies by category.

Commercial Advertising & Marketing Server

http://www.comcomsystems.com/search/en/welcome1.html

Search for a company, product, or service by name, category, or location.

Commercial Sites Index by Open Market

http://www.directory.net

Was the first Web site to concentrate on commercial sites (see Figure 3.11). It was started by Henry Houth from MIT and it grew so large and so quickly

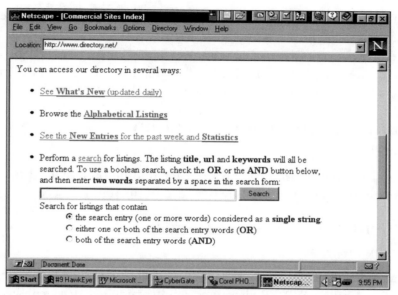

Figure 3.11 The Commercial Sites Index, aka "directory dot net."

that he turned it over to Open Market, a company that produces electronic commerce and Web server software. It's one of my personal favorites.

InterActive Yellow Pages

http://netcenter.com/yellows.html

Mike Mathiesen's NetCenter. Businesses can be found by category.

Internet Business Directory International

http://www.ibdi.com

Claims to have over 2 million listings. You may search by business name, city, state, zip code, and telephone area code. Of limited value since free listings do not link to a Web site nor have a description (IBDI charges $99 for a Web link and description).

Internet Mall by Dave Taylor

http://www.internet-mall.com/index.html

In February 1994, the first version of the Internet Mall was released via email as a Frequently Asked Questions (FAQs) document that contained just 34 companies. The Internet Mall idea came from research that Dave was doing for an article for *Internet World Magazine* about commercial ventures on the

Net. Since then it has grown to over 6,500 cybershops. The Internet Mall concentrates on products and services such as bookstores, insurance, food, etc. It receives an estimated 6,200 visitors each day. There is no charge to be listed in the Internet Mall. More details of getting listed here (and the many other places listed within this chapter) can be found in Chapter 5.

LinkStar Internet Directory

http://www.linkstar.com

This site is multipurposed and great for finding both general resources and businesses. Details were already provided in the previous section.

World Wide Yellow Pages

http://www.yellow.com

"The Yellow Pages for the Next 100 Years." Allows searching by heading, business name, or location. WWYP allows users to enter businesses that aren't online, so your results may include businesses that you cannot visit online for more information.

Virtual Yellow Pages

http://www.vyp.com

Find organizations through a simple search interface or browse categories.

Finding People (and Their Email Addresses)

In addition to general and esoteric information, the Internet has been used to find long lost friends and relatives. With the Net being populated by millions of people (with thousands joining daily), finding someone or someone's email address can be a challenge. The following utilities can help you in your quest. In addition to these tools, a great resource called "Finding an email address" can be found at **http://sunsite.oit.unc.edu/~masha/**, which will give you more in-depth tricks.

Four11

http://www.four11.com
Overall Rating: ★ ★ ★ ★

Four11 claims to be the largest white page directory on the Internet, with more than 4.6 million listings. It's great for finding someone's email address as long as you know their name. The creators have made it clear that the directory is not to be used to compile mailing lists and that their usage rules state that users should not contact anyone listed in the directory in a way that the person would find objectionable.

The directory is funded by a combination of sponsors and membership upgrades. Four11 receives listings from three sources:

1. Public sources such as people who post to Usenet
2. Voluntary registrations
3. Automatic registrations through Internet access providers

Four11 uses a very simple search screen, as well as an expanded search screen for those who have provided a listing (see Figure 3.12). You may enter your free email address (and Web page) listing by selecting the *Free Upgrade* link on the home page. You may also edit your listings via an online form on the site. Four11 features include:

- An alternative Names feature that allows you to be found by a nickname, maiden name, etc.

- A "Group Connections" option that allows users to enter information about themselves, such as past schools, locations, organizations as well as hobbies, Net hangouts, etc. This allows users to search for people who share similar interests or schools, organizations, etc.

- One email address per listing for security purposes. Email addresses are unique identifiers so no one can falsely register the address of another user.

- Four11 also acts as a PGP (Pretty Good Privacy) public encryption key server.

- Sleeper Searches. This is great. It allows you to store a search request in the system. You receive an email message whenever a match is found. For example, if you are looking for an old school chum or someone who shares similar interests as you, enter your search once and you'll be automatically notified if anyone registers with Four11 who matches your criteria. Although Four11 is free, this feature is only available to users who pay for the membership upgrade.

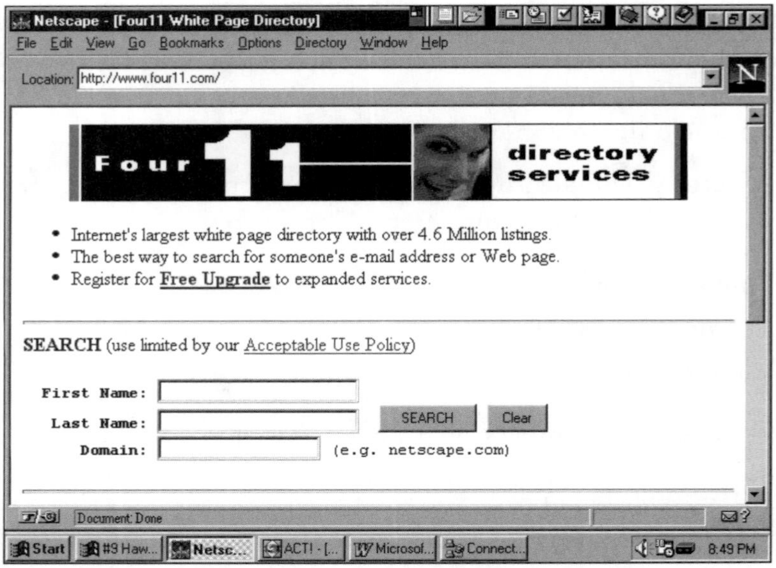

Figure 3.12 Four11's search screen.

Internet Address Finder

http://www.iaf.net
Overall Rating: ★ ★ ★ ¹/₂

IAF is giving Four11 a run for its money with over 3.6 million entries. It is free to add a listing and to search, as it is advertiser supported (see Chapter 6 for rates).

LinkStar Internet Directory

http://www.linkstar.com
Overall Rating: ★ ★ ★

You can find someone's email address by entering the person's name (or portion thereof). No need to remember anyone's email address so long as they are listed in LinkStar.

Netfind

http://www.ig.dk/ig/Netfind.html (Gopher Menu)
Overall Rating: ★ ★ ¹/₂

Netfind is an Internet white pages directory facility. You can search using the person's first, last, or login name. If you are looking for someone who is using a site that is not directly connected to the Net, Netfind probably won't be able to find anything.

InterNIC Whois

http://rs.internic.net/cgi-bin/whois
Overall Rating: ★ ★ $^1/_2$

This is a good source to use if the person you are looking for is involved in the Internet in some way. The Whois database primarily consists of information from Internet domain name applications (the successful ones). Whois helps you find email addresses and in some cases a phone number and address for a person and/or company. It acts as a distributed database system that is available on nearly all Unix machines. It is most often used to find domain names.

For example, if you are looking for the domain name for a certain company, you can enter the company name in the query box. If you are looking to see what organization owns a specific domain name, you can simply enter the domain name (i.e., coriolis.com) and you'll see something like the following.

```
The Coriolis Group, Inc. (CORIOLIS-DOM)
7339 E. Acoma Drive, Suite 7
Scottsdale, AZ  85260

Domain Name: CORIOLIS.COM

Administrative Contact:
 Duntemann, Jeff (JD131) jeffd@CORIOLIS.COM
 (602) 483-0192 x3 ext. 3
Technical Contact, Zone Contact:
 Fisher, William (WF17) bilfish@INDIRECT.COM
 602-274-0100

Record last updated on 24-Jun-95.
Record created on 28-Jun-94.

Domain servers in listed order:

NS1.INDIRECT.COM        165.247.1.3
NS2.INDIRECT.COM        165.247.1.17
```

Finger

If you have a Unix "shell" Internet account, you can use *finger* to find someone's name from an email address that you already know. Finger is available on just about every Internet access provider. To use it, you simply type "finger user@domain.ext" and if the computer they are using accepts finger connections, it will return any information the user permits to be seen (especially a *.plan* file if it exists). A *.plan* file can optionally be created by most Unix users and can contain whatever information they want to let the world know about (including an invitation to visit their Web site).

Finding Internet Mailing Lists (aka Email Discussion Groups)

Internet mailing lists (see Chapter 10) themselves contain a wealth of information about very specialized topics. But before you can benefit from the information exchanged within a specific list, you first need to find the list itself. There are a number of ways to find mailing lists that discuss a topic that you or your prospective clients are interested in. I'll list a few sources, but by far and away the best place to look is The Liszt.

The Liszt

http://www.liszt.com
Overall Rating: ★ ★ ★ ★

The Liszt was created by Scott Southwick and is a searchable directory of over 23,000 listserv, listproc, majordomo, and independently managed lists culled from approximately 500 Internet sites. If you create your own Internet mailing list (a tactic some people use to promote their company and/or Web site), be sure to promote it in The Liszt. There is a button for adding your list for inclusion (see Figure 3.13).

Cheat Sheet for The Liszt

- By default, Liszt uses substring matches and uses AND searches.

- Select *options* for a more refined search.

- Denote phrases by putting the words in quotes.

List of Publicly Accessible Mailing Lists

http://www.neosoft.com/internet/paml/index.html

Maintained by Stephanie da Silva, browsable by subject and name (there is no search option). Probably the oldest list of mailing lists.

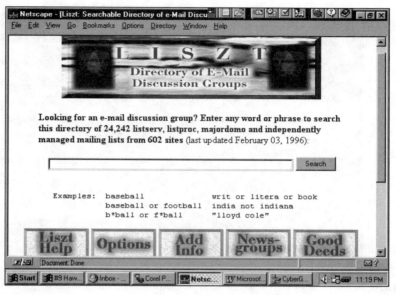

Figure 3.13   The Liszt is The Place to go for finding Internet mailing lists.

Usenet Newsgroups

With well over 13,000 individual Usenet newsgroups covering just about every topic imaginable, a needle can really get lost in the haystack. Before any search tools started indexing newsgroup messages, users had to browse particular groups for information of interest. If you were looking for a very specific type of information, it might be in a message on any number of groups. The problem was, it took too long to scour all the messages posted to all the possible groups where your target might be located. Today, you can ferret out desired information contained in the various Usenet newsgroups using several traditional search engines, but DejaNews is the defacto leader in Usenet searching. The benefit to using these engines is that you don't need to know which newsgroups contain what you are looking for. The bulk of Usenet consists of current information, and a smaller portion contains timeless information such as FAQs that are posted once a month. Here are the best ways to search Usenet newsgroup postings.

Alta Vista (Digital)

http://www.altavista.digital.com
Overall Rating: ★ ★ ★ ¹/₂

Offers a full-text index to more than 13,000 Usenet newsgroups and the articles posted on them. The database is updated in real time.

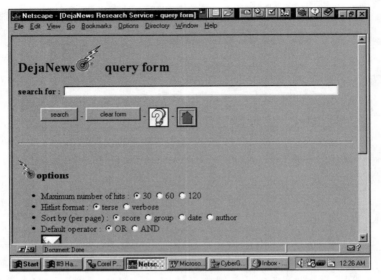

Figure 3.14 DejaNews: The most popular way to search Usenet newsgroups.

Deja News

http://www.dejanews.com
Overall Rating: ★ ★ ★ ★

DejaNews is the largest collection of indexed archived Usenet news anywhere (see Figure 3.14). It offers many search options as well as the ability to create a query filter to limit your search by newsgroup, date, or author. DejaNews is another sponsorable site where you can purchase a banner ad (see Chapter 6).

Excite

http://www.excite.com
Overall Rating: ★ ★ ★

Indexes over 10,000 groups and has another index you can search that contains only classified ads from certain newsgroups.

Infoseek Guide

http://guide.infoseek.com
Overall Rating: ★ ★ ★

Infoseek Guide provides Usenet searching, as well as Infoseek Professional (**http://professional.infoseek.com**), its subscription search service that indexes 10,000+ groups and keeps one month's worth of messages locally.

Stanford Information Filtering Tool (SIFT)

http://sift.stanford.edu

SIFT gathers tens of thousands of new articles which are posted in Usenet newsgroups, and filters them against topics you specify. The results appear on a personalized Web page that you can access with a username and password. The service is free, and is akin to a news clipping service.

Searching for Software

ARCHIE

ARCHIE is primarily used to search what's called *FTPspace*. It's a program that searches public file archives and returns a list of what files meet your search criteria and where those files can be found (i.e., what computer FTP address they are sitting on and where they are located within that computer). An Internet provider in England has compiled a list of ARCHIE servers available via the Web. By clicking on one of the listings, you'll be able to search for software and various other files via a Web-based interface. ARCHIE can also be used from the Unix shell by typing the word archie and then the name of the file (e.g., archie DOOM). The list of servers can be found at **http://pubweb.nexor.co.uk/public/archie/servers.html**.

"A complete reference to Anonymous FTP sites." (tile.net/FTP)

http://www.tile.net/tile/ftp-list/index.html

FTP sites are organized by each site's content. If a user is interested in PC software, the index contains entries for PC, and several FTP sites that have software for it. The sites are also organized into categories, such as by country or time zone, so that users can locate sites suited to just about any need. This is a browsable listing and not a searchable site.

In addition to these sources, if you are specifically looking for software, there are several companies that house large collections of titles within their sites and offer them for sale. The shareware.com site is one of them (**http://www.shareware.com**).

Searching "Gopher-space" with Veronica

Gopher is a hierarchical, menu-driven system that organizes information (which may be located anywhere in the world) by subject category. Menus and submenus contain directories and files of information. As you burrow deeper into the menu structure, you find more and more specific pieces of information. There are currently over 3,000 separate Gopher servers on the Internet. Gopher files can contain pictures and sound, but most of the information on various Gopher servers is text.

Veronica is the best way to search for data contained on various Gopher servers. Simply enter a keyword or two into the query box and a menu of results will be generated for you. From there, you can select each individual resource to view. Information on how to search using Veronica and a list of Veronica servers can be found at **http://www.cs.unh.edu:70/links/veronica**.

Possible Reasons Why You Couldn't Find What You Were Looking for When Using an Internet Search Engine

- The most probable reason is that your search was too narrow. Loosen it up and see if you get any hits. If that doesn't work, read on!

- If you are looking for a specific Web site or resource, it may not be indexed in the search engine you are using. The database of most search engines is built up through people submitting URLs and descriptions/keywords of the resource. If a site wasn't submitted to the search site, it won't show up in a search no matter how good a query you form!

- If the resource was submitted, it may not have been indexed yet. Yahoo! has had lag times of two to three weeks from the time a URL was submitted to when it was indexed and available in the database. Most sites require a few days (like Lycos).

- If you were using a Spider/Crawler type of search system, the Web page you were looking for probably did not contain any unique or meaningful words in the first few lines or title of the page. This is why it is important to place key words that people would use to find you in the beginning of your home page (see Chapter 5). Another reason may be that the server is using a *robots.txt* file to ward off automated search systems and so the resource was not indexed. Yet another possibility may be that the resource or Web page is located behind a firewall and therefore was never indexed due to security restrictions into the site.

10 Internet Searching Tips to Find What You're Looking For

Tip #1: Poor search results are usually due to a poor searcher!

If you have been around computers long enough, you've heard the acronym GIGO (Garbage In, Garbage Out). If you don't get enough or get too much or get totally unrelated information back from a search, it probably has more to do with what you asked for and how you asked for it rather than the search engine. Follow the steps below to ensure acceptable results when searching the Net.

Tip #2: Look in the right place.

Looking for a Web site that sells furniture with NetFind (a utility to find people) isn't going to work no matter how good a searcher you are. It's important to use the right tool for the job.

Tip #3: Learn how the search engine or tool works.

All search tools are not the same. Most of the tools you can use on the Net are customized to fit certain needs. They vary in default settings, syntax, etc. Most places you go to find things have FAQs or specific documentation on how to use it for best results. Take a few minutes and familiarize yourself with the particular search engine or tool that you want to use. I listed the important things in the various cheat sheets earlier in this chapter.

Tip #4: Use only discriminating terms (be specific).

The ideal query consists of terms (words or phrases) that can only be found in the documents that you seek. Unique words not found in other documents will yield more focused results. It is possible to "over focus" and get nothing back. For example, if you were looking for information about Ronald Reagan and you received a null set as the result of your search, you could try a search using words like president, politician, actor, or a phrase like "great communicator." Obviously, using his name is best because it's unique.

Tip #5: Start simply (add or delete search terms as needed).

After you see the results, pick a few and look for terms that are relevant. In the next iteration of your search, add the term or terms to what you used to get those results. This should help to narrow the results to a manageable level. By the same token, you may need to widen your search if little or no results were received.

Tip #6: Avoid common spelling mistakes (or any mistakes!).

Search engines don't have spelling correctors (at least not yet). If you misspell a word, you may still get a couple of documents back but only because the word was misspelled within those documents. For words that can be spelled multiple ways, you need to enter each possible spelling. You may want to do the search by separating each word with an "or." For example: *their* or *they're* or *there*. You'll find all documents that contain any of the variations. Also, don't forget about something that means the same thing but isn't spelled similarly, for example: *12* or *twelve* or *dozen*.

Tip #7: When necessary, use proper case and capitalization.

Some search engines require that you match the case while others do not. Some default to a certain case matching system and others offer case matching as a search option via a radio button on the query form. Proper names usually should be entered with the correct capitalization. Remember tip #3. For example, Infoseek will only return uppercase matches if you type uppercase (it will omit lowercase matches), but will return words with uppercase *and* lowercase if you typed the word(s) in lowercase.

Tip #8: Use variations and synonyms when necessary.

How many variations of CD-ROM are there? At least three (by my count), and that's not including the capitalization variations: CD-ROM, CDROM, CD ROM. Keep in mind that different people may use a different variation of a particular word. Therefore, in order to be sure that you've done a complete search, you'll need to search using the variations. The same goes for synonyms (words that are different but have the same meaning).

Tip #9: Wake up!

Some sites offer a simple search capability as well as additional search options (usually listed on a separate Web page). If you perform a more advanced search, there may be check boxes that are already checked (default settings). Wake up, and look at these boxes. I've conducted searches and scratched my head as to why the results weren't what I expected. Often times it was because I forgot about unchecking a box that defaulted to a certain search option such as matching case. The wrong options were right in front of my face, but I wasn't paying attention and just entered my search terms and clicked "submit." Be alert to additional ways to search for something or ways to describe what you are looking for. These become obvious when sifting through the results of your first attempt at finding something.

Tip #10: Computers cannot read minds.

Even those advanced computers used in the Star Trek series didn't have the ability to read the crew's minds. If you think through your search and follow the previous tips you should really be able to find almost anything on the Internet!

Hits vs. Hype: Tracking Your Progress

Chapter 4 Topics

How Do You Gauge the Success of Your Web Site?

What's Hot and What's Not on the Web

What's a "Hit" Anyway?

Glossary of Web Site Traffic Tracking Terms

Web Server Statistical Programs

Web Page Counters You Can Place on Your Pages

3rd Party Web Site Auditing Services

Tracking User Activity within Your Web Site

There are essentially two criteria that most organizations use to gauge the success of their Web site. One criterion is the actual number of responses received. I define responses to be:

- email messages
- online forms completed
- online orders
- responses/orders via telephone
- responses/orders via fax
- responses/orders via postal mail

The second criterion is the actual number of site visitors. Internet marketers face certain challenges when trying to *accurately* track these criteria.

Let's start with the first criterion—responses. I once ordered a videotape over the Net. It was *A Brief History of Time* by Stephen Hawking. I found the vendor through a cybermall called "Sell-It on the WWW." Although I'm not overly paranoid about providing my credit card information over the Internet, I still prefer to conduct business by telephone. I called the company on its 800 number (traditional studies have shown that 800 numbers have a tendency to increase response and sales) and proceeded to order the video.

Let's pause for a moment to look at my motivation for buying online in the first place by asking a few questions. First question: Why did I want to buy something from someone who is located halfway across the country from me instead of buying from someone who is located around the corner? Well, it's because I couldn't find the product around the corner! Second question: Why did I buy that particular product? Actually, it was an *impulse buy*. It was the holiday season, and I bought it as a gift for someone else. The recipient was reading the book, and I thought she would like the video as well. I wasn't looking for the video; I only thought to buy it when I saw the title listed in the online catalog. If impulse buying didn't exist, the shelves would be bare in the aisle next to the cash register at your local supermarket or department store. People see something at the last minute, grab it, and buy it. The Internet is no different.

Third question: How was the price? Pretty good actually. I spent about $25.00 including shipping. I doubt that even if the video was available around the corner, I could have done much better on price. So, my motivation for buying online in the first place was a combination of convenience and price. Also, I knew exactly what I was going to receive (a video is just that—a video). The product didn't require fitting (like apparel or jewelry), appearance wasn't important, etc. That's something you need to ask yourself. Is your product (if you are selling one) something that is conducive to selling on the Net?

Table 4.1 provides a look at what's hot and what's not on the Net. Please don't think that products and services in the Not category aren't selling on the Internet at all; they just aren't as popular as what's hot. As time goes on, just about any product or service may be viably sold on the Net.

Let's return to my story about purchasing the video. While conversing with the person who answered the phone, I was asked what product I wanted, how many, how I would like it shipped, and my billing information. Do you notice anything missing? *I wasn't asked how I found out about them!* This is a major *faux pas*! It's crucial to know what advertising is working and what isn't. I finally had to say, "Aren't you going to ask me how I heard about you?" The guy then said, "Sure, how did you hear about us?" This prompted a short discussion about Internet commerce. This all took place at the end of 1994. He said they were getting about two online orders a day. It just never occurred to him that people who learned about them on the Internet would call, fax, or

Table 4.1   Popular and Unpopular Internet Goods and Services

What's Hot	What's Not
Music CDs	Apparel
CD-ROMs	Jewelry
Books	Legal Services
Computer Software	Real Estate *
Computer Hardware	Furniture
Flowers and Gifts	Cosmetics
Travel Services	Building Materials
Videotapes	Automobiles (direct sales of)
Consumer Electronics	Printing Services
Adult-Oriented Products	Insurance Services
Unique or Niched Items	Drugs & Remedies

* Expected to be hot in the near future.

Table 4.2 Breakdown of Ordering Methods for a Web-Marketed Book

Online Order Form	65%
Telephone	15
Fax	15
Email	2.5
Snail Mail	2.5

mail their order! I estimate that the same number of Internet orders were coming from traditional channels. He was pretty happy with two orders a day as it was. My point is, that before you begin promoting your Web site, you should have a solid plan in place for tracking the response. Table 4.2 shows the breakdown of how my Web orders were conducted, in the period from June 1995 to December 1995, for *The Internet Marketing BlackBook.* The URL is http://www.legion.com/books/.

As you can see, the majority of my Internet orders were completed through an online order form. The second most popular ordering methods were phone and fax. Just a few orders were received through electronic or postal mail. I've received orders from around the world and have shipped books to England, Spain, Japan, Korea, Australia, Germany, Switzerland, and other countries. About half of my international orders have been faxed to me. Of the telephone orders listed in the table, about half actually filled out the online order form but checked "Call Me for Credit Card Data" instead of providing their credit card number and expiration date online. The statistics shown are for orders directly related to the Internet. I received more book orders through traditional sales channels. For me and most Netpreneurs, the Internet is simply an *additional* sales vehicle, not the *only* sales vehicle.

Hit Me!

There has been a lot of confusion about what a "hit" is. With some Web sites claiming hundreds of thousands of hits daily, the definition of what those numbers really mean has come under fire. So much so in fact, that while trying to come up with a title for this book, the title *Hits!* was rejected. After all, isn't that the goal of every Web site—to get hits? But what's a hit anyway?

A hit might actually be a file access, a page access, or a visitor access. What's the difference? The Web page shown in Figure 4.1 can be counted as three hits.

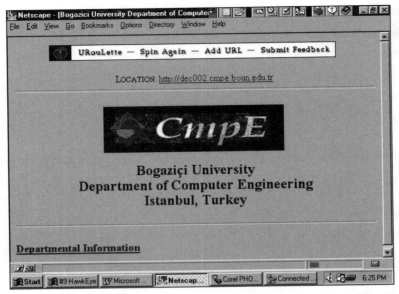

Figure 4.1   A Web page with 3 hits—1 for the HTML file itself and 2 for the two graphics files.

You may be asking, "It's just one Web page, doesn't it count as one hit?" The answer is no. Notice that there are two graphics on the page. In this case, we are defining a hit as a *file access* (which is the technical definition). Therefore, there are three hits: one hit for the HTML text file itself (which contains the "programming" for the Web page itself), and one hit for each graphic image that is requested from the server. In total, the server has received three individual requests for information. Each request caused a file to be accessed on the server's hard drive, which then was transmitted to your Web browser over the Internet via the HTTP (HyperText Transport Protocol). HTTP is the method used to transmit information between your Web browser and the server, over the Internet.

That same Web page can be counted as a single hit, but only if the statistical program ignores all file accesses except the one for the HTML file itself. No problem. Some programs can do this and, therefore, one hit equals one page access. Think about it, if you had 12,000 page accesses for the page in Figure 4.1, some servers may count that as 36,000 hits! What if there are three other Web pages associated with that Web page? That is, what if there are three other pages hyperlinked to the home page shown? Well, some of those 12,000 page accesses will choose link #1, some will choose link #2, some will choose link #3, and some will choose some or all of the links. This further complicates the issue of the total number of page accesses for the Web site. And if there are multiple Web sites on the server, you can see how a cybermall that boasts a certain number of hits can be deceptively representing its popularity.

There are many cybermalls and Internet presence providers that claim they get lots of hits (see Figure 4.2). This usually excites the prospective Web advertiser because if the advertiser can just get a small percentage of those hits, they will be in great shape. But this may not be a realistic way of looking at the situation.

Let me throw another scenario at you (as if this whole hit concept is not clouded enough already). You visit a company's home page and hit the reload button on your Web browser three times in a row. Does that count as four page accesses? The answer is yes. One page access for the initial loading of the Web page and then three more for each time you hit the reload button (which requests the Web page from the server again). But you are only one person. The statistics of how many visitors (who are different people) are now skewed! But wait, there's more. What if you visit that Web page two more times on the same day? This further confuses things.

Now you're really going to be angry with me. I am going to cloud this issue even more (good thing you can't see the sly grin on my face!). Some Internet providers and the consumer online services, (specifically America Online) *cache* popular Web pages. Caching is a computer term for loading information into memory and storing it locally, whether it be on a hard drive or in RAM (Random Access Memory). So, let's say that you have a popular Web page that many America Online (AOL) users visit and AOL caches your home page. If one hundred AOL users visit your Web site, *none* of them will be counted! This is because AOL downloaded your Web page previously (which counted as one page access) and stored it on their system. They do this to increase the speed at which the page is displayed on their users' Web browsers. When users request the URL (Web address) of that page, the locally stored file is sent in lieu of the page on your server. If your Web page isn't very popular, you won't have to worry about this particular wrinkle.

Suffice it to say, without very sophisticated statistical software, the best you can do is *estimate* how many actual living, breathing, distinct people visited your

Web site, unless you *actively* solicit some sort of information from visitors.

You're probably thinking, "What's he mean by actively solicit information from visitors?" Let's look at a popular Web site that charges a lot of money for advertising: HotWired. HotWired is more than great content. It's a virtual community. People learn, relax, and hang out there. You can check it out yourself at **http://www.hotwired.com**. When you join HotWired as a member, they ask that you fill out a survey form that requests various personal data. This demographic information helps HotWired attract advertising sponsors. Since HotWired is free to Internet users, quality sponsors are crucial to its operation. New users are given a subscriber code (see Figure 4.3). HotWired's programmers spent a lot of time creating a customized user tracking system. HotWired is continually evaluating what features within its Web site are working and what ones aren't. They know where people go and how long they

Figure 4.2 An advertisement for Penthouse's Web site in AdWeek. Who has had more actual visitors?

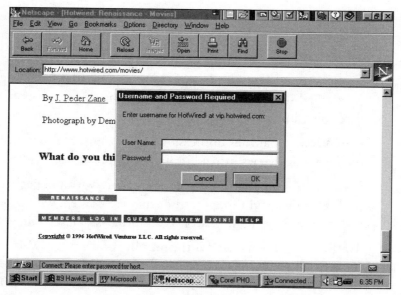

Figure 4.3   HotWired's Web site tracks visitors with their username (subscriber) codes.

stay. Before you get visions of Big Brother telling on you, realize that HotWired doesn't share its users' personal data with anyone. They only share the generic demographic information, not what your name is. This is important to mention if you ask users to register at your site. Many Internet users are concerned about their privacy.

Glossary of Web Site Traffic Tracking Jargon

This seems like a good time to clear up some online advertising definitions. Thus far, there isn't much of a universal set of these terms. The Internet is full of jargon, and understanding these terms will be especially useful. There is also a complimentary list for online advertising terms in Chapter 6.

Auditing   Attempt at recording and verifying the number of Web site visitors, often by an independent third party.

Hit   A general term for when a file or document has been accessed. Depending on how hits are counted, they may overstate the number of actual site visitors by as much as an order of magnitude (factor of 10). In most cases, a hit is one entry in a server log file and has no predictable relationship to how many people have visited.

Impressions   The number of times a particular Web page with an ad slot has been displayed. Online ad rates are often determined by the number of impressions made by visitors.

Page Views   Same as impressions. For example, Yahoo! uses the term page views instead of hits or impressions.

Session   A compilation of a user's activity within a particular Web site. Even though a user may access ten Web pages and 43 files in a single visit, it is counted as one session.

Traffic   A general term for the number of visitors a Web site receives. Internet marketers want to attract traffic to their sites. Cybermalls often use this term due to its use in traditional shopping malls.

Traffic Tracking   Analysis of user activity within a Web page or site. Traffic tracking is more in-depth than auditing, in that estimates of time spent on certain pages and areas within a site are recorded.

Unique Views   A unique view is termed as one person seeing one page one time. Some software filters out back-and-forth browsing produced by hitting the back button on your Web browser software thereby seeing the same Web page multiple times. This filtration yields a unique view rather than several views (which is meaningless to marketers).

User   One Web site session. Someone who visits your Web site today for 20 minutes is considered a user. If that person visits again in a few days, he or she is considered a user. Even though it is the same person, he or she is counted as two users.

Home Grown Server Statistics

A good reason for keeping track of your most popular Web pages is that you can get a good picture of server activity and can spot potential problems before they get serious. Other needs for tracking traffic are to:

- Satisfy your curiosity
- Justify a Web site to a manager or client
- Optimize your Web site

Web server software has its own built-in statistics capabilities. The problem with server-generated reports are that they can be difficult to interpret, can be ugly in format, and can often provide lots of extra, unneeded information. The raw data provided by your Internet provider's machine may not be any different and may not be real time (sometimes reports are generated on a daily, weekly, or monthly basis, and you need to wait for them to see how you are doing).

Internet marketers want statistical software with more flexibility, the ability to sort by various criteria and in many cases, would like to avoid the need to download and install perl scripts, or to ask their provider for *cgi-bin* access. The cgi-bin is a special, write-protected directory on Unix servers that contain various CGI scripts and processes. CGI and perl scripts are computer programs that perform certain tasks. Some programs require you to place them into the cgi-bin directory, but you need to have *write* access. Server administrators usually restrict who can write to the directory. If the software you want to run requires write access, your server administrator may need to install it for you. When you are renting Web space on someone else's server, this can be an inconvenience.

If you have your own server and don't have statistical software (or want to augment what you do have), there is additional software available to help you.

getstats.c, version 1.2

http://www.eit.com/software/getstats/getstats.html

Getstats analyzes the log file from NCSA, CERN, MacHTTP, and some other Web servers. The program can be licensed from EIT (Enterprise Integration Technologies), email **batson@eit.com** for more information. There is a companion, public domain addition called getgraph.pl that provides a graphical representation of server activity generated from getstats output. It can be obtained at **http://www.tcp.chem.tue.nl/stats/script/**.

MSWC: Multi Server WebCharts

http://www.ee.ethz.ch/~oetiker/webtools/mswc/mswc.html or
ftp://ftp.dmu.ac.uk/pub/netcomm/src/web/

MSWC consists of two perl (version 5) scripts written by Tobias Oetiker at the Swiss Federal Institute of Technology in Zurich and is distributed freely under the GNU General Public License. The software was designed to track the most popular pages on different servers. The software can create a graphical display of the distribution of page accesses. In addition to the URL of each page, the URL's title is also displayed.

WWWStat

http://www.ics.uci.edu/WebSoft/wwwstat

A perl program that processes NCSA httpd 1.2 (or later) log files and outputs a more readable summary in HTML. This allows you to make your statistics available to whomever you want, right there on your Web site. WWWStat was developed by Roy Fielding who modified previously revised versions of a multiserver statistics program created by Jonathan Magid. It doesn't require you to have write/execute access to the cgi-bin directory on the server, which is a plus. There is a graphic add-on program called gwstat available from **http://dis.umass.edu/stats/gwstat.html.**

Interse Market Focus 2
111 W. Evelyn Ave., Suite 213
Sunnyvale, CA 94086
Tel: (408) 732-0932
Fax: (408) 732-7038
info@interse.com
http://www.interse.com

If you don't know how you would implement any of the server statistics programs mentioned above or you don't own a server, this product might just be the ticket. Market Focus is Windows-based software that uses the log files (must be in CLF—Common Log File format) from your server or those of your presence provider. Web servers that use CLF are NCSA, Netscape, O'Reilly's Website, Appache, and some others. A number of reports can be generated into a Microsoft Word document that can be printed, edited, or used within other documents (assuming you have Microsoft Word 7.0 or higher). If your Web site is housed on someone else's server, all you need to do is FTP the log file to your PC! Market Focus will do the rest.

What's unique about this product is that it contains a database of over 70,000 U.S. Internet domains. The database is indexed by city, state, and zip code. They simply used InterNIC domain data that contains the geographical location for each domain name. For example, the domain **gate.net** is located in Deerfield Beach, Florida, 33442. What this software allows you to do is track regionalized advertising campaigns that direct people to your Web site! This is unique because it does not require that users of your Web site enter any personal information. I should explain that server software receives information from your access provider and in many cases, your Web browser software. All this information is exchanged behind the scenes, and the server records it in raw form. Market Focus is designed to make the raw data more useful.

Market Focus can help determine if the banners you place with organizations listed in Chapter 6 are really worth what they are charging. Reports can be used to justify cross-promotions with other Web sites, track regional visitor traffic, total number of users, URLs from which users have been referred (taken from the Web server's *referrer log*), and more. If you aren't very technical and want in-depth details of how well your Web site promotion campaigns are working, I highly recommend this product. You may think it's a bit pricey, but it's not when compared with I/PRO's product.

Market Focus 2 runs on a minimum of a Pentium CPU with 16 MB RAM (minimum), CD-ROM drive, and available hard disk space of 20 MB plus the size of any log files you want to analyze. Operating systems supported are Windows 95 and Windows NT 3.5.1. The product retails for $695 and carries a 30-day, money-back guarantee.

net.Analysis from net.Genesis
Tel:(617) 577-9800
http://www.netgen.com/products/net.Analysis
Somewhat similar to Interse's product. Pricing is $2,995 plus $495 for the accompanying reporting program.

Page Counters

A page counter is CGI script software that counts the number of times your Web page is accessed and displays that number on the page itself, for all to see. Figure 4.4 shows a page with a counter. Page counters aren't very accurate because most will count a reload as another access, as well as any hits you cause by loading your own pages. In addition, if you decide to use a counter on any of your Web pages, you'll need to contend with *counter terrorism!*

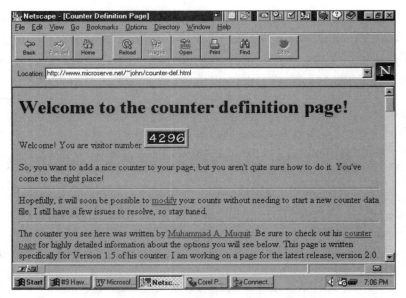

Figure 4.4　A Web page with a counter. The page has been accessed 4,296 times.

There's a lot of humor on the Net, most of it sarcastic. If you visit http://
www.netaxis.com/~pudge/ you'll see "The Counter Terrorist Page." When
you access the page, you'll be committing counter terrorism! The page links to
and accesses a number of other Web pages that contain counters. This causes
the counter on each of the pages listed on the terrorist page to increase by
one. This really screws up the accuracy of the victims' pages. To quote
Pudge, the creator of the page, "If you are feeling a bit malicious, come here
and give other sites a false sense of worth!" This Web site was selected as one
of the top "Useless Web Pages," a cool (uncool?) sites page (see Chapter 7).
If you know of pages that have a counter, you can suggest them to
pudge@eworld.com for inclusion. The creator got the idea from a meta-
index (see Chapter 8) for real life terrorism and crime resources. The real
site, appropriately titled "Links Related to Terrorism, Intelligence, and Crime"
had a page counter at the bottom. Pudge put two and two together and
created The Counter Terrorist Page.

Most counters are cumulative, so it's difficult for you to quickly track visitors
by day, week, or month. If you're not deterred from using a counter by now
(You shouldn't be, they are neat, but you shouldn't rely too heavily on their
accuracy.), here are some places where you can get your very own counter:

"How I put page access counters into my pages."
http://purgatory.ecn.purdue.edu:20002/JBC/david/how.html

This page provides a counter script written in C and details the steps to take to implement the page counter. The program runs on Unix servers running NCSA. I found the page in Yahoo under "How to Add Counters." The page was created by David Whittemore and was accessed more than 43,000 times by the time I got to it.

WWW Home Page Access Counter!
http://www.semcor.com/~muquit/Count.html

A counter program created by Muhammad Muquit that runs on Unix with any of NCSA, CERN, and Appache httpd Web server software. He also provides links to source code that will run on Windows NT and OS/2 machines. The program has an added feature to combat counter terrorism. The program allows you to enter terrorist URLs into a file, and ignores any accesses that come from those sources.

Yahoo's Counter Category Listings
http://www.yahoo.com

For more pointers to page counters, visit Yahoo! and go to the Computers and Internet:Internet:World Wide Web:Programming:Access Counts category.

Web-Counter
http://www.digits.com/web_counter/

If you don't know how to incorporate the above CGI scripts into your Web pages, you can still get a counter from the Web-Counter. All you need to do is fill out an online form and then add a line of HTML into the pages that you want to display a counter. There is no wait time for your counter activation; it will start counting your visitors once you've set it up. If you are a low-volume site (which after reading this book I hope you won't be!), the Web-Counter service is free. They define low volume as being under 1,000 counts a day. If you feel generous, you can pay for their commercial service even if your site is "low volume."

Initially, they planned on the service being free for everyone; however, the Web-Counter has been receiving over a half-million accesses and one gigabyte in data transfer each *day*. Therefore, they have instituted a commercial version. Subscription rates are subject to change, of course, and are listed in Table 4.3.

Table 4.3 Subscription Rates for the Web-Counter

Hits Per Day	Price/Month
0 - 49	$3
50 - 99	$5
100 - 999	$10
1000 - 1999	$28
> 1999	$10/month per 1000/daily hits

Payments can be made with a First Virtual or *ecash* account (electronic money services) as well as with old-fashioned personal and corporate checks.

What's interesting is that 0.3 percent of Web-Counter's users account for over 50 percent of their system load and bandwidth with the top 40 sites accounting for over 150,000 daily accesses. There are over 13,000 Web pages using Web-Counter. The "80-20" rule strikes again.

Web-Counter was created by Gray Watson and Jason Galanter. Web-Counter permits over a dozen different character sets (even Arabic numerals!), a query page for additional statistics, and segregated top-10 lists (adult and non-adult/family oriented sites). If you'd like to keep the number of visitors secret, there is an option for you to know the statistics but hide them from everyone else. The Web-Counter site contains a substantial FAQ (Frequently Asked Questions list) and all the additional information you need to sign up.

Whom Do You Trust?

In the real world of magazine and newspaper publishing, publications that sell advertising have their circulation numbers audited by a third party. This not only helps the advertiser by knowing how many potential readers may see their ads but also helps the publication in measuring its success in getting new subscribers and readers. Two organizations who have been involved in traditional auditing have been investigating Web auditing, BPA International and the Audit Bureau of Circulations (**http://www.accessabc.com**). As you'll see in Chapter 6, knowing how many people that can see your banner is important before you plunk down a chunk of change on an ad.

Fortunately, there is an electronic equivalent of a circulation audit bureau. A number of companies have sprung up to offer an unbiased account of how many page accesses a site receives. Aside from providing tons of tips, tricks, and techniques for promoting your Web site, my goal is also to provide tons of resources for you as well. What follows are the major third-party Web site auditing companies and what they charge.

Internet Audit Bureau (IAB)

2159 India St., Suite A
San Diego, CA 92101
(619) 238-5396
iab@internet-audit.com (general info automated reply)
contact@internet-audit.com (human response)
sponsor@internet-audit.com (advertising info)
http://www.internet-audit.com

Internet Audit Bureau was the first independent Web site auditing service to market (see Figure 4.5). Initially dubbed "iaudit," the company changed its logo and domain name to avoid confusion after Internet Profiles came out with a product of the same name. The IAB was first conceived by Paul Colton and Brent Gutekunst when their clients kept asking them about the number of visitors their sites were getting. Counters and server statistics software are hard to implement for Net novices, so they created an easier way. IAB began testing in June 1995 and has been rapidly growing ever since.

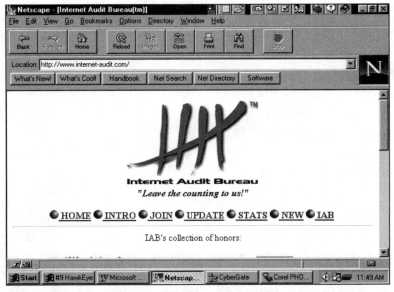

Figure 4.5 Leave the counting up to the Internet Audit Bureau.

Nearly 5,000 sites signed up in the first three months of operation. 1995 year-end access statistics had over 11,000 subscribers tracking 15,000 Web pages, and there were over two million weekly accesses. IAB defines an access as each time its logo appears on a member page. I just love the company's logo and byline: "Leave the counting to us!"

Statistics are updated on a regular basis (at least every 48 hours), and plans are in the works to update daily. IAB is working on providing statistics on which Web browser software was used to access audited Web pages, security features, domain name filters (to remove your own accesses from the stats), and more. IAB is free to use. They make money through sponsorships (see Chapter 6 for rates). IAB reserves the right to provide its sponsor's logo on your Web page. If you don't like this additional advertising taking up space on your Web page, IAB isn't for you. A fee-based service like Web Audit may suit you better; however, IAB is working on a "plus" version of its service that would be fee-based.

LinkStar Counts!

662 S. Military Trail
Deerfield Beach, FL 33442
(954) 426-LINK (5465)
counts@linkstar.com
http://counts.linkstar.com

Similar to IAB and Web Audit, LinkStar Counts! was created to provide a faster and more reliable third party auditing service. Fees start at $4.95 per month.

NetCount

1645 N. Vine St., Level 4
Los Angeles, CA 90028
7000NET or (213) 848-5700
info@netcount.com
http://www.netcount.com

NetCount provides precise site traffic information, broken down by Web site, page, subject, day, and hour. NetCount is designed to monitor traffic both within a site and between sites. Prices for the NetCount Plus service range from $125 to $2,400 per month depending upon the number of average daily hits and the number of "report units" (50 or 100 per month). Report units are simply the number of reports you can request from NetCount. That is, if you want to check your stats every day of the month, you would use up 30 report units. NetCount offers a free basic service that provides you with a few reports each month. To try their free service, you must fill out a contract (available on its Web site). Specific software is required to be run on the Web server computer. If you have your own Unix or Windows NT based Web server, you can install the software. If you are renting space, you'll need to contact your service provider and/or NetCount to get started. Like Internet Audit Bureau and WebAudit, a small icon will be added to any Web pages you want tracked. NetCount's Web site traffic monitoring services first became available in October 1995.

If you choose to do any banner advertising (see Chapter 6), the AdCount service is available to track the effectiveness of your banner ads. Each time someone clicks on your ad and visits your site can be tracked. If you are already a NetCount subscriber, the fee is $250 per ad per month, and $375 per ad per month if you are not a subscriber. You'll receive weekly, monthly, and quarterly reports for the life of your AdCount subscription.

Web Audit

Janzten Beach
243 N. Hayden Bay Drive
Portland, OR 97217-8301
webaudit@wishing.solid.net
http://wishing.solid.net

Web Audit provides real-time statistics of up to 10 Web pages for their shareware account and up to 25 Web pages for their Deluxe account. You can sort your pages by name, hits, daily, weekly, and monthly totals, and more. There are some differences between the shareware and Deluxe account. Visit the Web Audit site for all the details.

Randel and Bob, two guys located thousands of miles apart (one in Oregon, the other in Hawaii) initially developed Web Audit to track the hits of several Web sites they created that were housed on different servers (it's easy to track multiple sites on the same server). The software they created allowed them to see the results of all their sites on a single Web page. The concept worked so well for them that they thought others could use it, too.

Web Audit is built on the shareware "try before you buy" concept. If you like their service, they ask that you pay for it with a small donation ($3 to $6 a month). I set up a lot of my Web site promotion customers with Web Audit. I feel the small sum they ask for is quite a bargain and encourage you to support their efforts should you use their service. They ask for a little more money if you receive more hits, as this requires more of their system resources. If you expect a lot of traffic (1000+ page accesses a day), would like to track more than 10 Web pages, want to restrict who can see your stats, or require more sophisticated statistics, they offer a Deluxe account for $25.00 a month. The Deluxe account is good for sites that get 10,000 page accesses a day or fewer. They accept checks, cash, credit cards—even foreign currency!

To sign up for Web Audit, visit **http://wishing.solid.net** and read through their information. You'll need to fill out an online form, provide some contact information, and answer some questions about your Web site. You will receive your Web Audit account number by email within 30 minutes, as well as instructions for checking your stats. Paste the three lines of HTML code provided to you in email to each Web page you want to audit (Web Audit recommends you do this near the top of each page). Load each page that you want to track. You should see a small [WA] logo on your page. The logo was designed to be attractive but not to detract from the purpose of your page (see Figure 4.6). Then check to make sure everything works by entering the URL

Figure 4.6 A Web page using Web Audit. Notice the tiny WA logo in the upper left corner.

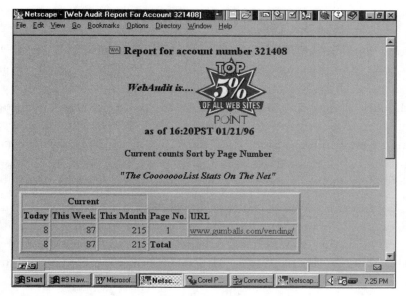

Figure 4.7   Web Audit statistics for the page in Figure 4.6.

they gave you in email or visit the Web Audit site and go to the stats page and enter your account number. You should receive a screen similar to Figure 4.7. The entire process takes less than an hour.

WebStat Auditing Service from WebTrack

Kevin Henderson
(212) 725-5328
http://www.webtrack.com
info@webtrack.com

WebStat allows subscribers to gather and analyze a number of data sets to receive a comprehensive view of site activity and traffic, some of which are:

- *Advertiser's links.* Monitor where the links are coming from.

- *Hot Page Analysis.* Rank pages in order of most popular to least popular.

- *Visitor Session Counts.* Compare hits, unique views, and session timing distributions.

- *"Whois" Data.* Learn basic geographic locations of site visitors as well as what domain type (com, gov, edu, etc.).

The service costs $100/month and was under beta test as of this writing.

To Register or Not to Register

Asking your site visitors to complete a registration form in order to enter your site can be a great way of not only tracking your traffic but tracking what they do once inside. By filling out a form, your users indicate that they may be more inclined to come back and are more committed to your site. Few commercial Web sites require registration, however. Sites that are online publications or virtual communities are the most likely to require registration. Even though registration is free for most sites, there can be huge drops in site users if you require registration. Some surveys I've seen indicate a drop of up to 50 percent!

It takes time for users to fill out an online form. Remember what I mentioned in Chapter 2 about online forms. The more questions people need to answer, the less likely they will fill it out to begin with. Also, some people are paranoid about filling out forms (due to privacy concerns). I know I am. In most cases, you can get away with fudging some of your personal information except an email address. Also, it's tough to tell if one person has registered as several users. This can lessen but not necessarily negate the value of the information you compile on your users. One solution to reduce the hassle of registration among various Web sites is provided by I/PRO's I/CODE system (described in the next section).

Who, What, When, and Where

In addition to tracking the popularity of various ordering methods and how many people visited their Web site, more and more Netpreneurs want to know what parts of their sites are popular, how long people stayed, and what their demographics are. The problem has been that this information wasn't possible to obtain with traditional Web statistics software. Leave it to the pros at A.C. Neilson to solve that problem. Actually, a company called Internet Profiles Corporation (I/PRO) solved the problem and has partnered up with Neilson. I/PRO's clients include Yahoo!, Microsoft, CompuServe, USA Today, Ziff-Davis Publishing, and other high traffic sites. I/PRO has created four products that are of interest to Internet marketers, as follows.

I/AUDIT

I/AUDIT provides independent auditing of Web site usage. The product is geared toward Internet sites that sell advertising. I/PRO charges a monthly or quarterly fee for this service. I/AUDIT reports are stored as Adobe Acrobat PDF files and require the Adobe Acrobat reader. There are three "frequency charges" for I/AUDIT: $1,500 for *each* monthly report, $3,000 for each quarterly report, and a flat $5,000 for a single report. With I/AUDIT, sites that sell advertising can show their advertisers:

- The number of visitors each month

- When they visited (popular times during the day or evening, etc.)

- The average length of their visit

- Geographical location of visitors and type of domain (com, edu, mil, etc.)

- Average number of pages per visit

- And more

I/COUNT

I/COUNT essentially does the same thing as I/AUDIT with the exception that I/COUNT isn't considered audited. You run reports through an online form at I/PRO's Web site. Fees are dependent upon the number of file requests made each day. Prices range from $200/month for fewer than 5,000 daily file requests to $5,000/month for 600,000 file requests.

I/CODE

I/CODE is a universal registration system that stores a user's demographic information in a central database. The demographic information is obtained through an online registration form that each user fills out. The user then receives his or her I/CODE. The benefit to I/CODE is that users don't have to fill out form after form or remember tons of passwords for the many different Web sites that require registration. For example, what if there were ten sites like HotWired that were totally unrelated to each other? An Internet user that wanted to interact with each site would need to fill out ten forms and would have ten user codes and passwords. With I/CODE, the user would have just one password and an I/CODE code. The user could use that code to log in to each of the ten sites, assuming they were I/CODE subscribers, and not have to separately register with them. Web sites with I/COUNT and I/CODE can track things like

- What percentage of men and women clicked on a certain product image?

- Did more single, married, or divorced people click on a certain Web page?

- Were less-affluent users more likely to enter online contests?

I believe that this universal registration system will become very prevalent with those sites that require users to join or sign in upon visiting.

I/MAIL

I/MAIL was being beta tested as of this writing. It will allow Internet users to request advertising messages to be sent to them via email according to their specific interests. Users will even be able to control the amount of messages they receive over a certain period of time. The I/MAIL service requires users to subscribe to it; therefore, they will not be offended by receiving email messages.

Internet Profiles Corporation
785 Market Street
13th Floor
San Francisco, CA 94103
Tel: (415) 975-5800
Fax: (415) 975-5818
info@ipro.com
http://www.ipro.com

Concluding Comments

Don't believe that instituting a third-party auditing system or a service like Web-Counter is a one-time setup. These services are in continual development. As visitor-counting services get more popular, they need to upgrade equipment and software that may require you to sign up again or edit your Web pages to insert new HTML. I had to do this twice with Web Audit (for multiple clients). And of course there are hard costs involved with rapid growth, such as the need for more servers and bandwidth. Expect prices to go up as these services are flooded with accesses from thousands of Web sites.

Don't take the statistics you get from any source to be 100 percent accurate. Many services cannot filter out things like your visits, repeat visits and the reloading of pages. They also may ignore users with text-based Web browsers because the graphic that's used to do the counting doesn't appear on the screen. The use of security firewalls further compounds the problem. In many firewall cases, you can't tell if the same person visited your site 50 times or 50 different people visited. A firewall causes everyone to look the same.

As a rule of thumb, I assume any access statistics are 75 percent accurate, so I just multiply the visitor number by .75 and use that as my count of actual real, live people who have visited. This may or may not be accurate but that's what I use as a likely conservative number.

If you want to get some of the smaller places like Web Audit on the phone, good luck. Trying to get a phone number out of some of the auditing services was difficult (they did not list any telephone numbers on their Web sites). Even after sending email requesting a phone number, there was a long delay.

Overall, I think these services are a great idea and are sorely needed. But the usefulness of them is greatly diminished if you don't *evaluate and use* the information they provide! Investigate which method is going to be best for you. In this chapter, I've provided lots of pointers to more information about the services. Be sure to follow them.

Registering with the Internet Directories and Search Engines

Chapter 5 Topics

General Tips for Submitting Your Listing

Tips for Submitting to Spiders and Crawlers

Tips for Submitting to the Indexers

Editorially Reviewed Directories

Search Sites That Automatically List Submitted Web Sites

International (Non-USA) Directories

Additional Resources That List Even More Search Engines and Directories That You Can Submit To

The first thing many new (as well as experienced) Internet users do when they start up their Web browser is to visit a search engine or directory to look for a specific type of Web site or subject. If you read Chapter 3, you learned how search engines work and know how to find almost anything on the Net. That information will be helpful here as we work to make sure *your site* can be *found*. In this chapter, I show you where to list your site and give tips to ensure that your listing is as prominent and useful as possible. Unfortunately, all too many people who have Web sites have limited their promotion campaign to getting listed in the top dozen or so search engines. There's no question that you need to be listed in as many search services as possible, especially the major ones. However, that's just the tip of the iceberg. That's why this book has many more chapters than just this one! It's the combination of many Web site promotion techniques that will make your site one of the top destinations on the Net, assuming that it's a well-designed site (Chapter 2) and that there's a reason for people to return to it (Chapter 15).

Except for some of the Spiders (see the discussion later in this chapter), in order to be listed in a search engine, you need to *submit* your site information and address. This is accomplished by visiting all the places you want to be listed in and filling out a form that requests information such as your Web address (URL), name of your site, description, and perhaps other information. Once the form is filled out, you click on the submit button and the information is sent to the appropriate party for review or automatic inclusion. You can manually submit information about your Web site to the places in this chapter one by one or go to Chapter 14 and either hire someone else to do it or use an automated service like Submit It!, The PostMaster, or WebPost. Please note that the directories and sites that these services submit to vary and may not include some of the sites listed in this chapter.

The sites listed in this chapter do not charge you for adding your site to their database (a few may charge for extra information associated with your listing, but the base listing is still free).

General Tips for Submitting

Keep a log

Track what sites you submitted your URL to, with what information, and when you did it. Include a box for any authentication information (password) required to update your information. You may want to create something like Figure 5.1 for tracking where you've submitted to.

Use a good descriptive title

Bookmarks (hotlists) within most Web browsers use the title of the Web page. Most Web browsers such as Netscape display a document's title in the top-most line of your screen (probably in blue). That one-line description is located within the <TITLE> and </TITLE> tags in the HTML (HyperText Markup Language) file for your Web page. Try adding your Web page to your bookmark list. Does the title instantly identify to someone who isn't familiar with your page what it's all about? A title like "The Home Page" is terrible. A better one would be "ABC Company's Home Page." An even better one may be "The ABC Company Plumber's Internet Resource Center." This last example assumes that ABC Company is a plumbing supply business or something similar. I think you get the idea. Simply choose a title that will appear in a bookmark list that clearly describes the site. Keep in mind that long titles get chopped (try it and see).

Be prepared

Gather the information required to be listed in the various sites into a text file on your hard drive. When you visit the site, simply cut and paste data from

Site Name	Date Submitted	Date Verified	Password
Lycos	19-Mar-96	25-Mar-96	
LinkStar	19-Mar-96	19-Mar-96	k239bz6
Yahoo	20-Mar-96	10-Apr-96	
WebCrawler	20-Mar-96	24-Mar-96	
NetMall	20-Mar-96	27-Mar-96	abc123*

Figure 5.1 A simple form to track your Web site promotion activities.

the file using your word processing program (I use Microsoft Notepad) into the appropriate boxes on the screen within your Web browser. This will save you time and avoid any typos.

Proofread your listing (repeatedly!)

I cannot stress this enough. Trying to change your listing after it has been submitted can be difficult and frustrating in many cases. Very few search engines permit you to instantly and securely change your listing (LinkStar does). The most critical portions of your entry are the URL and then the title; so be sure to double check those.

Fill in all the blanks

When submitting your site to a search engine or directory, fill in all the blanks that are appropriate (some may not be). Some sites will reject your entry if you leave out certain information. Most are pretty self-explanatory and will say what fields are required, but you really need to be aware of this rather than hurriedly enter information into boxes.

Read the instructions!

Please, do yourself a favor and read the URL submission guidelines (or some such document that tells you what's acceptable). It can take five minutes of your time, but each site has a different way of accepting new Web sites for inclusion. The Web is still like the Wild West in this respect. There just isn't much uniformity among the various search sites—each one is different. Maximize each promotional opportunity by making the most of your listing.

Perform sample searches before submitting

One way to see what type of description is good or to prepare your site for indexing by a Spider is to look at how other people listed themselves. Learn from their mistakes and learn from those that catch your eye. Adjust your site submission accordingly.

Get listed near the top

Many people ask how to get their Web site listed first on a search results page. The sarcastic answer is that the only way to guarantee prominent exposure in a search result is to purchase a banner ad (if the site offers this option, see

Chapter 6 for more) that appears on the top of that page. Some sites list you alphabetically, others by the chronological order that the site was submitted in, while others use a combination of criteria. There's no one sure-fire way to cut to the front of the line. For alphabetically arranged listings, you can use a number as the first character in your title. I once used *1st Edition: The Internet Marketing BlackBook* rather than *The Internet Marketing BlackBook*. The former ensured that it was listed as one of the first few because of the number 1 being the first character, whereas the latter was pushed down to the "Is" or the "Ts" depending upon whether the word "The" was ignored or not. By being listed closer to the top, I received more visitors.

Get multiple listings

Some Web sites contain many different products or subject areas. These are accessible from the home page. These additional areas are called second-level pages or product-specific pages. One way to get your site listed in a directory is to list it many times but under different URLs. For example, suppose your company deals in software, and you have three products—one has to do with accounting, the second is a word processor, and the third is a game. Well, you can list your site under the category of software with the home page URL and perhaps list the types of software you offer in your description so someone searching for those subjects can find you. In addition, it is possible to list the accounting product separately since it has a different URL than the home page and can be described with a different subject (accounting rather than software, even though it can be categorized as either). You can do the same for the other two products. By doing this, you have quadrupled the number of listings that lead to your Web site. Sure, it took a few extra minutes to submit the other pages, but it's probably worth it. This may seem a bit anti-promotional, but it's important to abide by *netiquette*. In some search sites, the previous practice of submitting multiple submissions is acceptable and maybe even welcomed. In others, it is considered abuse and is discouraged. Use your judgement on this one.

Tips for Submitting to Spiders and Crawlers

Contrary to what I may have said in Chapter 1, you can build it and they may actually come without you actively promoting your site. You won't get massive response, but it is possible to be indexed in a few places automatically. Spiders and Crawlers (which are essentially the same thing) quietly access your Web site and index the information they find. You can speed up the process of being found simply by submitting your URL to them—kind of like priming the pump.

If you don't want your Web page to be included in the index of a Spider, you need to create a file called robots.txt and place it on your server (with a "world readable" file permission). In the file, include the URLs of the pages that you do not want indexed. Any Spiders adhering to the robot exclusion standard will ignore these pages. Here are some more tips.

Check to see if you are already listed

Spider engines can find your site regardless of whether you actually submitted it. Although it only takes a minute to submit your URL, take a moment to search for your site before submitting it. This practice keeps the Spiders busy adding new sites to their databases rather than wasting resources. Some Spiders will check to see if your site is already listed before accepting your submission and will let you know that when you try to submit your site.

Use a good descriptive title

Spiders like WebCrawler index and list your site with the <TITLE> within each Web page. Implementing this tip can generate significantly more traffic than ignoring it. Spiders merely request a URL and seek out and index the Web page associated with that URL (as well as other pages that are linked to it). When a Spider adds your page to its database, it uses the title found in the <TITLE> of your HTML page.

Be "index-friendly"

A Spider typically indexes a Web page in one of two ways. It will either index a portion of the page, or it will index the entire page. In either case, it is important that your home page (which is essentially the front door to your site) has text that adequately explains what your site's purpose is and contains numerous keywords and synonyms that people who are looking for you would use to find you. To give you an idea, InfoSeek uses the first 250 characters of the Web page for its description, whereas Lycos uses the first 200 in the description yet indexes the 100 most statistically important words from each document. If you want your site to be listed higher up in a search result, keep these things in mind. WebCrawler, for example, will give your site a higher rating (place you higher in the list) if the word the user is searching with (florist, computer, car, whatever) appears many times in the first paragraph or so of the page.

You can compare the description of a Web site that appears in the results of a search with the page itself. Print out both and you'll see how the Spider extracts information from a Web page and displays it to the user in the search results. From this, you'll have an idea of what will happen after you submit your site and it's indexed. Ask yourself, does this description adequately explain my site? Does it entice the user to click on my entry to visit? If not, you'll want to rewrite the portion that gets indexed.

Remember, query engines only work on words, not images. Highly graphical pages aren't likely to be pulled up due to the inability to index any significant information.

THE SPIDERS
Alta Vista
Site Address: http://altavista.digital.com
URL Submission Address: http://altavista.digital.com/cgi-bin/query?pg=addurl
Corrections Address: N/A

Alta Vista is Digital's search engine. It's fast and extensive but often provides way too much information for a search. It's quick to submit your site (just requires a URL), but if you list in some of the other Spiders, Alta Vista will probably find you on its own.

Excite
Site Address: http://www.excite.com
URL Submission Address: (click on suggest site) or use
http://www.excite.com/cgi/comsubhelp.cgi?display=html;path=/
    query.html;section=search;Suggest+Link=Suggest+Link
Corrections Address: N/A

Excite (see Figure 5.2) indexes the entire page for each URL submitted instead of partially extracting information for indexing. This provides a more accurate representation of what's in the page and ensures that relevant pages aren't left

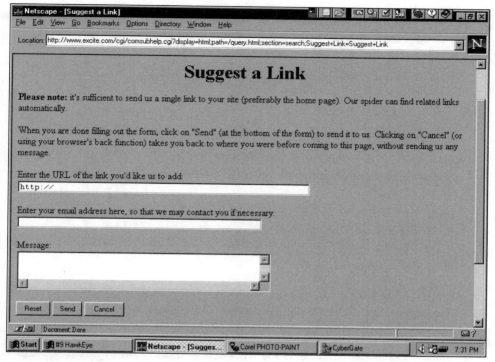

Figure 5.2 Suggest your link to Excite.

out of a search. In addition to Excite's database of over 1.5 million Web pages, it also provides over 50,000 Web site reviews.

Infoseek Guide
Site Address: http://guide.infoseek.com
URL Submission Address: www-request@infoseek.com
Corrections Address: N/A

Infoseek updates its index every few weeks or so. It uses the title from your <TITLE> and uses the first 250 characters that appear on your Web page as the description of your site.

Inktomi
Site Address: http://inktomi.berkeley.edu
URL Submission Address: http://inktomi.berkeley.edu/addurl.html
Corrections Address: N/A

A lesser-used search engine, probably because it was created by an educational institution and is not currently a commercial venture. It's fast and only asks for a URL.

Lycos
Site Address: http://www.lycos.com
URL Submission Address: http://www.lycos.com/register.html
Corrections Address: http://www.lycos.com/register.html (deletion)

Lycos is one of the oldest—and most used—Spiders (see Figure 5.3). It takes a few days before your site is added to the database.

Open Text Index
Site Address: http://www.opentext.com/omw/f-omw.html
URL Submission Address: http://www.opentext.com/omw/f-omw-submit.html
Corrections Address: N/A

Open Text uses this site as a test bed for its new search products. Open Text's primary market is *intranet* applications (internal networks).

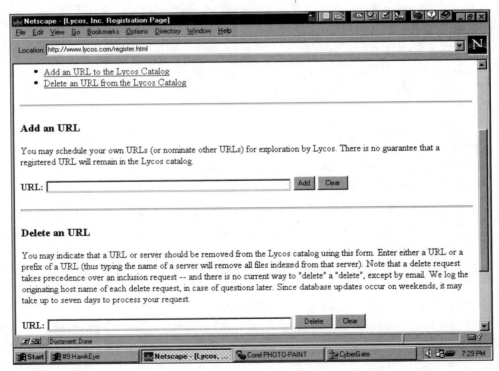

Figure 5.3 As simple as it gets—Lycos requires just your URL. It'll do the rest.

WebCrawler
Site Address: http://www.webcrawler.com
URL Submission Address: http://www.webcrawler.com/WebCrawler/SubmitURLS.html
Corrections Address: N/A

WebCrawler permits up to 10 URLs to be submitted at once. It takes about a week before your site is indexed and the system updated.

World Wide Web Worm
Site Address: http://wwww.cs.colorado.edu/wwww/
URL Submission Address: http://wwww.cs.colorado.edu/home/mcbryan/WWWWadd.html
Corrections Address: N/A

Oliver McBryan's WWWW contains over three million URLs and was voted as Best Navigational Tool in the 1994 Best of the Web Awards. The submission form asks for the URL and a brief description containing keywords. It may take up to several weeks after submitting before your site is indexed.

Tips for Submitting to the Indexers

As discussed earlier (and in Chapter 3), the indexers are sites that require you to submit to them. These include editorially reviewed sites (the first section) as well as sites that automatically list yours (the second section).

Reconsider using unrelated words to describe your site

One way to ensure that your site appears in search results more often is to expand the number of words by which people can find you. However, if you add words for the sake of adding them, and they are not related to the content of your site, this procedure can be rather counter-productive. The reason being, that if someone typed in "games" to search for sites that have something to do with games, and your site is a set of pages about your plumbing supply store, the people who visited on the premise of your site having something to do with games will likely be very disappointed. If you are not in the habit of disappointing your customers, you'll want to honestly represent your Web site.

Although sex is a popular topic on the Net, you'll want to be careful about adding in sex and many related words (like adult, XXX, etc.) if they don't apply to your site. If you are a sex therapist, then by all means, use the word. Some directories have started putting Web sites that abuse this on a *stop list*. This means that your site won't be listed until you shape up. Infoseek does this in certain cases. The act of adding words to the description or keyword lists of search sites is called *skewing*. As you can see, skewing can indeed create more awareness of your site, but it can backfire on you as well.

Use a good descriptive title

User-defined titles are used for listings within directories like Yahoo! and are critical to your promotional success. My first book was published by my own publishing company. Rather than list the Web site under "Legion Publishing Corp.," I decided to list it under "The Internet Marketing BlackBook." People seeing the former title who were looking for what I have to offer on the Web site (a book about Internet marketing) would never actually click on the hypertext link! Simply by changing the title—to one that an interested user can instantly identify with—made all the difference.

Use HTML if they accept it

Most sites do not permit you to use HTML in your site description, but a few do (Commercial Sites Index and Gold Site Europe, for example). Using HTML to emphasize certain items or words within your description or announcement helps your listing stand out better than the rest. Figure 5.9 (shown later) illustrates what one listing looks like with HTML (labeled as "Closeout") and some others that don't use HTML. As you can see, the one with HTML is much more readable and jumps out at you more than the others, which are rather "flat." The site's submission guidelines page will state if HTML is accepted. You'll also be able to tell by looking at the listings within the site.

Editorially Reviewed Directories

These sites don't automatically list you in their directories. A real, live person reviews your submission for various factors, which may include appropriateness for the directory, quality of the site, and that the submitted site is indeed up and running. These services are under no obligation whatsoever to list your site! I've often had a hard time explaining this to clients who would complain that they are not listed in Yahoo! even though they submitted their site information. You can't twist their arms until they list you (although a little pestering won't hurt!). Don't give up at first, but after submitting three times and not being added to the database, there's a good chance that your site just isn't appropriate and you should invest your energy elsewhere.

BizWeb
Site Address: http://www.bizweb.com
URL Submission Address: submission@bizweb.com
Corrections Address: submission@bizweb.com

BizWeb has a very specific set of guidelines for submitting your site. These guidelines can be found at **http://www.bizweb.com/InfoForm/infoform.html**.

Infoseek Guide's Web Site Reviews
Site Address: http://guide.infoseek.com
URL Submission Address: http://guide.infoseek.com/IS/AddUrl?DCaddurl.html
Corrections Address: N/A

Infoseek's free search service, Infoseek Guide (See Figure 5.4).

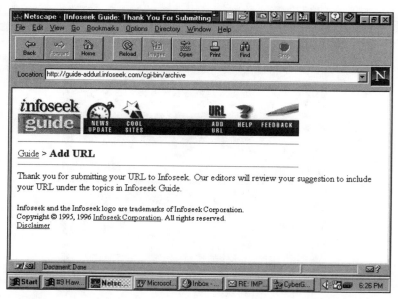

Figure 5.4 *Submitting to Infoseek Guide—maybe you'll get in, maybe you won't.*

Internet Mall

Site Address: http://www.internet-mall.com/index.html
URL Submission Address: http://www.internet-mall.com/howto.htm
Corrections Address: taylor@netcom.com

If your Web site provides additional information about a tangible product or service and potential customers can order it, it is appropriate for Dave Taylor's Internet Mall (see Figure 5.5). The mall is divided up into eight "floors" containing sites containing anything from automotive-related products and books to clothes and professional services. The Internet Mall excludes Internet-related services (access and Web page publishing), as well as things like multi-level marketing.

Magellan (McKinley's Internet Directory)

Site Address: http://www.mckinley.com/
URL Submission Address: http://www.mckinley.com/mckinley-txt/220.html
Corrections Address: feedback@mckinley.com

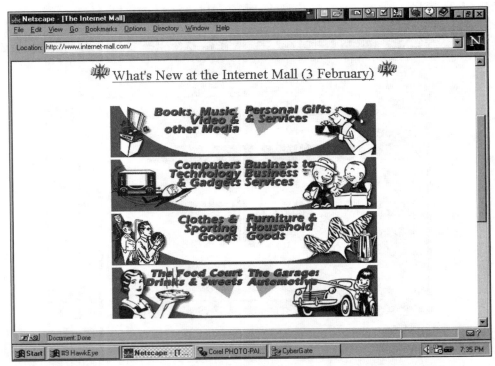

Figure 5.5 The Internet Mall is more like a directory than a cybermall.

As you may have guessed, the name of the directory came from Ferdinand Magellan, a Portuguese explorer who sailed the seas in the 1500s. Magellan is an online directory of reviewed and rated Internet sites. Their writers review and rate thousands of new sites each month. In addition to the reviewed sites (numbering less than 100,000), over 1.5 million nonreviewed sites are searchable in their unrated database. Some of those sites may be reviewed at a later date.

When you submit your site, there is no guarantee that it will be reviewed and listed. The rating system awards from 1 to 10 points in three areas (as excerpted verbatim from Magellan):

- Depth: Is it comprehensive and up-to-date?

- Ease of Exploration: Is it well organized and easy to navigate?

- Net Appeal: Is it innovative? Does it appeal to the eye or the ear? Is it funny? Is it hot, hip, or cool? Is it thought-provoking?

The resulting point total is converted into a star rating with the highest being four stars. Many sites that achieve a rating of three stars or more display a graphic "badge of honor," if you will, on their site. Much like sites that are reviewed in the Point survey (shown next).

Point
Site Address: http://www.pointcom.com
URL Submission Address: http://www.pointcom.com/gifs/submit/
Corrections Address: N/A

Even though this site is mentioned in Chapter 7, it falls under this heading as well. The difference is that Point will only list your site if they think that your site is in the Top five percent of all Web sites. They rate your site on a scale of 0-50 for content, presentation, and experience.

Scott Yanoff's Internet Services List
Site Address: http://www.uwm.edu/Mirror/inet.services.html
URL Submission Address: http://www.uwm.edu/Public/yanoff/feedback.html
Corrections Address: http://www.uwm.edu/Public/yanoff/feedback.html

This list is one of the oldest subject lists on the Net (originally distributed via email and now available on the Web) and contains many useful sites. It is restricted to free services only. Scott does not accept sites that sell or promote a product, that are advertisements, or that are adult oriented. Check out what's already on the list to see if your site fits in.

Trade Wave Galaxy (formerly EINet Galaxy)
Site Address: http://www.einet.net/galaxy.html
URL Submission Address: http://www.einet.net/cgi-bin/annotate?Other
Corrections Address: galaxy@einet.net

An Internet directory "old timer" that has been around for awhile. It has a rather extensive list of categories that your site should fit into, but if it doesn't, the Trade Wave personnel who review each entry will create one that's appropriate.

Yahoo!
Site Address: http://www.yahoo.com
URL Submission Address: http://add.yahoo.com/bin/add?
Corrections Address: http://add.yahoo.com/bin/change

In order to add your site to Yahoo!, shown in Figure 5.6, you need to choose the appropriate category. Your entry will be rejected without providing a

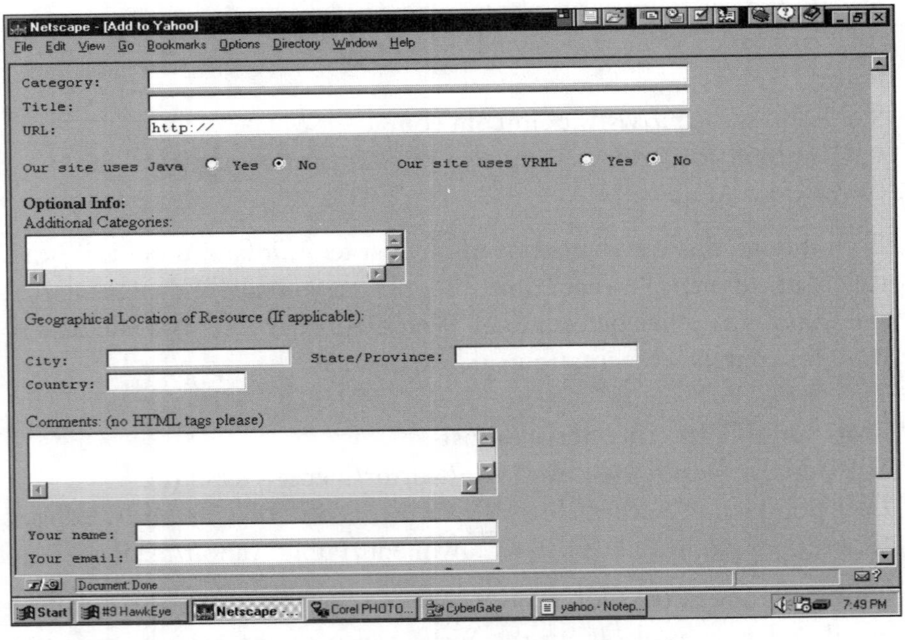

Figure 5.6 You've just gotta submit your site to Yahoo!

category when filling out the Add URL form. Unfortunately, it can take several weeks before your listing is added to Yahoo! On numerous occasions I submitted a site and it was not listed. Yahoo! does not list every new site suggestion it receives, but I knew these sites should be listed. After resubmitting one or two more times, the sites finally got listed. If you have this trouble, you can call Yahoo! and ask to submit the site via email (they will give you an address to send it to). You'll need to provide all the information normally required in the online form. Once you finally get listed in Yahoo!, you'll receive a letter like the one shown in Figure 5.7. Even though Yahoo! is one of the most popular sites on the Net, don't expect to receive tons of visitors just because you are listed. Yahoo! will add to your traffic count, but unless you purchase advertising, you're not likely to get massive amounts of additional traffic. I can say, however, that I did get sales of my first book from people who found the site's tiny listing in Yahoo! (Yahooooo to that!).

Search Sites That Automatically List Submitted Web Sites

555-1212.com
Site Address: http://www.555-1212.com

```
Date: Sat, 25 Nov 1995 14:18:02 -0800
From: Aaron Bromagem <aaron@yahoo.com>
To: Bill Brock <lti@laser-tone.com>
Subject: Yahoo Addition

Hi,

The URL you submitted <url:http://www.laser-tone.com/usa/> has been added
to Yahoo! It will appear in Yahoo on the next update, which will likely occur
within the next 24 hours. You can find your listing by looking through the
"What's New" listing or by doing a keyword search after the next update.

We appreciate you taking the time to add your site to Yahoo. We rely on users
like yourself to make Yahoo as complete and comprehensive as possible. In
order to keep Yahoo accurate as well, please let us know of changes to your
listing in the future.

Thanks again...

The Yahoo Team
```

Figure 5.7 Email confirmation from Yahoo! of a Web site addition.

URL Submission Address: http://www.555-1212.com/addbiz.html
Corrections Address: correction@555-1212.com

Specializes in being a World Wide Web business directory and therefore does not list personal home pages or those that are subject oriented. In addition to companies, 555-1212.com does list schools, government, products, and organizations.

Apollo Advertising
Site Address: http://www.apollo.co.uk
URL Submission Address: http://apollo.co.uk/place-usa.html
Corrections Address: http://apollo.co.uk/place-usa.html

Apollo recently started charging a modest $8/year for businesses and organizations (see Figure 5.8). Personal listings are still free. A listing may be up to 300 characters and for $15 extra, you can get a small banner (100 by 64 pixels)

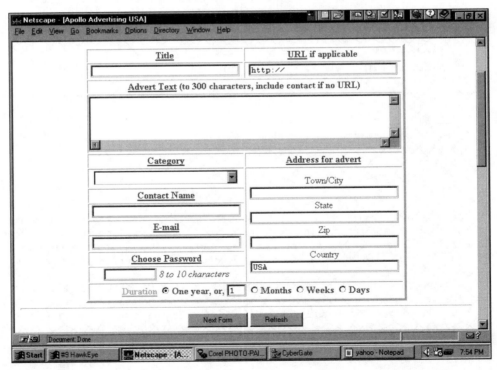

Figure 5.8 Apollo is one of the first directories to start charging for certain types of listings.

displayed with your listing. Payment may be made by credit card online. Since Apollo has been around a very long time (in "Internet time," that is) and since it's quite popular, I'd say it's worth the $8/year they are asking, especially if you are selling a product or service. The submission address I listed above is for sites within the USA. Apollo has other areas if your site is located elsewhere in the world.

Commercial Advertising & Marketing Server
Site Address: http://www.comcomsystems.com/search/en/index.html
URL Submission Address: http://www.comcomsystems.com/search/en/welcome2.html

Corrections Address: http://www.comcomsystems.com/search/en/welcome2.html

Accepts product and service Web site listings only. You may provide a one-line description and up to 40 keywords when submitting your listing.

Commercial Sites Index (by Open Market)
Site Address: http://www.directory.net
URL Submission Address: http://www.directory.net/dir/submit.cgi
Corrections Address: http://www.directory.net/dir/submit.cgi

Listings are restricted to companies, institutions, or organizations with a Web presence and not individual products or services. This is one of the few sites that contains a specific box for keywords. There doesn't appear to be any restriction on the number of keywords it will accept, so be sure to enter all that you think are necessary. After submission, your listing will appear in the new announcements area of the site and will also be searchable. Announcements are posted to a What's New page on the site. The page is updated daily (see Figure 5.9).

You can use HTML in your announcement, and I highly encourage you to do so (as your announcement will stick out while anyone is scrolling though the What's New page). You are permitted up to 100 words for your announcement, and this is what is displayed (when your site meets the search criteria) and shown in the results page. This is one of the few sites where the words within your announcement are *not* indexed (the keywords and title are). Listings appear in alphabetical order, so you may want to consider creative ways to name your site. It takes up to a few days before your listing is added. Although Open Market says that your site submission needs to be reviewed for approval,

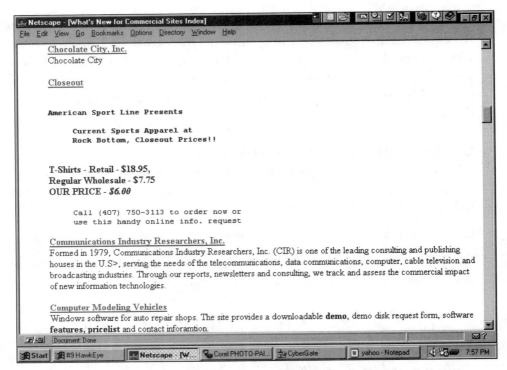

Figure 5.9   Some What's New announcements in the Commercial Sites Index—
which one stands out?

they don't stringently filter listings like McKinkley or Yahoo! Therefore, I list
it in this section.

Entrepreneurs on the Web

Site Address: http://www.eotw.com
URL Submission Address: http://www.eotw.com/gather.html
Corrections Address: eotw@eotw.com

EOTW primarily lists company sites.

Gold Site Europe

Site Address: http://www.gold.net
URL Submission Address: http://www.gold.net/gold/gold2.html
Corrections Address: http://www.gold.net/gold/gold2.html

Created by CityScape Internet Services Ltd., gold.net is one of Europe's busi-
est sites, with over 2.4 million accesses per month. Its database contains
information on over 18,000 sites. You may enter several pages of description

(more than anywhere else I've seen), and your description may contain HTML codes. I recommend using a "mailto:" anchor for the places where you may enter your email address. This will make your email address "hot," and users can click on it and send you mail right there from your listing. You can do this by replacing "you@yourdomain.com" with the email address you want to list, for example: <A HREF="mailto:you@yourdomain.com">you@your-domain.com</A>

LinkStar Internet Directory
Site Address: http://www.linkstar.com
URL Submission Address: http://www.linkstar.com/linkstar/bin/doform?form=ecard
Corrections Address:
http://www.linkstar.com/linkstar/bin/form-builder?form=ecard&MODE=UPDATE

Linkstar, shown in Figure 5.10, is one of the few sites where you can provide contact information with your listing. People wanting to call or mail you have all the information they need. In addition, a 50-word description and up to eight categories may be selected to describe your site. Be sure to provide the keywords in your description. After submitting your "e-Card" (electronic business card), your listing will be indexed and available within three hours.

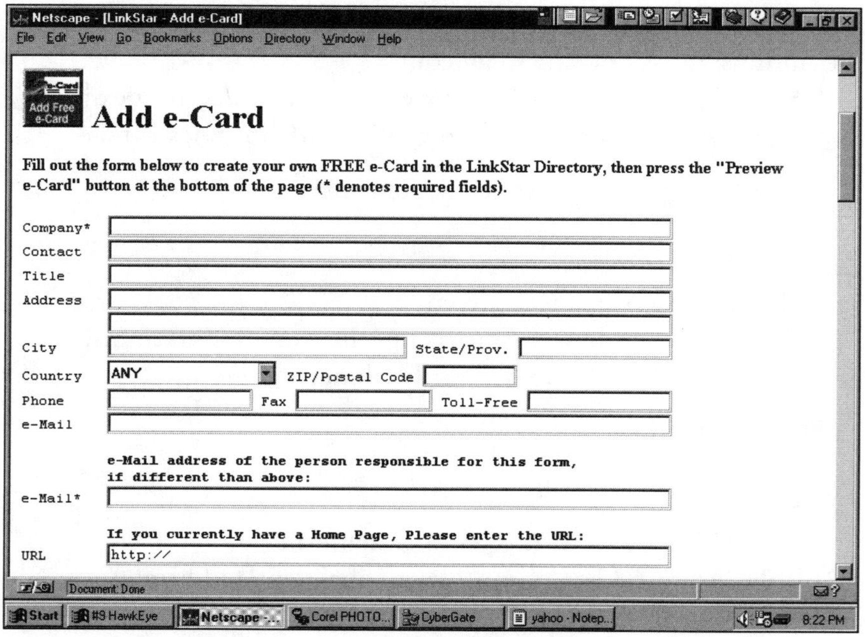

Figure 5.10 LinkStar requests typical business card information and more.

Manufacturer's Information Net
Site Address: http://mfginfo.com
URL Submission Address: http://mfginfo.com/htm/infoform.htm
Corrections Address: webmaster@mfginfo.com

Lists manufacturers and related services. Visit this site to see if you fit in.

Navigate dot Net
Site Address: http://www.navigate.net
URL Submission Address: http://www.navigate.net/add.html
Corrections Address: navigate@navigate.net

Quick and easy searching and listing.

Nerd World Media
Site Address: http://www.nerdworld.com/index.html
URL Submission Address: http://www.nerdworld.com/nwadd.html
Corrections Address: dstein@nerdworld.com

An Internet Subject Index with over 30,000 links.

NetMall
Site Address: http://www.netmall.com
URL Submission Address: http://www.netmall.com/add/index.html
Corrections Address: http://www.netmall.com/add/index.html

A fast growing, popular place to list your site.

The HUGE List
Site Address: http://thehugelist.com
URL Submission Address: http://thehugelist.com/addurl2.html
Corrections Address: 3mwedia@earthlink.net

It's HUGE all right!

Tribal Voice
Site Address: http://www.tribal.com/search.htm
URL Submission Address: http://www.tribal.com/add.htm
Corrections Address: update@tribal.com

Yet another place to submit your listings and do searches.

Virtual Yellow Pages
Site Address: http://www.vyp.com
URL Submission Address: http://www.vyp.com/yp/additions.html
Corrections Address: jtito@vyp.com

Claims to be getting more than three million "hits" per week (you *did* read Chapter 4 regarding what a hit is, didn't you?).

Wandex—The World Wide Web Wanderer Index
Site Address: http://www.netgen.com/cgi/comprehensive
URL Submission Address: http://www.netgen.com/cgi/addhost
Corrections Address:

Matt Grey and net.Genesis' "Comprehensive List of Sites." As you can see in Figure 5.11, you'll probably have to wait a while before your site is indexed.

World Wide Yellow Pages
Site Address: http://www.yellow.com
URL Submission Address: http://www.yellow.com/cgi-bin/online
Corrections Address: listing@yellow.com

Created by Home Pages, Inc. and dubbed as "The Yellow Pages For The Next 100 Years." You may choose up to five categories (search the site for ones that

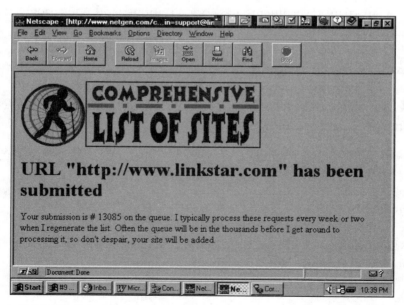

Figure 5.11 Don't hold your breath waiting to be added after submitting here!

apply to your situation and use those) and enter a 25-word description that will accompany your listing (no HTML permitted). You may also enter an 80-word announcement (HTML permitted).

International (non-USA) Directories

These directories restrict submissions to Web sites that are located in their respective areas. If your site is located outside the U.S., one or more of these may apply.

Asia Business Connection
Site Address: http://asiabiz.com
URL Submission Address: http://asiabiz.com/addwww.html
Corrections Address: intercon@singnet.com.sg

"Your Guide to Business Resources in Asia." The company doesn't accept any listings from outside of Asia.

The Canadian Internet Business Directory
Site Address: http://cibd.com/cibd/CIBDHome.html
URL Submission Address: http://cibd.com/cibd/add.html
Corrections Address: http://cibd.com/cibd/add.html

Lists Canadian government sites, organizations, and educational institution sites (as well as businesses).

Canada Net White Pages
Site Address: http://www.visions.com/netpages/cnwhitep.html
URL Submission Address: http://www.visions.com/netpages/cnwpform.html
Corrections Address: info@visions.com

The first searchable database of Canadian email addresses and URLs available on the Web. Restricts listings to Canadian sites only.

CiberCentro
Site Address: http://www.cibercentro.com
URL Submission Address: http://www.cibercentro.com/contribuir/
Corrections Address: webjefe@cibercentro.com

Spanish language directory with search capability (see Figure 5.12). It takes a few days before your entry is added. Only accepts sites that are in Spanish. "CiberCentro" means "CyberCentral" in English.

Nihongo Yellow Pages

Site Address: http://www.nyp.com
URL Submission Address: http://www.nyp.com/HTML/quickEntry.html
Corrections Address: feedback@nyp.com

Listings geared toward Japanese market (but will accept listings in English or Japanese).

But Wait! There's More!

There are literally hundreds of directories and searchable sites on the Net where you can list your site. Since it doesn't make sense to list every possible

Figure 5.12 If you have a Spanish language version of your Web site, list it with "CyberCentral."

site here, I've listed many of the more significant ones that are likely to provide the bulk of your traffic from search sites. New ones have popped up since this book has gone to print. To remedy this, I'm providing you with a number of valuable Web site promotion resources that contain lists of sites where you can submit your Web site URL and associated information.

A1's Directory of 574 FREE WWW Web Page Promotion Sites

http://www.vir.com/~wyatt/index.html

At last count, 574 was the number. By the time you get to it, there should be many more! (See Figure 5.13.)

A Big Ol' List of Places to Submit Your URLs To...

http://www.shout.net/~whitney/html/gopublic.html

An alphabetical listing created by Whitney Proffitt.

Internet Promotions Megalist

http://www.2020tech.com/submit.html

Figure 5.13 A1 is a great resource that will point you in the direction of more sites to list with!

A listing of not only search engines and directories but many other types of Web site promotion related sites.

Pointers to Pointers

`http://www.homecom.com/global/pointers.html`

HomeCom Communication's comprehensive listing was probably the first of its kind.

Online Media Buying, Banner Ads, and Sponsorships

Chapter 6 Topics

Who's *Really* Making Money on the Internet?

Web Advertising Jargon

Basics of Banner Advertising

Types of Banner Ads and Sponsorable Web Sites

How to Avoid Getting Ripped Off with Banner Ads

Graphical Design of Effective Banner Ads

Internet Directories and Search Engines You Can Advertise On (with Rates)

Jupiter Communications, a company that specializes in providing research and reports for the online arena, found in a study released in January 1996 that online advertising revenue is expected to grow to $4.6 billion by the year 2000. In 1995, online ad revenue totaled $55 million. Table 6.1 shows some of the top Web publishers based on ad revenues. The primary way this ad revenue is being generated now is through *banner ads*. Simply put, a banner ad is a mini-billboard that takes up a small amount of screen real estate on the Web page that it is placed on. Banner ads are the number one way to create awareness of your site *online*. Chapters 12 and 13 deal with creating awareness of your site *offline*. Before I get into the nuts and bolts of banner ads, which is what this chapter is primarily about, let's review the lingo of Internet advertising.

Internet Advertising Lingo

Ad Click Rate—See "Click Through."

Ad Slot—Also called a slot. A position space on a Web page that has been reserved for a banner or button advertisement. A Web page may contain more than one slot.

Table 6.1 Top Web Publishers Based on Ad Revenue (4th Quarter 1995)
Source: WebTrack's InterAd Monthly (January 1996)

1.	Netscape	$1,766,000
2.	Lycos	1,296,000
3.	Infoseek	1,215,000
4.	Yahoo!	1,086,000
5.	Pathfinder	810,000
6.	HotWired	720,000
7.	WebCrawler	660,000
8.	ESPNET SportsZone	600,000
9.	GNN	594,000
10.	clnet	540,000
11.	Playboy	325,000
12.	CMP's TechWeb	313,000
13.	ZD Net	295,000
14.	Riddler	267,000
15.	IUMA	263,000

Auditing—An attempt at recording and verifying the number of visitors to a Web page or site, often by an independent third party.

Banner—A rectangular graphic displayed in billboard fashion on a Web page. Banners can be any size, but many sites standardize the size. The most popular banner sizes are from 460 to 480 pixels wide by 60 to 80 pixels high, with 468×60 pixels being the de facto standard. Banners provide some of the most prominent exposure possible on the Web. Interested users click on banners and are subsequently connected to the advertiser's Web site.

Button—A smaller, more square-shaped online ad. A button can be considered a mini-banner.

CPM—Cost per thousand. A cost term often used in print advertising. Print publication ad rates are typically based on a CPM. Online publications seem to be adopting this standard as well. The average CPM for a banner ad is $20 to $30.

Click Through—The number or percentage of users who actually click on the banner of an advertiser (to visit that Web site). The real-life analogy is the number of people who call an 800 number displayed on a short TV spot. In both situations the viewer is self-qualified, is believed to be interested in the advertiser's product or service, and took action to get additional information.

Impressions—The number of times a particular Web page with an ad slot has been displayed. Online ad rates are often determined by the number of impressions potentially seen by visitors.

Linking—The act of buying, bartering, or begging for a hyperlink listing on a Web page. The more links you have to your site, the more traffic you are capable of getting.

Middle Page—A Web page that appears after an Internet user clicks on a banner ad but before the actual site is displayed. It is used to better track click throughs. A middle page typically has a paragraph of information and a link to the advertiser's Web site.

Online Media Buying—The act of placing banner ads in the appropriate Web sites for maximum exposure or to suit other goals of the advertiser. More and more, there are third parties who offer this as a service, much like traditional advertising agencies do for traditional media.

Page Views—Same as impressions. For example, Yahoo! uses the term page views instead of hits or impressions.

Pixel—A unit of measurement on a computer monitor. A pixel is an abbreviation for picture element. Banner and button ads are created to be a certain size measured in pixels.

Unique Views—A unique view is termed as one person seeing one page one time. Some software filters out back-and-forth browsing produced by hitting the back button on your Web browser software (thereby seeing the same Web page multiple times). This filtration yields a unique view rather than several views (which is meaningless to marketers).

Who's Using the Web Anyway?

One of the things advertisers of traditional media ask before placing an ad is: "What type of people are watching, reading, or listening to the programming or content who would be exposed to my ad?"

The answer to this question for Web advertisers isn't so easily determined or available as yet. Sure, there are demographic studies of Internet/Web users, which I'll share with you in a minute, but it's still early in the game and the dynamic nature of the online environment and its users makes it difficult to pin down who's out there. In addition, online surveys are conducted online. I personally feel that the results of these surveys may be biased and skewed. In my opinion, the users who are comfortable participating in and who take the time to fill out these long Web-based survey forms are not typical of the average Internet user. How much of a difference this makes, if any, is anyone's guess. In addition to possible biases, various surveys often conflict with each other with regard to how many actual Internet users there are out there and who they are. Perhaps the safest bet is to take the results of several surveys and average them. The good news is that the demographic picture is getting clearer all the time. What's safe to say is that Internet users are more technologically-literate, make more money, and are more educated than nonusers. These are exactly the types of people many advertisers are interested in reaching. Check out these surveys yourself to get a firsthand idea of who, and how many people, are out there.

GVU World Wide Web Survey

http://www.cc.gatech.edu/gvu/user_surveys/

Georgia Institute of Technology's Graphics, Visualization & Useability (GVU) Center biyearly Internet demographics study. The first large-scale Internet demographics study.

CommerceNet/Nielsen Internet Demographic Survey

http://www.commerce.net

CommerceNet is a nonprofit consortium of organizations that seek is to promote electronic commerce. The final report is over 300 pages and is available for $5,000. The proceeds fund additional CommerceNet activities. For additional information or to order, call (415) 617-8790 or email survey@commerce.net. Some of the results were

- 17 percent of people age 16 or older in US homes had access to the Net, and 11 percent had used it within the past 3 months.

- People spent an average of 2.5 hours a week online, although 15 percent of them accounted for 50 percent of the total online usage.

- 48 percent had household incomes of $40,000 or more.

- 60 percent were age 35 or older.

O'Reilly & Associates Survey

http://www.ora.com:80/survey/

O'Reilly's "Defining the Internet Opportunity" claims to be the first statistically defensible study of US Internet users. The survey was conducted with Trish Information Services and used the RDD (Random Digit Dialing) methodology. The survey was conducted in three phases, utilizing direct mail as well as telephone interviews. The survey found that there is a total of 5.8 million adult Internet users within the US (approx. 1 user per 1,149 households). The survey compared Internet and online service users and found fairly close correlations between the two. Some of the results were

- 66 percent of Internet users are male.

- 74 percent make over $35,000 a year.

- Most (80 percent) are between the ages of 18 and 44.

The full text of the results is available to the sponsors of the survey. If you're interested in being a sponsor contact Florence Kanuk (florence@ora.com) or call (707) 829-0515 ×231.

Yahoo! User Survey

Yahoo! teamed up with Jupiter Communications, a company that tracks online media, to conduct a survey of its users. The survey was completed in October 1995 and had over 62,000 respondents. The survey found

- 63 percent use Netscape as their primary Web browser.

- 22 percent had America Online accounts.

- Less than 10 percent access the Web through an online service.

- The average age of Yahoo! users is 35.

The full report is priced at $2,495 and is available from Jupiter at (800) 488-4345.

Internet Users in England

NOP Research Group conducted a face-to-face survey of Internet users from the UK. The findings: 66 percent are male, 65 percent are between 15 and 34 years of age, and 35 percent make $40,000 or more a year.

Banner Ads 101

From the definition list, you know what a banner ad is. Figure 6.1 shows an example banner ad for InterLotto, a Liechtenstein Government, state-controlled lottery ad that was placed on clnet (http://www.cnet.com). In my opinion, banner ads are the best way to create or enhance the awareness of your Web site with Internet users.

Before you start buying ad slots all over the Net, there are a number of things you should know about. This section will get you up to speed and help to ensure that you don't waste your money creating a poor banner and placing it in the wrong place for too much money.

Figure 6.1 A banner ad for InterLotto placed on a page within clnet's Web site.

Types of banner ad slots

Banners ad slots come in three flavors:

1. **Static.** Static banners remain constantly on the same Web page until they are removed. Every single user who views the particular Web page will see your banner. These are often found on lower traffic sites.

2. **Rotating.** These are banners that rotate among different Web pages on the same site. Most of the search engines and high-traffic sites offer this type. There is space made on each Web page and a CGI program randomly (or in some cases not randomly) chooses a banner from a list and places it in the slot. Remember that at any one time, dozens of Internet users can be looking at the exact same Web page. With a rotating banner situation, some users would see one particular banner while others would see another, etc. Some sites have their banners rotating because there are just too many slots, and no single advertiser has the money or wants to spend the money to monopolize the site. Therefore, the ad space is divided up among numerous advertisers.

3. **Scrolling.** This is a very new type of slot. It's reminiscent of those real-life billboards that have many vertical panels. They all turn at once to show a

different billboard every 10 seconds or 20 seconds or whatever—thereby making it possible for the same person viewing that billboard to see more than one ad. A scrolling banner ad slot permits Web publishers to sell more ads in the same space since two or more ads can be seen by the same person while that person is viewing the same Web page.

Audience-specific Web sites

There are essentially three types of audience groups that different Web sites cater to:

1. **General Audience Sites.** These Web sites offer you the ability to reach a "mass" audience. Examples are major directories and search engines and sites that consistently attract large volumes of users. None of these sites is solely dedicated to a specific subject or audience.

2. **Niche or Subject-Specific Sites.** Offers the ability to target the audience due to the demographics or special interests of the users. Meta-indexes (see Chapter 8) and publications catering to a certain hobby or interest are good examples of niche sites. The downside is that niche sites have lower traffic counts; however, the goodside is that their users are more likely to buy certain products or services. Sites that cater to a certain demographic on average have lower traffic counts than general audience sites, but there are some real powerhouses out there like ESPNET SportsZone, SportsLine USA, Playboy, and Penthouse (young and middle-aged male audiences). These are good if your Web site offers information that is of interest to the user demographic of the site that you would place your banner on.

3. **Geographically Oriented Sites.** This is a new breed. Certain sites like The Virtual Tourist (**http://www.vtourist.com/webmap/**) or City.Net (**http://www.city.net**) are arranged in a geographical format. There are quite a number of cybermalls and marketplaces that use their geography in their names. These typically house Web sites that are located in the area. Users of most geographically oriented sites are either interested in visiting or moving to a particular part of the planet or already live there. Since the Internet is no longer a single global market (because of its rapid expansion and the self-grouping of users by their interests), this is likely to be a growth area as far as banner ad placement is concerned.

Objectives of banner ads

The main objective of most Web advertising is to boost traffic to the Web site of the advertiser. Secondary objectives would be to create or enhance the awareness of the site's existence (by putting the URL on the banner), awareness of the brand (like a banner I saw for Honda), and/or awareness of an event (like a DCI Web World conference where the date and location of the event is displayed on the banner).

It's important to know what your objectives are before you create the banner ad itself. Your objectives will determine the overall look of the banner, what information is written on it, how many different types of banners you'll need, where you will place them, and for how long.

Most Web site promotion situations fall into one of the following two categories:

- *Short-term traffic burst*

   The types of scenarios which apply to a short-term approach are:

   > Case #1: Launch of a new Web site

   > Case #2: Announcement of an event such as a seminar, conference or exposition

   > Case #3: Announcement of a product

   > Case #4: Promotion of a contest or giveaway

   > Case #5: Announcement of a major face lift of your site

- *Long-term traffic building*

   The types of scenarios which apply to a long-term approach are:

   > Case #1: Continuous flow of visitors to an existing Web site

   > Case #2: Building up of a subscriber base (where you require users to register)

   > Case #3: Followup to short-term cases 1, 3, and 5

SHORT-TERM PROMOTION APPROACH

You just created your Web site, launched a new product, organized an upcoming event or something similar, and you want the world to know about it in a hurry. You want to have a "grand opening" and line them up waiting to get in.

You'll probably want to concentrate on high traffic sites, and purchase a banner slot for as short a time as possible. Most sites are negotiable, but the typical minimum placement time is one full month. Yahoo!'s Web Launch for $1,000 is a no brainer in this situation. That will get you one week's worth of good exposure. Obviously, you see that your budget capacity will be the final decision maker. You'll want to place your banner in lots of places for a very short time. If you purchased a banner from a site that charges on a per-impression basis (a method that's getting more and more popular), they may be able to accelerate the number of times it is seen (as these are almost always rotating slots). LinkStar, for example, can assign a higher "weight" to a particular banner ad. This will cause the banner to be displayed more often in the rotation. The end result is that the number of impressions is higher per unit of time. As an event draws closer for example, the weight of the ad can increase as well. Therefore the banner will be seen more often by more people. If you've ever noticed the ads that are run in the newspaper before a big event in your area occurs, you've seen that they often start small a month or two before the event, and gradually get larger and run more frequently until the day of the event. A similar approach can be accomplished on certain Web sites.

LONG-TERM PROMOTION APPROACH

The goal of the long-term approach is that you want to increase the daily traffic to your site on a consistent basis. Lower-traffic sites as well as higher-traffic sites are appropriate for this approach. The difference is that you'll want to use multiple banners and move those banners from site to site as time progresses. Use the tools from Chapter 4 to track the effectiveness of different banners in different locations. See which ones are most effective. As time goes by, you'll find a core of reliable sites that get a satisfactory number of click throughs on a regular basis. These are the ones to stick with, but always keep placing banners in new "test" locations to find even better sites and keep changing your banners within the sites that work.

Is Web advertising a better deal than other media?

Some people have questioned whether Web advertising is a good deal as compared to print (or other media). I've seen arguments to the effect that Web advertisers are paying from 40 to several hundred times more CPM (cost per thousand) for banners than print advertising. I disagree with their logic. Obviously, no one wants to throw his or her money away, so let's discuss this for a minute before moving on.

The way the naysayers figure the online CPM is by how many people actually click on the banner, not how many people see the banner. The act of clicking brings users to the Web site, which they consider to be the actual ad (I on the other hand, consider the banner to be the ad). Therefore, they divide the number of click throughs by the cost of the banner for a set period of time. This gives a CPM amount that is grossly exaggerated and therefore inaccurate in my opinion.

The problem with this logic is that when I place an ad in a magazine, for example, most readers see my ad. Not that many actually respond to the ad by calling or writing for more information. Therefore, online CPM should be determined by how many people see the banner, not by how many respond to it (by clicking through). This is a more equivalent comparison between advertising in the two media, and the Web wins hands down.

Comparing effectiveness between the media is more tricky. You can gauge effectiveness by counting how many people respond to an ad or by how many sales were generated due to an ad. It can be difficult for certain companies to track exactly how many people responded to a print or TV ad because they aren't equipped or able to ask all the respondents how they heard about them. It's definitely do-able though. I'm sure you've seen things like "don't forget to ask for Dept. 5" or "call and ask for extension 300" or some cryptic code in the fine print on a response card or coupon. The Web however, has increasingly more tools available for you to accurately track ad response (some of which were mentioned in Chapter 4).

How to avoid getting ripped off with banner ads

As you'll see from the resources listed at the end of this chapter, there are many Web sites where you can spend your money to place a banner ad on a company's pages. Before you do, there are some considerations you'll want to make. Obviously you want your banner to be seen by as many people as possible for the lowest price possible. In most cases, however, the reason you are placing the ad to begin with is to get people to actually click on it to visit your Web site (click through).

BANNER AD FACTORS

- **Exposure time**—How long do people see your banner? I've noticed that when I use Lycos (a search engine), I enter my search term and hit "submit" before the banner has had time to download and display on the screen. Therefore, I'm exposed to it for zero seconds, an essentially worthless impression.

- **Impressions**—The more impressions you get, the more people who are likely to see your ad.

- **Unique visits**—Most people in newspaper advertising say that more small ads will get you better results than fewer big ads. Repetition. Repetition can be good and bad. On the Net, it's very difficult to tell how many of the impressions that you paid for were seen by the same exact person. Ideally, you want to get as many unique people to see your ad as possible. I remember seeing an ad for Honda on Yahoo! at least seven times before I actually clicked on the darn thing. I just got tired of seeing it and not knowing what the site was like. I spent a few minutes in the site and then went back to Yahoo! to continue my search. In this case, repetition was good because that's what it took before I actually clicked.

- **Position of banner on the Web page**—The higher your banner is, the more click through you are likely to get. The only good thing about being lower on the page is that it's less intrusive. Check to make sure that your banner appears in the top third of the screen. (See Figure 6.2 for an example of poor placement.)

- **Position of banner within the site**—Different parts of a site attract different types of people. If you are selling cosmetics, you don't want your banner to appear on a page where 90 percent of the users are male. Since Web sites consist of many different pages, some pages may be more popular than others or attract different types of users. Find out where your banner will be placed within the site before committing to a contract.

- **Hyperlink route**—Where does your banner lead to? You can direct traffic to a specific place within your site or to the home page. You can even add on an extra page that welcomes them from the previous place (called a middle page). If you have banners running in several types of sites, you can direct users from one site to an appropriate page within your site and other users from another site to a different page within your site.

- **Click throughs**—In most cases, this is what it's all about. If increasing traffic is what you want, then you want click throughs. When aren't click throughs as critical? A good example is for a conference. For example, DCI's Web World conferences occur in different cities throughout the year. In April of 1996 it was in Orlando, Florida, and in June it was in Chicago, etc. The important thing to them is that people are aware of the event, the date, and the location. The banners they placed on the LinkStar search site contained this information. Therefore, any users who saw the banner for the Chicago event, could quickly decide if they were interested and able to go. If there was a chance, they would click the banner to visit the DCI Web site to get more information. Therefore, click throughs (although great) aren't critical in this situation. It's the information on the banner that's important. Regardless of whether click through is important to you or not, it's probably the most popular way of determining the value of a banner. It's a yardstick.

How to determine the value of a banner ad

1. Determine the total number of impressions to the page or pages that your banner will be placed on.

2. Determine the price per impression.

3. Multiplying 1 by 2 gives the total price.

4. Determine the estimated (or actual if you've been running the ad) click throughs. This is the number of times your ad was actually clicked on.

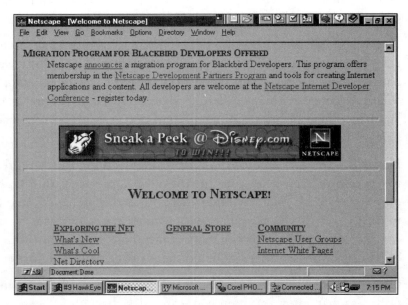

Figure 6.2 Disney's banner ad on Netscape's site is located in the middle of the page (not ideal).

Some sites have the capability to give this data to you, and depending upon how you are tracking your statistics on your Web site, you may be able to determine this yourself (or your Webmaster can).

5. Divide 3 by 4 to get cost per interested lead (or alternatively, Web site visitor).

As we just discussed, click throughs aren't necessarily critical, but that's really what most sites want to see—a high click through rate. Very few Web publishers charge only on click throughs. If click throughs are important to you, try to negotiate on the basis of expected or actual click through. See if the site will reduce the price per impression if you don't receive a certain number of click throughs. Or, another scenario is to ask them to reduce the price per impression, but offer to pay extra for each click through.

There are currently two predominant pricing models for banner ads:

- *One model is based on a per month or per quarter (or more) basis.* There is a fee associated with placing your banner on the site for a certain length of time. The price is fairly well set. It's based on an *estimate* of the number of impressions for that time period. For example, Yahoo! charges $20,000 for a banner to be placed in certain locations (specified on its rate sheet) for just one month. Yahoo! estimates that the number of impressions received (it calls them page views) is about 1 million. For example, the actual number of page views may be 750,000 or may be 1,500,000, but your price is still the same. Maybe you come out ahead, maybe you don't. The price is based on a $20 CPM (two cents per impression but in actuality it may be a little higher or lower).

- *The other pricing model is based on the actual number of impressions.* If you buy a banner for 100,000 impressions, it may take a week, a month or several months before all those impressions are used up. Regardless of the actual amount of linear time it takes, you pay on a per-impression basis. This model is becoming more popular because advertisers know what they are actually paying for, not an estimate.

An even newer model has begun to emerge that combines the two models. You can purchase a month's worth of advertising for a certain amount of money, and you are guaranteed a certain number of impressions.

A good example of banner ad value is when Interse Corporation, a producer of Web site hit-tracking software, did its own study. It placed a banner on

InfoSeek and Netscape. The value of each ad was $15,000 for 30 days. Interse found that the ad on InfoSeek generated a higher click through rate than the exact same banner on Netscape. Why is this you may ask? Well, these are two different classes of sites even though they both cater to a general audience. InfoSeek users go there by choice, while some of Netscape's users go there by default. They go to Netscape by default due to Netscape's URL being the place where new users of Netscape end up after starting the software. Even though Netscape was the highest grossing site in ad revenue for the 4th quarter of 1995, it's probably not as good a buy as search and content sites because not all the users make a concerted effort to visit it. For some of these people, your banner is wasted. In addition, most banners are located in the middle of the Web page. Some of Netscape's Web pages fill many screens. Not everyone scrolls down on every Web page they see.

If your site receives enough traffic, you can trade banners. If you have something of value to another site that has decent traffic, you can barter for the banner. In the beginning of 1995, bartering for banners used to be the primary way slots were filled because no one would pay for them. Today, people see the value and pay.

Graphical design and information elements of a banner ad

How a banner is designed can have a significant impact on the number of click throughs that are achieved. And click throughs are usually the main objective of placing the banner in the first place. Different sites accept different sized banner ads. The most common size, however, is 468×60 pixels. Obviously, smaller banner ad sizes restrict the amount of space for your message. Some sites also restrict the file size of the banner. The only way you can get the file size down without resizing a banner is to reduce the number of colors. If you're not skilled in creating graphics, the information in this section should be directed to your graphic artist who will design a banner for you. Some Web publishers will create a banner if you advertise with them. They may charge extra, but try to negotiate it for free. Most banners should cost under $150 with the average being around $75.

You can only fit so much in a banner. Most banners contain a logo and perhaps a tag line of some sort. Figures 6.3 through 6.6 contain some banners I've collected from various sponsorable Web sites. I don't claim that they all are good and work. I present them for you to compare and to give you ideas for how to design your own. Take note of how the information is organized, how good the readability is, whether you would click on it, etc. Unfortunately, you'll be seeing them in black and white. A banner that's just a logo isn't very compelling. Free offers of software or contest giveaways are quite effective as they tend to appeal to a user's curiosity if nothing else.

If you are advertising with the same site for more than one month, replace your banner each month as a minimum. If users see the same thing too often, they will stop paying attention to it. The Discovery Channel, for example, uses several banners simultaneously within the same site at the same time. Its banners are very effective at getting users to click through. An example is shown in Figure 6.3 (it's the 5th one down that says "who is this?"). The Discovery Channel banners appeal to a user's sense of curiosity by displaying a blurred image with some text to the effect "do you know who this is?" or "do you know what this is?" Psychology can play a big part in banner ad click through effectiveness. Some of the highest click throughs LinkStar received were with its banner that said "Don't Click Here," and that's it. As obvious as the ploy was, people still clicked on it.

Figure 6.3 *Banners I've collected from various Web sites.*

Figure 6.4   *More banners I've collected.*

Next generation banner ads

Static banners are the first generation of Web ads. Sites (like c|net) that collect user preference data have the capability of directing different banners to different users. For example, if a user has a PC compatible with Windows 95, that user will not receive ads for Macintosh software. Another example is that if you came from an educational site (with *.edu* extension) you may receive an ad geared to students or stating some academic discount program. There aren't many sites capable of this as I write this chapter, but more Web publishers will be able to selectively target ads to users. It's good news to Web advertisers, too. Technology like this greatly reduces the number of wasted impressions that an advertiser pays for. I don't know how many times I've seen a banner for Adobe PageMil software (Mac-based), and I use a PC.

Duracell broke the mold of Web advertising "going beyond the banner" as they say. The approach was to create a graphic for one of their batteries that

Figure 6.5 Yet more banners I've collected.

looked like it was bursting through the Web page. The graphic was made to look like it was actually part of the Web page it was placed on. This is interesting enough, but when you clicked on it, a page was displayed that looked like you had clicked *behind* the page the graphic was placed on. The middle page looked like a reversed mirror image of the page the graphic was placed on and had some Duracell batteries drawn to look as if they were powering the Web site you were using. This is hard to visualize without seeing it, but the idea was innovative enough to win Duracell one of the five "1995 Tenagra Excellence in Internet Marketing" awards.

Sun's Java language will be used to create animated banners where clicking on different parts of the banner may yield a different reaction. Sounds can be integrated into a banner as well, so when it is clicked you receive an audio message. As Web technology advances, expect to see more innovative ways of getting people to click through.

Figure 6.6 Yet even more banners I've collected.

Content-Oriented Sites

Some of the more prominent sites that attract Internet users due to their content are listed in this section. Content is what motivates us to tune in to a certain TV show or radio station. Content is what motivates us to subscribe to a particular magazine. The difference between a print magazine and an online one is that online publications rarely charge for a subscription. This may change soon, but for now, there is a lot less overhead associated with publishing online, and therefore, publications can survive solely through advertising support. As the Web advances, I suspect some of the higher quality sites will begin to charge for subscriptions, or at the very least, charge for value-added features. As I write this, the *Wall Street Journal* announced it was going to start charging users $10/month for using its online version.

Each publication or content-oriented site has users that fit certain demographics and have certain interests. The easiest way to waste your interactive advertising dollar is to purchase banners indiscriminately. If you know your audience and the audience of the sites where you are interested in purchasing banners, you'll help to ensure that you are not throwing your money away. Please note that I list ad rates in this section and in the following ones. These rates are of course subject to change. Don't start budgeting for placement until you contact the sites and receive their latest rate card. You'll get a pretty good idea of the types of rates that are out there from these listings, and most of them probably won't change their rates too much from what I have listed.

Avion On-Line

http://avion.db.erau.edu

The online extension of Embry-Riddle Aeronautical University's (my alma mater!) *Avion* newspaper. Niche based in the area of aviation. Sponsorships vary from $50/week to $350/month depending upon exposure.

CMP's TechWeb

http://www.techweb.com

TechWeb claims to be the "leading technology resource on the Web" with more technology advertisers (35+) than any other Web site. TechWeb offers online versions of a number of its print publications. All advertisers are listed in the TechWeb Ad Index, which provides a text link to the advertiser's site. If you make a special offer, such as free software to download, you'll also be listed in the TechMall (a special advertiser section). TechWeb comprises three groups, each of which contains different publications and rates.

The CMP Personal Computing Group consists of *HomePC, NetGuide* and *Windows Magazine* with a combined print magazine subscriber base of more than 1.4 million. These publications are primarily focused on the consumer market. The online versions of these publications generate more than 1 million page views monthly. Advertisers are guaranteed 750,000 banner impressions. In a unique move, these publications also charge $.50 per click through up to a maximum of $500/month. Additional information can be obtained by calling (214) 661-5673.

Publication	Rate (1 month)
HomePC	$1,000
NetGuide	$2,500
Windows	$3,900

Table 6.2 Major Advertisers and Where They Are Linked

Source: WebTrack's InterAd Monthly (August 1995)

AT&T	HotWired, Netscape, Pathfinder
IBM	HotWired, MecklerWeb's iWORLD, Mercury Center Web, ZD Net
Saturn	HotWired, Pathfinder
Zima	HotWired, Point Communications, Riddler

CMP Enterprise Computing Group publications are geared toward IT (Information Technology) professionals. The associated Web sites provide industry news, trending information, product reviews and articles related to IT and online. Discounts apply to advertisers who purchase three or more banners in the same quarter. Additional details can be obtained by calling (617) 487-7534.

Publication	Home Page	Edit Rotation
Communications Week Interactive	$4,000	$1,666
Information Week Online	$5,000	$2,333
Interactive Age Digital	$5,000	$2,333
Network Computing Online	$3,333	$1,666

CMP Channel Group publications consist of *Computer Reseller News, Computer Retail Week, MAX* and *VARBusiness*. Rates for a position on the home page for a three-month period are $5,000 (with the exception of Computer Retail Week, which is $3,500). Rates are about 30 percent lower for placement within the Edit Section of each publication's Web site. Call (617) 487-7528 for more details.

CMP OEM Group publications consist of *Electronic Engineering Times, Electronic Buyer's News,* and *OEM Magazine*. Various sponsorship levels exist with rates starting at $10,000 for three months. Call (516) 562-5742 for more details on rates.

Condom Country

http://www.ag.com/condom/country

Safe sex information and products. Averages 20,000+ visitors/week. Sponsorships vary from $550 to $750/month depending upon exposure.

c | net

http://www.cnet.com

clnet, first launched on June 24, 1995, is the "first full-function online service devoted entirely to computers, multimedia, and online services." By all accounts, it's the largest original content site on the Web. clnet the computer network augments the clnet TV show called *clnet Central*, which airs on the Sci-Fi Channel and USA Network six times a week. clnet is free to users and (as you may have guessed) is sponsor supported. clnet's initial sponsors were the movie *The Net*, Hewlett Packard, and MCI. In just the first two weeks online, clnet attracted over 30,000 users.

As I write this, clnet has over a half million registered users. Features include daily news features, links to mailing lists and newsgroups, columns and reviews, and lots more. clnet performed a survey of its users and found that approximately 75 percent of respondents accessed the service from home with 21 percent accessing it while on the company clock. The survey showed that the vast majority of its users are male (92.6 percent) and the average wage was about $50,000 a year.

Advertisers can sponsor different areas of the site. Sponsor banners link to a page located on clnet (for example, a middle page), which in turn has a link to the sponsor's site. clnet charges on a per impression basis. Contact clnet at **sponsor@cnet.com** for rates.

ESPNET SportsZone

http://espnet.sportszone.com

The online takeoff of the ESPN cable network, SportsZone (see Figure 6.7) offers the broadest, deepest, and most up-to-date sports information on the Net. The site is huge, containing over 10,000 pages. Over a quarter of a million individual users visit monthly with 96 percent being male. The site receives over a million and a half "hits" a day.

Sponsors receive an exclusive position in one of its main areas called franchise positions (rotated on a weekly basis), rotation among all its nonfranchise pages, and a listing in the sponsor index.

13 Weeks	*26 Weeks*	*1 Year*
$100,000	$175,000	$290,000

Figure 6.7 ESPNET's SportsZone.

HotWired

http://www.hotwired.com

HotWired is more than just a publication, it's a virtual community. It benefits greatly from the cross-promotion of its sister print publication, *Wired Magazine*. The content of each supports the other. A four-week minimum sponsorship commitment is required; rate is $15,000. HotWired has over 250,000 subscribers.

IUMA (Internet Underground Music Archive)

http://www.iuma.com

This site features independent and unsigned bands, sound clips, product sales, and more. It has over 75,000 registered users and receives an estimated 150,000+ visitors a month. A one-month sponsorship, which gets you a prominent link on its home page, is $14,000—with the price going down to $10,000/month for a year-long contract.

MacSense

http://www.macsense.com

A monthly electronic magazine focusing on the Macintosh computer market. Receives an average of 20,000 visitors a month. Sponsorships range from $400 to $1,800 depending on exposure.

MecklerWeb

http://www.mecklerweb.com

A product of MecklerMedia, the producer of *Internet World Magazine*, the site benefits from the cross promotion. Three-month sponsorships range from $1,500 to $7,000 depending upon exposure. One month sponsorships are available. MecklerWeb receives over 50,000 visitors/month.

Mercury Center Web

http://www.sjmercury.com

The online companion to the *San Jose Mercury News*. This site was one of the first newspapers to venture onto the Web and offer advertising. Rotating ads are $100/day with a one year contract. About half the users are based in Silicon Valley.

NCT Web Magazine

http://www.awa.com/nct/

"The information source for people who buy computer equipment and supplies." NCT contains over 700 pages of news and reviews. Sponsorships range from just $25/month for a simple link to $300/month for a home page sponsorship.

Netsurfer Marketplace

http://www.netsurf.com/nsm/

The companion to the popular Netsurfer Digest and Netsurfer Focus email publications. Covers news and interesting Internet places. Sponsorships range from $700 to $2,000 with discounts for multiple insertions.

NewsPage

http://www.newspage.com

NewsPage was developed by Individual, Inc. NewsPage is a customized news delivery service whose sources include over 700 trade journals and newspapers. It was ranked 12th by *Interactive Age* magazine in its list of "The 100 Best Business Web Sites." NewsPage claims to have placed the highest number of advertising sponsorships of any Web site and has over 1,000 ad positions available.

The site uses a "Dutch Auction System" where Web marketers bid on placing banners in various areas within the site. Whoever bids highest for a specific area wins the opportunity to place their banner in that slot. These are static banners and exclusive positions. An advantage of the system is that advertisers pay only the amount of the second highest bid. To submit a bid, you need to request a NewsPage auction kit. Visit the site for more details.

Pathfinder

http://www.pathfinder.com

Combines Time Warner magazines like *Time, Fortune, People,* and *Sports Illustrated* into an online publication (see Figure 6.8). Receives over 10 million "hits" weekly. Sponsorships are $36,000 per quarter. Marketplace listings are a lot less, priced at $1,250/month.

Playboy Magazine

http://www.playboy.com

Not much needs to be said here (see Figure 6.9). Sponsorships are $30,000 per quarter. Monthly sponsorships are available, but you'll incur a 15 percent surcharge.

SnoWeb (formerly SkiWeb)

http://www.snoweb.com

Skiing-related site, featuring ski reports, links to ski resources, and more. Site traffic exceeds 4,000 visitors per day in season. Sponsorships are very reasonable at $50 to $100 per month.

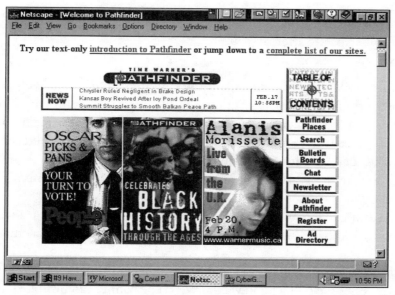

Figure 6.8 Time Warner's Pathfinder combines multiple print publications into one online publication.

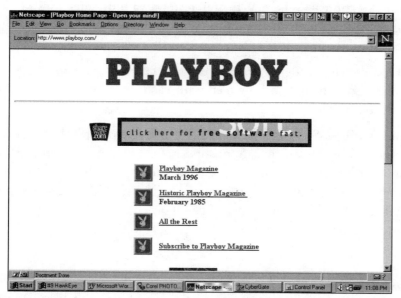

Figure 6.9 Playboy's site gets over 750,000 "hits" a day.

WEBster

The Cyberspace Surfer
http://www.tgc.com

Features breaking Web news, product releases, and latest Web technology. Subscription and advertiser supported. Demographics summary of its readership is 75 percent USA, 12.6 percent Europe, nearly 50 percent are aged 36-40, 70 percent have a household income over $50,000, 95 percent use email daily, 90 percent either plan to launch, upgrade, or expand their Web sites. Additional demographic information is available on its Web site.

Circulation: Each Web issue receives about 40,000 article or advertisement accesses, and over 20,000 copies of WEBster are circulated via email.

Front Page Banner—Provides highest visibility and will be seen by every person who accesses the publication via the Web. The banner can by linked to your site. The ad is also in the same prominent position on the Table of Contents which is sent via email. Front page banners are sold on a per-issue basis.

Hotlist Sections—Where WEBster reviews various categories of Web sites. Your ad will appear at the top of the section above all the reviews and is sold on a per-month basis.

INFOmercials—Provide a place to post current company news and press releases. Content may be changed with each issue but ads are sold on a per-month basis.

Sponsorships—Sponsor ads are linked in a sponsorship box that appears at the bottom of every article. Sponsors also receive one free Front Page Banner plus a 10 percent discount on all other ads. Sponsorships are sold on a six-month and yearly basis. Sponsors have included SGI (Silicon Graphics, Inc.) and DCI (Digital Consulting, Inc.—The company that puts on the Web World conferences).

Rates:
Front Page Banner (per bimonthly issue)

Frequency	1x	3x	6x	12x
Rate	$3,450	$3,300	$3,125	$2,925

HOTlist Sections (per month, 2 issues)

Frequency	1 Section	2 Sections		
Rate	$1,000	$1,750		

INFOmercials (per month, 2 issues)

Frequency	1x	3x	6x	12x
Rate	$1,475	$1,350	$1,200	$1,025

Sponsorships

Half-year (6 months):	$7,000
Annual:	$10,000

World Wide Web Tennis Server

http://arganet.tenagra.com/Racquet_Workshop

As you may have guessed, tennis is the center of attention here. Every-thing from a calendar of events to pictures of players, general tennis information and tips, links to other tennis information, and more. Spon-sorships vary from $150/month to $400/month. Boasts over 16,000 visitors a month.

ZD Net

http://www.zdnet.com

Features Ziff-Davis publications, including *PC Magazine, PC Computing, MAC User, PC Shopper,* and more. Sponsorships range from $10,000 to $25,000 per quarter depending upon exposure.

Internet Directories and Search Engines

According to WebTrack InterAd Monthly, the top category of Web publish-ers in terms of revenue generation is search engines and Web directories, which for the 4th quarter of 1995 accounted for 35 percent of the total Web advertising market. It's only natural when you think about it. Due to the decentralized nature of the Web, there is a clear need for services that help users find things. The people who are using search engines are seeking to visit Web sites (for the most part) and are likely to be receptive to visiting a

Web site that they weren't necessarily looking for but catches their fancy—which they see in the form of a banner placed prominently on the search results page or other pages within the site.

Many search engines offer you the ability to "purchase" keywords for a period of time. The price is a lot more affordable than purchasing an ad that everyone sees. If you are in the computer business, then you may want your banner ad to appear *only* when people type words like "computer," "laptop," "software," etc. If you are 1-800-FLOWERS, you'd want your banner to appear anytime someone typed in "flowers," "gift," "florist," etc. Before you invest in any banner advertising on a search engine, inquire about keyword sponsorships! This may very well be one of the most effective ways to reach your audience on the Net.

DejaNews

http://www.dejanews.com

The Usenet newsgroup search site. Cost is a bit higher than other search sites at three to four cents per impression. Although, you can receive a discount for paying in advance, which will get the price down to a competitive level. DejaNews receives 2 to 3 million page views on its results page each month.

Excite

http://www.excite.com

A relatively new search engine that has become very popular, very fast. It offers Web site searches, site reviews, and Usenet newsgroup searching. Rates are as follows:

Impressions/month	Discount	Gross Cost	Directory Spots	Keywords
500,000	2.5%	$11,700	2	2
1,000,000	5%	$22,800	4	4
1,500,00	10%	$32,400	6	6
2,000,000	15%	$40,800	8	8
3,000,000	17.5%	$59,400	12	12

LinkStar

http://www.linkstar.com

A next generation search engine widely considered to be one of the most accurate on the Net. Banners rotate throughout the site and are purchased on a per-impression basis. Unlike most other search engines, LinkStar offers affordable options to advertisers with small budgets. In addition to rotating banner ads, placement on its Hot Web Sites Page is just $75/week or $250/month. Banner ad design/creation is $100 each. Banner rates are among the lowest of the search engines as well, $10 CPM if purchased in quantity. Keyword and subject category sponsorships are available as well.

Impressions	Price (US Funds)
1,000	$100
5,000	375
10,000	500
25,000	1,000
50,000	1,500
100,000	2,500
250,000	5,000
500,000	7,500
1,000,000	10,000

Liszt

http://www.liszt.com

Scott Southwick's Internet mailing list search site. Contact him at scott@bluemarble.net for rates. Liszt has reasonable rates and is very flexible with advertisers.

Lycos

http://www.lycos.com

Initially developed at Carnegie Mellon University, Lycos went commercial and is owned by CMG Information Services. Since then, it has welcomed advertising on its site.

Locations	# of impressions	Price/month
Results page/Home page	1,000,000	$20,000
Results page/Home page	750,000	$16,500
Results page	500,000	$12,000
Results page	200,000	$5,000
Results page	60,000	$1,500

You can purchase keywords as well starting at $500 and their "New2Net" announcement page starts at $750 for one week and goes down with the purchase of multiple weeks. You can also contact them about advertising on Point, the Web site rating company that Lycos acquired. Rates are similar at $20 CPM.

Open Text Index

http://www.opentext.com/omw/f-omw.html

Open Text is very flexible and offers various options from keyword sponsorships to rotating banner placement. For 1 million impressions: $20,000 ($20 CPM). Other options are available, and more information can be obtained by emailing advertising@opentext.com.

The HUGE List

http://thehugelist.com

A big directory of categorized Web sites, which is also searchable. Rates are $1,750/month to $2,500/month depending upon exposure. Discounts apply for six-month sponsorships.

WebCrawler

http://www.webcrawler.com

Now owned by America Online, you can send email to info@webcrawler.com and ask about advertising rates. WebCrawler's rates are comparable to the other search engines listed here.

Yahoo!

http://www.yahoo.com

Yahoo! attracts more top advertisers than any other search engine. Its Web Launch (see Figure 6.0) is just $1,000 for one week. They don't allow the

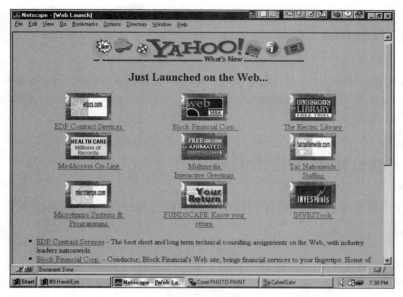

Figure 6.10 Yahoo!'s Web Launch—great exposure for $1,000.

same site to advertise in Web Launch for more than one week. You'll be one of nine advertisers with a small button graphic and short text description of your site. Rotating banners typically run $20,000 per month for an average of a million impressions. You can even purchase keywords and categories so that when someone types in the word "gift" in a search, your banner can be displayed (assuming that you sell gifts or something like that).

Entry Portals

These are Web sites that are primarily the first place people go when their Web browser is started. That's because most Web browsers permit the user to choose which Web site acts as their "home" (default) page. When someone downloads a new copy of Netscape and runs that copy for the very first time, it automatically takes you to **http://www.netscape.com**. Users visiting the Netscape site are considered to be a general audience. Internet access providers are also entry portals. Most access providers program in their own home page URL into the Web browsers that they give away to their users. This generates lots of traffic to the access provider's home page. The bulk of visitors to Internet access provider Web sites consists of their users. For local and regional access providers, those users are located in the same region as the provider. Most providers, however, don't offer banner opportunities on their pages. The ones that do provide an excellent way to promote to a geographically specific audience.

Netscape charges between $20 and $30 CPM. Using Netscape Servers, Netscape's Web site serves more than 40 million hits a day and more than 1 billion hits a month.

Geographical Sites

Target your market geographically with these resources

City.Net
http://www.city.net
http://www.city.net/forms/advertise.html
Architext Software
2701 NW Vaughn St., Suite 411
Portland, OR 97210

Email: info@city.net
Phone: (503) 229-0792
FAX: (503) 229-0793

Acquired by Architext Software, the company that brings you the Excite search engine, City.Net currently supports city and regional information, including travel, entertainment, government and community services. Things like restaurant listings, movie guides, and so on are likely to be listed. To submit your site for a free listing, go to the geographical area that your site concentrates on and choose the link for submitting your entry, and fill out the registration form. There is no guarantee that your site will be listed, but if it is applicable it should be added.

The Virtual Tourist

http://www.vtourist.com

The Virtual Tourist does not offer sponsorship opportunities since it is used as a way to promote the maintainer's business (Kinesava Geographics, a custom mapping company). However, it will lead you to the right place to list your site for free. By clicking on the maps, progressively narrowing down the geographical location to your neck of the woods, you'll end up at the appropriate page within the World Wide Web Consortium's (W3C) list of World Wide Web servers. There should be a link to a form where you can list your Web site. The criteria for getting listed are that your site be physically located within that part of the world and that it reside on your own server. They will not list individual Web sites that rent space on another server.

Other Sponsorable Sites

BigEye
http://www.bigeye.com

A big hotlist for all intents and purposes. It was featured in *Newsweek's* CyberScope page in November 1995. Rates vary from $85/week to $300/month.

Click of the Week
http://www.eshnav.com/click.htm

A site that rates other sites. Featured as the Starting Point's Hot Site. Rates are $30/day or $180/week.

Consummate WinSock Applications List
http://cwsapps.texas.net

This popular site contains lists of HTML authoring tools, Internet software applications, and more. It receives 100,000 users a day. Rates vary from $150/month to $8,000/month depending upon exposure.

EOTW—Entrepreneurs On The Web
http://www.eotw.com

EOTW has been featured in *PC Magazine* (as one of its top 100 Web sites), in *PC Week,* and others. The site averages about 2,000 visitors a day. Exclusive front-page sponsorships are $125 for one week to $400 for a month.

Internet Tools

http://www.itools.com

Paul Sarena's site offers sponsorship on its main page as well as on each of its popular sites (Find-It!, Research-It!, and Promote-It!). Promote-It! contains lots of free Web site promotion resources and can be found at **http://www.itools.com/promote-it/promote-it.html**. I encourage you to take advantage of this resource to promote your site as it is updated more regularly than this book. Advertising rates are as low as $20/month for certain pages within the site up to $940/month for the main Find-It! page. Your banner size should be 234×60 pixels.

Matt's Script Archive

http://worldwidemart.com/scripts/

One of the more popular sites that offers free CGI scripts for downloading. In comparison to some of the other sites listed in this chapter, Matt's Script Archive is a low-traffic site but still worth advertising on. Remember, an eyeball is an eyeball. Just keep in mind that different eyeballs have different

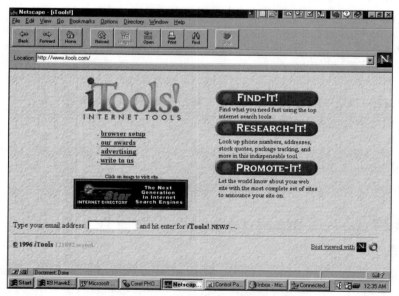

Figure 6.11   "iTools!" features lots of great resources to find things on the Net and promote your site.

interests, and make sure you place your ads appropriately. Rates vary from $25 for 1,000 impressions to $360 for 20,000 impressions.

NetCreations

http://www.netcreations.com

Ryan Scott and Rosalind Resnick's site is chock full of useful things for the Web promoter and marketer. From The PostMaster (see Chapter 14) to Pattern Land, a site that offers background patterns for Web pages, there's a spot that's appropriate for most anyone. Rates vary from $250 for 10,000 impressions to $15,000 for a million. You can also choose a click through purchase plan where each click is from thirty to fifty cents depending upon quantity.

NetMall

http://www.netmall.com

Operated by American Information Systems, Inc. The NetMall was declared as one of the "top shopping spots on the Web" by *Kiplingers Personal Finance Magazine*. NetMall offers keyword sponsoring and sponsoring a particular page or pages within the site. Rates vary from $600 per quarter to $6,000 per quarter depending on exposure.

Riddler

http://www.riddler.com

An interesting site that offers cash prizes to players of its free Web-based games. Riddler guarantees a million impressions each month (audited by Nielsen/IPRO) for $16,000. Riddler does offer a $0.25 per click through sponsorship option with a minimum $5,000 commitment.

Wave of the Day

http://www.marketsquare.com/wave/index.html
Sponsorship Info URL: http://www.marketsquare.com/wave/sponsor.html
Sponsorship Contact: Phillip Winn, pwinn@winn.com

A popular "cool site" page providing interesting sites for Web surfers since June 14, 1995. Rates are as low as $20/week or $50/month. Your banner (500×100 pixels or less) will be displayed on the WotD page.

What's New Too!

http://newtoo.manifest.com

The popular What's New listing site (see next chapter for more). Sponsorships are $250/week. Email **sponsor@manifest.com** for more information.

Where to Find Sites That Offer Sponsorship Opportunities

New online advertising opportunities are springing up every day. It's very difficult to keep up with them all. In the previous pages, I provided you with a variety of options to suit a variety of Web site types and budgets. An entire book can be created to list all the places where you can purchase a banner slot. The following meta-indexes contain lists of sites that sell links and offer sponsorship opportunities. If your site sells banners or offers online advertising opportunities, you'll definitely want to promote your site in these locations. If you are looking for places to promote your site, these sites will point you in the direction of hundreds of places that offer sponsorship opportunities.

Interactive Publishing Alert's Online Ad Index

http://www.netcreations.com/ipa/adindex/index.htm

A great resource for finding appropriate sites to purchase banner advertising on. The IPA Ad Index page offers a powerful search interface that allows you to search by category, rate, hits, keywords, and more. There is an online form for adding your resource if you offer sponsorship opportunities. IPA reviews all submissions for appropriateness, thus ensuring that you'll find serious, useful places to advertise.

SRDS Interactive Advertising Source (Print)

http://www.srds.com
(800) 851-7370 or (708) 375-5079

Quarterly print publication featuring Web site content providers, service providers, and online sponsorship opportunities, including rates. Price for the book is $179/year. If you offer any of these services, you can submit your listing using an online form at the Web site. The book goes out to over 3,000 advertising agencies and departments.

WebTrack's AdSpace Locator

http://www.webtrack.com/sponsors/sponsors.html

WebTrack, the publisher of InterAd monthly, provides a solid listing of places that offer banner slots. The criteria for submission to the AdSpace Locator include sites that offer visitors with some sort of professional service, that they substantiate access statistics, they have adequate bandwidth, and the sites must not contain "offensive" material. If your site offers sponsorships, simply fill out the online questionnaire form with the description of the site, who is currently sponsoring it, your rate card, traffic statistics, the profile of the audience, and contact information. The AdSpace Locator is updated every few weeks or so.

Concluding Remarks

One emerging class of available sites where you can reap some traffic is events sponsorships. For example, InterAct '96 is the first virtual conference and exposition where companies will exhibit in virtual booths and speakers will make their presentations available on the Web site. By the time you read this, InterAct '96 will have passed but visit the site anyway. It may be the first of many virtual trade shows to come. The site's address is **http://www.interact96.com**. You can also sponsor electronic mailing lists and various email based services. See Chapter 10 for more. If you are confused by all the sponsorship choices, check out SponsorNet. They will do all the work for you and get you a discount to boot! Visit the SponsorNet site for more information (**http://www.sponsornet.com**). As I write this, new software programs are becoming available to help companies sell more ads.

NetCreation's "AdMagic" provides sites that offer advertising the ability to have scrolling ads. Scrolling ads with AdMagic only work with advanced Web browsers. That is, users who visit the site using Netscape 2.0 or higher would see the banners scroll by, while those using a browser that is not capable of viewing the scrolling will just see the first banner that appears. More information about AdMagic can be found at **http://www.netcreations.com**. NetGravity offers its AdServer which can help sites better manage their ad slots. Yahoo! now uses the

AdServer and has increased its ad spots from 200 to over 12,000! More information about the AdServer can be found at **http://www.netgravity.com**.

If you don't have the budget to pay for banners nor have the traffic to barter them out, the next chapter can help you. If you have an attractive Web site, you can submit it for consideration as a "cool site." If your site is chosen, you are likely to get a significant increase in traffic—at least for awhile. Use "Cool Site's" pages, "What's New" pages, and other places to promote your site for free.

"Hot" and "Cool" Links Sites, What's New Pages, and More

Chapter 7 Topics

Things You Can Do to Make Your Web Site "Cool"

Submitting Your Site to the What's New Pages

"Hot" and "Cool" Sites Pages You Can Submit To

Reciprocal Links Pages

Random Links Pages

Free for All Pages

Having your site selected by one of the many "sites of the day or week" (SOTDs) or "What's New" pages will do more than give you an ego boost. It's likely to give you a substantial boost in traffic (albeit short lived) as well. Many of these sites receive 5,000 to 15,000 or more individual daily visitors. Thousands of people program in their favorite what's new or cool site page into their Web browser so they can check out what's new or what's cool every day they start up their browser.

When there were fewer Web sites around, maintainers of these types of sites had to search all over creation to find something to write home about. Today, email and Web-based form submissions by other Internet users are the primary way sites are found. In addition, some of the maintainers use search engines, scour Usenet newsgroups, keep an eye out for press releases, and get candidates through word of mouth.

Some maintainers provide an associated review of the site they select while others just take users to the selected site without any warning. I prefer the sites that review what they select since the opinions are often insightful and occasionally humorous. I really respect these site maintainers (if they are doing a good job). It can be surprisingly difficult to choose a neat site every single day. Imagine every day having to wake up to 50 email messages with all those people clamoring for your attention and selection.

Unfortunately, getting listed in some of these sites isn't very easy. The more popular a site is, the more selective it is likely to be. But don't worry, all is not lost. If your site adheres to most of the tips I gave in Chapter 2 and it fits the description of a cool site, it may just make it. Good luck!

What Makes a Site "Cool" Anyway?

Cool can be in the eye of the beholder, but sites that adhere to the following guidelines greatly increase the chances of receiving some sort of cool site award:

- Professional-looking graphics that capture the browser's attention
- Quality content that is dynamic, useful, and interesting
- A speedy display time (anything over 25 seconds to load and you're uncool)
- Uniqueness is a plus, even to the point of being a bit weird or off-beat
- Fun features (something fun to interact with)

- Web browser independence
- Ability to alleviate "Web anxiety" and keep the user within the site

Web browser independence is particularly important. If your Web site has a Dr. Jekyl and Mr. Hyde look to it—due to using Netscape-specific HTML tags and such, some "coolmeisters" may reject it. Then again, some may not.

How to Get Your 15 MegaBytes of Fame

Make sure your site is cool and then submit, submit, submit! Just having a "cool" site isn't going to get you listed automatically. You'll have to submit your URL to wherever you want to be reviewed. The rest of this chapter contains sites where you can submit your site. If you aren't sure if your site is good enough, try anyway! You can't win if you don't play (I've been watching too many lottery commercials!). Please note that most sites recommend that when you make a submission via email (most offer a Web-based form), you place the URL on a separate line and provide some details about the site. Many have a submission guidelines page (usually guidelines are written on the same page where the form is located). Be sure to read the guidelines to ensure that your site has the best chance of being selected.

What's New Pages

The perhaps obvious purpose of these is to inform Internet users of new Web sites that have recently gone online or have been updated. Promote your site with these places as soon as it goes online and is fully functional.

NCSA's What's New

http://www.ncsa.uiuc.edu/SDG/Software/Mosaic/Docs/whats-new.html
http://www.ncsa.uiuc.edu/SDG/Software/Mosaic/Docs/whats-new-form.html
Submission email: ncsa-wn@gnn.com (need to fill out all fields, see site URL for more info.)

The Grandaddy of them all, the NCSA What's New page (see Figure 7.1) receives tens of thousands of visitors each day. The NCSA What's New page was created by the National Center for Supercomputing Applications (NCSA)

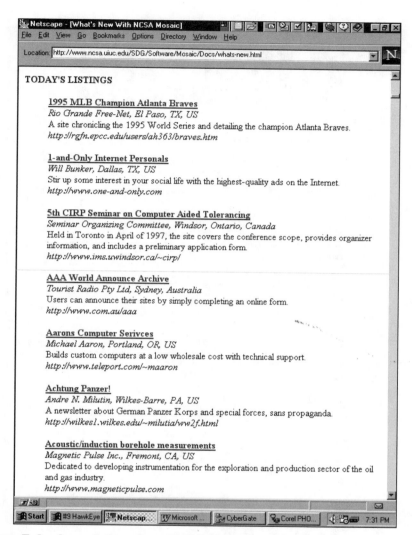

Figure 7.1 Some listings from NCSA's What's New page.

at the University of Illinois. In 1995, it partnered with O'Reilly & Associate's GNN, which was later acquired by America Online.

NCSA's What's New receives about 1,500 submissions each week. After submitting your URL and associated site information (see Figure 7.2), it takes approximately two weeks before your entry appears. In fact, there is no guarantee that your entry will appear at all since the site does not accept submissions from personal home pages nor those that contain material that may be deemed offensive. It also rejects pages that are single product promotions,

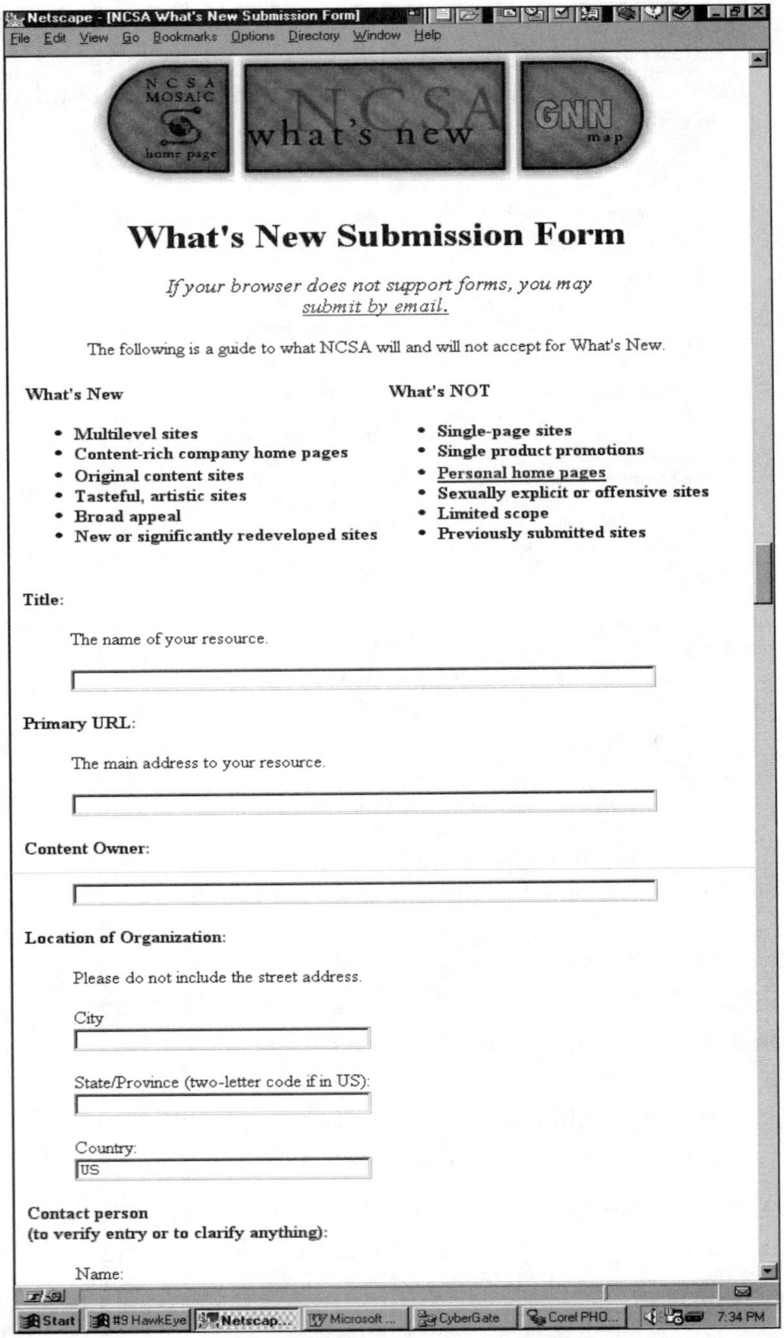

Netscape - [NCSA What's New Submission Form]

File　Edit　View　Go　Bookmarks　Options　Directory　Window　Help

NCSA MOSAIC home page

NCSA what's new

GNN map

What's New Submission Form

If your browser does not support forms, you may submit by email.

The following is a guide to what NCSA will and will not accept for What's New.

What's New

- Multilevel sites
- Content-rich company home pages
- Original content sites
- Tasteful, artistic sites
- Broad appeal
- New or significantly redeveloped sites

What's NOT

- Single-page sites
- Single product promotions
- Personal home pages
- Sexually explicit or offensive sites
- Limited scope
- Previously submitted sites

Title:

The name of your resource.

Primary URL:

The main address to your resource.

Content Owner:

Location of Organization:

Please do not include the street address.

City

State/Province (two-letter code if in US):

Country:

US

Contact person
(to verify entry or to clarify anything):

Name:

Start　#9 HawkEye　Netscap...　Microsoft ...　CyberGate　Corel PHO...　7:34 PM

Figure 7.2　The URL Submission Form for the NCSA What's New page.

single-page Web sites, and sites of a "limited scope." Preferred sites are those that are rich and original in content, have a broad appeal, and contain many pages.

NCSA What's New lists sites alphabetically. There is an advantage to being near the top since the page can span dozens of screens. If there is any way to begin your site title with a number, do so. This will cause your entry to be listed near the top so long as your submission is not edited (they reserve the right to reject or edit any submission). Check out the titles for the first few listings for several day's worth of What's New pages. By doing so, you'll see the pattern of what characters or numbers are used to get listed higher on the page. If appropriate, you can alter your title accordingly.

The page is updated daily (Monday through Friday). There is also a searchable archive of past selections. Of all the things I did to promote the Web site for my first book, none provided me as many visitors in so short a time as the NCSA What's New page did! NCSA's What's New also offers sponsorship opportunities (see Chapter 6).

Netscape's What's New

http://www.netscape.com/home/whats-new.html
http://www.netscape.com/home/submit_new.html

Rather than feature each and every new Web site, Netscape's What's New selects sites that are not only new but are "neat." That is, sites that make use of advanced Netscape features, Java, or advance the technology of the Net in new ways. Therefore, few sites that are submitted are selected. The good news is that if you are selected, you'll receive a greater share of visitors than you otherwise would if they accepted just any submission.

Point Now

http://www.pointcom.com/now
marks@pointcom.com

A companion to Point's Top 5%, for announcements of high quality Web Sites.

What's New in Europe

http://www.ukshops.co.uk:8000/whatsnew
http://www.ukshops.co.uk:8000/whatsnew/announceit.html

If your Web site is located in Europe, this is the place to announce it.

What's New Too!

http://newtoo.manifest.com/WhatsNewToo/index.html
http://newtoo.manifest.com/submit.html

What's New Too! posts more than 700 new sites a day. New announcements are posted within 36 hours of submission. The database is searchable and What's New Too! offers sponsorship opportunities (see Chapter 6). When I started promoting the site for my first book, my first order came from someone who saw the listing in What's New Too! I had posted less than 24 hours before. So within one day, I had my first order, which was from someone who lived in Canada.

World Lynx What's New

http://www.cei.net/comp/newmonth.html
webmaster@cei.net

An Arkansas Internet provider that gathers a listing of new Web sites of interest to its customers.

Hot and Cool Pages

These sites are quite picky. They choose Web sites that they like and let the world know about them. There's definitely a market for these types of sites as dozens have popped up in a short amount of time. Everyone seems to think they are qualified to judge what's cool. I've listed many of the older and respected places as they tend to generate respectable amounts of traffic that you can benefit from if your site is listed.

The BigEye

http://www.bigeye.com
stewart@netline.net

With little online and no offline promotion, the BigEye miraculously was one of the featured sites in *Newsweek's* November 20, 1995,Cyberscope column. BigEye also offers affordable sponsorship opportunities (see Chapter 6).

Bottom 95% of Sites on the Web

http://coos.dartmouth.edu/~jaundice/bottom95
guaraldi@dartmouth.edu

Created by Peter A. Dutton, Jr. as a "cunning comeback to Point's Top 5% of the Web spot," the only criteria for your site being listed here is that it hasn't received Point's honor. The site is now maintained by Ben Guaraldi, Mike Banulescu, and Benjamin Hill who are undergraduates at Dartmouth.

GEnie's HotSpots on the Web

http://www.GEnie.com/hotspots/picks.html
sysmom@genie.com

Even GEnie (the consumer online service) has gotten into the act.

Justin's Links from the Underground

http://www.links.net
http://www.links.net/int/

Justin Hall has more than just interesting links to Web sites here. It's truly one of the weirdest yet most interesting sites around. I hate to admit that I spent at least a couple of hours here without leaving to visit the outside links. From Web site creation tips to his "unauthorized autobiography," you'll find useful tips and lots of wry humor. Every time I visit I seem to end up "trapped" for longer than I intended to stay.

Justin's Links from the Underground site has been up since January 1994 and receives over 15,000 daily readers. It has been cited in *The Wall Street Journal*, *The New York Times*, *Rolling Stone*, *New Yorker*, *Playboy*, *Wired*, *Internet World*, and *The San Francisco Chronicle*. Justin was one of the founding members of the *HotWired* editorial staff and knows how to build an engaging site that people return to over and over.

Links Ahoy!

http://www.imagesmith.com/imagesmith/links_ahoy/index.shtml
links@slugs.com

NETLiNKS!

http://www.interlog.com/~csteele/netlinks.html
csteele@interlog.com

"Your Online Cyberspace Guide."

What's Hot and What's Cool

http://kzsu.stanford.edu/uwi/reviews.html
http://kzsu.stanford.edu/cgi-bin/uwi/feedback?10:1:0:reviews
Submission email: jon@kzsu.stanford.edu

DOES NOT ACCEPT COMMERCIAL SITES! Submit your site only if it has to do with experimental-art, fringe, bizarre, underground, avant garde, and "Random Cool Things." Remember, if your site sells a product or service, this list is not for you.

Sites of the Day, Week, Month, and Year

In 1995, more than 1,000 sites were selected as being cool. What's interesting to note is that very few were selected as being cool by more than one of the predominant SOTDs (sites of the day or week). Personal taste plays a factor. A probably unproductive yet interesting technique to get listed in one of these sites is to visit some of the sites that have been selected by a particular SOTD and look for a pattern. Perhaps you can see certain design features that the selector prefers and model or modify your site to fit the mold. There's a meta-index (see next chapter) of cool sites pages called Mart's MetaPicks that you can use to keep abreast of new places that you can submit your site to, the address is **http://www.euro.net/5thworld/metapick/** and another one is Promote-It! at **http://www.itools.com/promote-it/promote-it.html.**

Above and Beyond Cool Site of the Day

http://www.abmall.com/cv/csod.html
cwells@abmall.com

This site typically has a featured topic for each month. Check back each month to see if your site fits the current month's topic. When it does, be sure to submit your URL. For example, the January 1996 topic was "pages with live photo shots that update frequently."

Barbara's Best Bookmark of the Day

http://www.shsu.edu/users/std/stdkco/pub2/best.html
stdkco@shsu.edu

Barbara is a wife and mother of three who, when she has time, shares some of her best bookmarks with the Internet community. She typically does not accept sites that sell something or that are commercially oriented.

BAT's Catch of the Day

http://batech.com/catch.html
techs@batech.com

BAT's does not accept URLs that are commercial advertisements, that have a single graphic image over 50 K on the page, or no email address to contact the owner. BAT's accepts sites that are funny, contain useful information, and appear quickly.

BesT in the BiZ Web Site of the Week

http://www.mindspring.com/~dmonline/BIZ/BiZ.html
dmonline@mindspring.com

"Every Monday, the BesT in the BiZ is awarded to the business site that combines superior Web design with savvy marketing and sales smarts." Submit your site if you think it's worthy.

Click of the Week

http://eshnav.com/click.htm
click@eshnav.com

Computer Life Online's Hot Site of the Day

http://www.zdnet.com/~complife/filters/site.html
clmatt@aol.com

The online version of Ziff-Davis' *Computer Life* magazine where they "surf the Net like a bad habit."

Cool Site of the Day

http://cool.infi.net
cool@infi.net

Originated by Glenn Davis, the Cool Site of the Day (see Figure 7.3) is definitely one of the most popular cool sites pages on the Net. The site's popularity helped propel Glenn to cybercelebrity status. In 1995, InfiNet, an Internet access provider took over the reigns of the CSotD. Currently, Richard Grimes chooses what's cool.

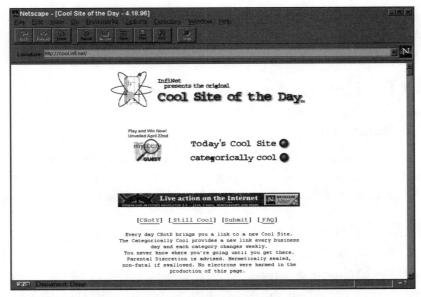

Figure 7.3 The ever-popular Cool Site of the Day page.

Cybertown Site of the Week

http://www.directnet.com/cybertown/spider.html
cybermail@cybertown.com

The "pickers" from this site know what they are talking about—the Cybertown Site of the Week page has won a lot of awards itself. I suppose it takes one to know one.

Dynamite Site of the Nite

http://www.netzone.com/~tti/dsotn.html
tti@netzone.com

See Figure 7.4.

Egotistical Site of the Week

http://www.bibiana.com/ego.html
cayton@bibiana.com

"Every week a totally new, totally self-serving Web site will be featured."

Funky Site of the Day

http://www.realitycom.com/cybstars/index.html
funky@realitycom.com

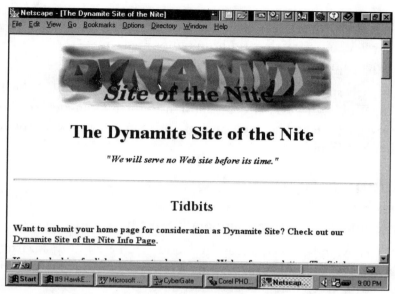

Figure 7.4 *The Dynamite Site of the Nite:* serves no Web site before its time.

If your site fits the definition of "funky" (of which I'm not even sure), submit your site here.

Geek Site of the Day

http://chico.rice.edu/~indigo/gsotd/index.html
http://chico.rice.edu/~indigo/gsotd/mail.html

GSotD has been featured in *GNN, NY Times, PC Novice,* the Useless WWW Pages Web site, the *London Times,* and a few other places. If your site is geeky (you know who you are!) or one that geeks would be interested in, be sure to let Scott Ruthfield know about it via the submission URL or via email at indigo@rice.edu.

Ground Zero

http://www.ground.com/zeros.html
http://www.ground.com/submit.html

Rated as one of the Top 5%, Point said "Why choose just one cool site each day when you can pick six? Each day brings visitors six new sites worth visiting." Submit your site here and you have six times the chance of being selected as comparable cool sites pages.

Hot Site of the Nite

http://www.euro.net/5thworld/hotnite/hotnite.html
lynx@neturl.nl

Their page states that they were inspired by Cool Site Of the Day "But Willing To Play It Less Safe," an allusion to their willingness to choose more controversial sites. The Hot Site of the Nite is sponsored by Euro Net Amsterdam (Holland).

Humor Site of the Every Other Day

http://bird.taponline.com/yourmom/HSotEOD.html
http://bird.taponline.com/yourmom/HS/submitsite.html

On every Monday, Wednesday, and Friday, a new funny, bizarre, or goofy Web site is selected for your viewing enjoyment. If your site fits this description, getting listed here probably can't hurt!

Loads-a-Links

http://www.aber.ac.uk/~ngd2
Halted submissions.

Neil Dodd's Loads-a-Links has been operating since May 1995 and receives about 100 submissions a week of which only one makes it. As of this writing, he posted a message stating that he is just too busy to keep up with new submissions and will not accept new ones. I list it here to illustrate how hard it can be for these poor old site maintainers! Give Loads-a-Links a look to see if he has started accepting submissions again.

MecklerWeb's Web Pick of the Day

http://www.mecklerweb.com:80/netday/sotd.html
johnh@iw.com

Meckler Media's *Internet World* site offers a SOTD feature. It's compiled by John Harmon and provides a few-paragraph review and description of the site, as well as convenient information at the beginning of the page stating the URL, developer, and subject area of the site.

Mediocre Site of the Day

Site URL: http://pantheon.cis.yale.edu/~jharris/mediocre.html
Submission URL: http://pantheon.cis.yale.edu/~jharris/submit.html

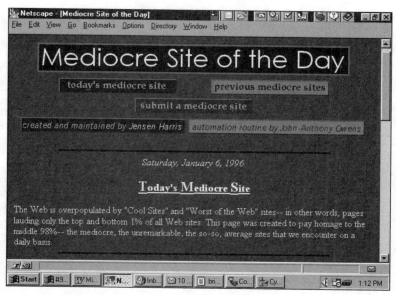

Figure 7.5   Mediocre Site of the Day. I hope your site isn't chosen, but if it is, the bright side is it's a free link.

Jensen Harris, the site's creator/maintainer writes, "The Web is overpopulated by "Cool Sites" and "Worst of the Web" sites—in other words, pages lauding only the top and bottom one percent of all Web sites. This page was created to pay homage to the middle 98 percent—the mediocre, the unremarkable, the so-so, average sites that we encounter on a daily basis." If you're intimidated by the prospect of being cool and are all stressed out trying to make your site hot, then maybe you should relax and submit your site here. (See Figure 7.5.)

Same Site of the Day

http://pnx.com/falken/samesite.htm
http://pnx.com/falken/submitit.htm

For a little humor, check out The Same Site of the Day, a place where you are *guaranteed* that the selection is just as cool as the previous day's (no more, no less). For an exercise in futility, you may submit your site at the above submission URL.

The Spider's Pick of the Day

http://gagme.wwa.com/~boba/pick.html
boba@wwa.com

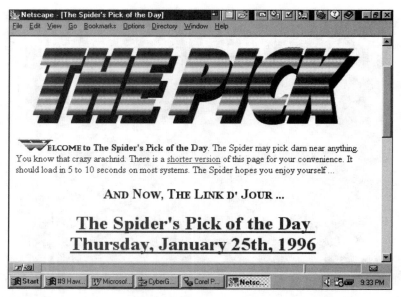

Figure 7.6   Being selected as The Spider's Pick of the Day has become a holy grail for many Web site developers.

Bob Allison's extremely respected site has been announcing cool selections since November 1994, making it one of the oldest SOTD pages. It's another one of those "holy grail" sites for Web developers (see Figure 7.6). If you think your site is cool, submit it to the Spider! If you are going to submit your site to SPotD, be sure to read his submission guidelines at **http://miso.wwa.com/~boba/submit.html**.

Tabitha's Groovy Site of the Day

http://www.mtnlake.com/people/holtz/cool.html?
holtz@medius.com

Another site with lots of mentions in the press. If your site is cool, it's groovy, too.

Today's Cool Place

http://www.teleport.com/~blay
http://www.teleport.com/~blay/comments.html

Brandon Lay's Cool Place.

Unusual or Deep Site of the Day

http://vvv.com/adsint/freehand/deepsite/
sswitzer@vvv.com

"We're all a bit weird...we're all a bit twisted...we're all a bit overweight. The sites you'll find here are guaranteed to appeal to the weird, twisted, and overweight side in you." So says the DSotD. If your site is normal, forget about submitting it here!

Wade's Weekly Web Picks

http://www.teleport.com/~wnorton/pick.shtml
wnorton@teleport.com

Wade Norton's weekly picks.

Wave of the Day

http://www.marketsquare.com/wave/
http://www.marketsquare.com/wave/about.html

Phillip Winn and The Winner's Circle publish a weekly newsletter that used to feature some favorite links each week. It was a popular feature that led to the WotD being created. If you are interested in a very inexpensive sponsorship opportunity, this is the place. See Chapter 6 for rates.

Web Site of the Week

http://www.duke-net.com/wsw/
wsw@duke-net.com

Provides a review of the site they choose along with the link to the site. (See Figure 7.7.)

X Site of the Day

http://www.holli.com/~rhingst/homer2.html
rhingst@holli.com

ZonE oF tHe WeEk

Site URL: http://www.ualberta.ca/~bsowa/zow.html
Submission URL: http://www.ualberta.ca/~bsowa/nomination.html

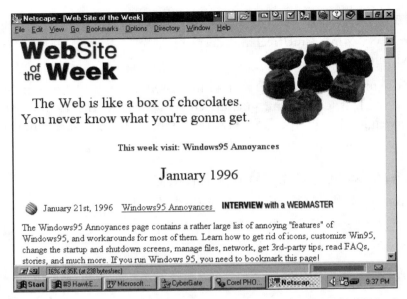

Figure 7.7   The Web Site of the Week. Forrest Gump's favorite Web site.

Reciprocal Links Pages

There are a number of Web sites that will list your site on their page or in their database *if and only if* you list them. This cooperative approach to promoting your Web site can get you lots of links. In order to do this, you need to have a place within your Web site where you can list URLs. Some Web sites are designed in such a way that there really isn't any place to provide reciprocal links. If you haven't built your Web site yet, you may want to consider designing in a spot for reciprocal linking within your Web site. The sites listed in this section offer reciprocal linking. After you build in a link to them, you need to let them know that you've listed them on your site. In most cases, you just send them email (I listed their email address as "notification address" in the listings below).

In many cases, while you are surfing around the Net, you'll find places whose users are similar to the types of users who would be interested in your site. When you find these, they may be good candidates to approach for a reciprocal link. All you need to do is ask. The worst thing that can happen is they say no. Simply send off an email message saying how your sites are complementary and that you would like to offer a reciprocal linking arrangement.

Digiratti

http://www.digiratti.com/suckup1.htm
julian.loren@sbaonline.gov

PageHost A-Z

http://www.pagehost.com/url_list.html

This site used to be called Hendrik's Reciprocal URL Collection. Submit your URL in the correct category.

Seeress of the Web

http://www.cyberzine.com/seeress/daily.html
jmra@ix.netcom.com

Vivek

http://yoyo.cc.monash.edu.au/~vivek/friends.html
vivek@halls1.cc.monash.edu.au

Random Links Pages

These pages are great for people who like surprises or who are in the mood for an adventure. It's like being taken for a ride through cyberspace blindfolded. Random links pages take users to a random Web site. When a user clicks the appropriate hyperlink, a CGI script chooses one of the URLs in the database and activates it. The user, who has no clue where he or she may end up, is then taken directly to the random site.

From a Web site promotion standpoint, I recommend adding your URL to these pages when you have completed most of the other promotional techniques listed in this book. The problem with most of these pages is that there are so many URLs in their databases that the odds of your URL being chosen at any time are very slim (on the order of several thousand to one). For example, if one of these pages has 3,000 URLs in its database, and it receives 3,000 visitors a day, on average you will receive about 30 hits a month by listing with a random links page. One may argue that is 30 more hits than you had without being listed. This is true, but you have to prioritize where you list your site. Random links pages and the Free For All pages listed in the next section should be low on your list. But if you have the time, definitely add your URL. A few hits here and a few visitors there all add up.

The RIMNET Random Link Server

http://www.st.rim.or.jp/~hirono/rlink/rlink.html
http://www.st.rim.or.jp/~hirono/rlink/addlink.html

MagicURL Mystery Trip

http://www.netcreations.com/magicurl/index.html
cool@netcreations.com

Ryan Scott from NetCreations hand selects the URLs for this site. It eliminates 99 percent of the junk that you'll see in other random site generators. It has won a number of awards, such as Spider's Pick of the Day, WinMag, and Net Guide HotSpot.

URouLette

http://www.uroulette.com:8000/

The first and most well-known of the random links pages. URouLette was created by Matthew J. Angell and Matthew T. Abrams, two of the developers of the Kansas University Campus Internet Association. (See Figure 7.8.)

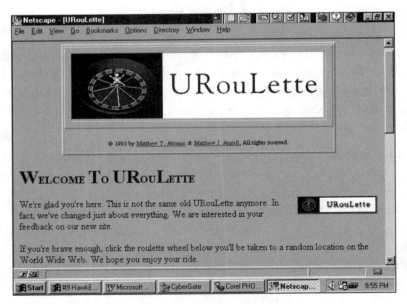

Figure 7.8 Take your chances with URouLette.

Vivek's Random URLs

http://yoyo.cc.monash.edu.au/~vivek/random.html

The links in the database are from his Reciprocal URL list (see previous section), from his hotlists, and from other places he liked on his travels.

Web Autopilot

http://www.netgen.com/~mkgray/autopilot.html
http://www.netgen.com/~mkgray/mkgray.email.html

A unique site that will transport you to a new Web site every 12 seconds (or time period you select). It contains over 8,001 URLs. Give Matt Gray a compelling reason to add your site and he may just do it.

Free For All Pages

"Free For All" pages permit anyone to add anything to their database. Most of the pages have some sort of disclaimer that they do not screen URL additions. The promotional value of adding your Web site to a Free For All page is questionable. The main reason people visit these pages is to add their URL and not to see what neat stuff may have been added (unlike a What's New page). Therefore, you have lots of people adding their URLs but not as many looking through the listings for places to visit. Nonetheless, Free For All pages are indeed free, and if you have already pursued many of the other Web site promotion avenues in this book, submitting your URL to these sites won't hurt. The good thing about Free For All pages is that it takes only a few seconds to add your URL as most have a box for your URL and a one-line or short description of your site.

Add a Site Superpage

http://www.henge.com/superpage
http://www.henge.com/superpage/addsite.html

Cornelius' Hot Links Page

http://www.fn.net/~jmayans/newlinks.html
http://www.fn.net/~jmayans/addlink.html

The LinkList

http://www.comp.vuw.ac.nz/linklist/index.html
http://www.comp.vuw.ac.nz/linklist/linklist.html

Matt's Free For All Page

http://worldwidemart.com/scripts/demos/links/links.html

MegaMall's Free For All Links Page

http://infotique.lm.com/links.html

Probe's Free For All Links

http://www.cs.utexax.edu/users/usamaw/links.html
http://www.cs.utexax.edu/users/usamaw/addlinks.html

Recyclinx: The Link Recycler

http://www.amsmain.com/cgi-amsmain/recyclinx

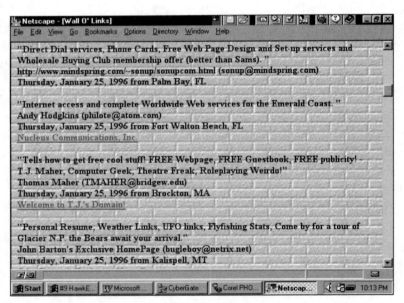

Figure 7.9 Listings from the Wall O' Links Free For All Page.

The Revolving Door

http://www.galcit.caltech.edu/~ta/cgi-bin/revdoor-ta

The Vortex

http://www.cen.uiuc.edu/~ehrhart/Vortex/Vortex.html
http://www.cen.uiuc.edu/~ehrhart/Vortex/VortexAdd.html

Wall O' Links

http://www.ahoynet.com/~jamie/guestbook.html
http://www.ahoynet.com/~jamie/phpl.cgi?guestadd.html

An example of a typical Free For All page can be found in Figure 7.9 for the Wall O' Links.

Meta-Indexes: Information about Information

CHAPTER 8 TOPICS

WHAT IS A "META INDEX" ANYWAY?

SOME EXAMPLES AND PLACES THAT MAY BE RIGHT FOR YOU

AFFINITY PROMOTION

The term "meta-index," when used in the context of the Net, is a list of Internet resources pertaining to a specific subject category. Meta-indexes are intended to be useful resources for Internet users who have an interest in a specific topic. Since information is scattered everywhere on the Net, it's very difficult and time consuming (more time consuming than difficult actually) to seek out varied sources of information about any single topic.

A meta-index is simply a collection of URLs for related Internet resources, all arranged on a Web page by their titles. You can create your own meta-index by using various search engines, directories, and other sources (from Chapter 3) to find Web sites that center around the topic of your index. For example, one such topic may be Salvador Dali art. A search may find that 14 different Web sites contain information about Dali art. These sites are most probably spread out all over the world. To create a meta-index of Dali art, you would record the titles and URLs of each site, and perhaps summarize what each site contains about the subject. You would then take that information and create a Web page that lists these resources along with hyperlinks to them. People who are interested in Dali art can now visit your meta-index and use it as a launching pad to any one of the fourteen other Web sites that contain information on the topic.

Now, if you were compiling this meta-index, wouldn't you like to know about other Dali art Web sites so you could list them in your meta-index? By the same token, what if you were an art dealer selling Dali art, wouldn't you like to be listed on the "Salvadore Dali Art Meta-index?" Obviously people visiting the meta-index are interested in Dali, and low and behold, you sell Dali art. Some of these people will click on the hyperlink to visit your Web site and, who knows, they may even buy some art from you.

As you can see, meta-indexes are a great way to get people who are interested in the topic of your Web site to visit, so long as you are listed on them.

Meta-Indexes Where You Can Submit Your Site

This section contains a select list of meta-indexes covering a wide range of topics where you can request that your Web site be added. It is very important to realize that most of the people who maintain these lists do it for the fun of it, and they are under absolutely no obligation to list your resource. It is also important to submit your site only to those meta-indexes where it is appropriate. That is, if your site is all about coin collecting, it is inappropriate to submit it to a meta-index that lists wine resources. Those that I list here will give you an idea of the types of sites that are out there and what they contain. Some of them may even be applicable to your situation, and I encourage you to submit your site where appropriate. Obviously the list is by no means complete. There may be many meta-indexes that "compete" on the same subject. Getting listed on some will yield you more visitors than others.

If you want more exposure than being one of many listed on a page, you can inquire about adding a more prominent link or banner on the page. Most meta-index sites aren't set up for this and don't actively solicit advertisers; however, I've found that if you approach them about the idea, many are open to it. There's minimal work involved in them adding the HTML to the page. I usually send an email message to the maintainer stating that I really like their site. (Don't lie, but if there are features you like about the site, be sure to let them know.) If you have some constructive suggestions, don't be afraid to give them as well.

In the introductory message, I say something like, "I see that you don't have any sponsors for your page and perhaps you don't want any, but I like what you've done here and was wondering if you are open to the idea." More often than not, you'll get a positive response back. At that point, it comes down to what you are willing to pay for it. Most of these people aren't money mongers, and for a small fee you can get a logo or prominent text link saying something like, "sponsored by ABC Co., makers of blah blah blah, please support our sponsors by visiting their sites."

The maintainer of the site may or may not know how much traffic it is getting. The more traffic, the more valuable the link is. But even a small number of visitors, if they are keenly interested in the subject, are very likely to visit your site if it fits in. And aren't those people more important than just anyone who stumbles onto your site? If you've ever taken any seminars on negotiating, you know to never make the first offer. Ask them how much money they would want to place a graphic logo (or banner) of yours on the site. If they don't want any graphics taking up the space, perhaps they would accept a prominent text message. For most sites, a fair price would be from $50 for a month on up to several hundreds of dollars a month. If you know you are getting a good deal, offer to commit for several months and prepay.

Or, if the price is a little high, make a lower counter proposal and offer to give them three months in advance and call it a "frequency discount." You don't know unless you try.

As far as submitting your site for a typical free listing, be sure to provide your URL on a separate line, a short description of your site, and why your site should be added to the list. Provide some contact information in case the maintainer has questions. State that you have a suggestion for an addition to the list in the subject line of your email message. The theme of your message should be that of a request not a demand. As I stated earlier, the maintainers are under no obligation to list you. You'll greatly increase the chances of being listed if you tell them that you are going to add their site to your page. Some of these people are very busy, so give them a couple of weeks to respond before sending a reminder message.

Albany On-Line

http://www.albany.com
http://www.albany.com/addlink.shtml

Over 100 links to information, businesses, and organizations located in Albany, NY. There are many regional meta-indexes. Using your search knowledge from Chapter 3, do a search for your region and see if there are any sites that accept listings, and then submit your site to them. If you are located in Albany, start with this one.

All Inclusive Radio Database

http://www.xnet.com/~dfleming/radiochr.html
dfleming@polar.bowdoin.edu

Doug Fleming maintains this site which includes "Every single CHR, Hot AC, Dance, Urban, New Rock, and Hard Rock Station in the U.S.A. 98% accurate!" including links to radio station Web sites.

Beer Info Source

http://www.beerinfo.com/~jlock/wwwbeerb.html
http://www.beerinfo.com/~jlock/wwwbeerb.html

Maintained by John Lock, the Beer Info Source is "Your One-stop Shop for Internet Beer Info." Contains links to everything from breweries to commercially oriented sites to beer-related software.

Bicycle Racing Links

http://www.worldmedia.fr/tour/otherlin.htm
cattoire@cnam.fr

Maintained by Gilbert Cattoire, this site contains bicycle magazine links, racing results, racing event calendars, and links to other meta-indexes on the topic.

Broadcasting Link

http://www.algonet.se/~nikos/broad.html
nikos@algonet.se.

Maintained by Nikos Markovits, this site contains selected links to broadcasting-related Internet resources, which are arranged by subject and country. He also maintains a meta-index of Journalistic Resources. You can get to that link from the Broadcasting Link page.

ChiroWeb

http://www.chiroweb.com
chiroweb@earthlink.com

If your site has anything to do with Chiropractic (information, business, etc.), then this is the place. If they like your site, they will list it free. There are also some fee-based options. If you want to find a chiropractor in your area, there's a search capability available to you free of charge.

Coin Universe

http://www.coin-universe.com/index.html
coin-master@coin-universe.com

You guessed it, everything about coins and coin collecting. See Figure 8.1.

Cool Medical Site of the Week

http://www.hooked.net/users/wcd/cmsotw.html
wcd@hooked.net

I wasn't sure whether this should go into Chapter 7 or this one. Since it's so subject specific I opted for this chapter even though it is not technically a meta-index. If you have a medical site, be sure to submit it here!

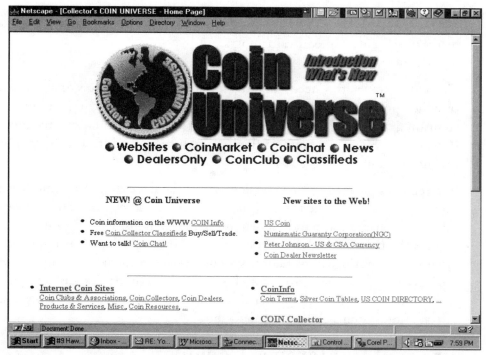

Figure 8.1 The name says it all.

Directory and Registry of Java Resources

http://www.gamelan.com
http://www.gamelan.com/add.shtml

Maintained by Earthweb's Gamelan. If your site has Java on it, you are a Java developer or you are involved with Java in some way, this is the place to promote your site.

GreekSource

http://www.greeksource.com
http://www.greeksource.com/sub_form.htm

A list of fraternities and sororities that are on the Web, including announcements and information of interest to "Greeks."

Information Systems Meta-List

http://www.cait.wustl.edu/cait/infosys.html
joeh@proserv.wustl.edu

Created to meet the needs of information systems professionals, this list provides pointers to information systems resources on the Internet. It is sponsored by the Center for the Application of Information Technology (CAIT). Joe Haspiel maintains the list and his email address is shown above for submissions.

Subject areas on the list include client/server databases, database middleware, transaction monitors, client/server client application development tools, Graphical User Interface tools and guidelines, data warehousing, software engineering/CASE analysis and design tools, distributed computing, distributed object oriented computing, information systems service companies, computer vendors, operating systems, processor chips, software companies, distributed systems and network management, groupware, computer publishers, and information systems conferences and shows.

Internet Conference Calendar

http://www.automatrix.com/conferences/
http://www.automatrix.com/conferences/submit.shtml

If you are putting on an Internet-related event, you can promote it for free here.

Interesting Places for Kids

http://www.crc.ricoh.com/people/steve/kids.html
steve@crc.ricoh.com

Stephen Savitzky maintains this list of pointers to sites that may be interesting to kids.

J-LINKS Meta-Index

http://www.islandtel.com/j-links.html
mkeegan@st.rim.or.jp

Maintained by Myles Keegan, J-LINKS is an index to indexes of Japan-related information.

Maserati Launcher

http://stone.america.com/maserati/html/launch.html
spdracer@america.com

Not only Maserati cars but other high performance car resources are listed.

Metal Band List

http://www.netlab.co.uk/rwoolley/band.html
woolleyr@westhert.demon.co.uk

This site is maintained by Rob Woolley and lists famous and not-so-famous heavy-metal rock bands that have Web pages.

Music Festivals

http://www.timeinc.com/vibe/mmm/music_festivals.html
Link to submission form is available on the site address page.

Vibe magazine's music festivals list.

Nursing and Health Care Resources on the Net

http://www.bath.ac.uk/~exxrw/nurse.html
r5-ward@uwe.ac.uk

Maintained by Rob Ward, this site contains United Kingdom links and world-wide links separately for nursing and health care related sites including psychology & social science resources, midwifery & early child health, mental health & learning disabilities, alternative/complementary therapies, general medicine, and condition-specific links.

Nursing Related Web Servers

http://www_son.hs.washington.edu/www-servers.html
webster@son.washington.edu

Maintained by Brian Parkhurst, includes listings for Gopher and FTP servers, Telnet sites, and Web sites.

Real Estate Sites on the Internet

http://www.human.com/proactive/links2.html
http://www.pacificrim.net/~proactiv/linkdeal/

Maintained by the Consumer Mortgage Information Network, your real estate related site can be added if you add a link to their site. Details can be found at the submission address.

Woodworking Catalog

http://www.woodworking.com
info@woodworking.com

Anything from lumber, hardware, power tools, schools and workshops, stores, furniture manufacturers and designers, associations, woodworking companies and more are here (see Figure 8.2). Extremely good resource even though I don't know much about woodworking myself. This site is a great example of a meta-index.

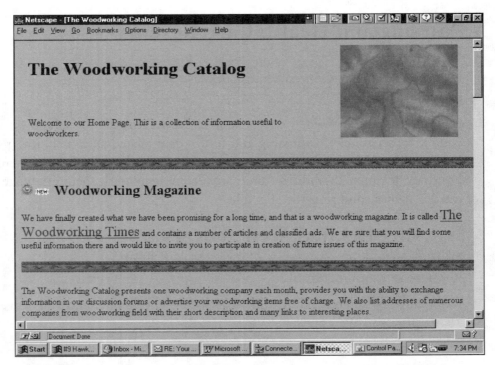

Figure 8.2 The Woodworking Catalog. Comedian Tim Allen from TV's "Home Improvement" would love this site!

Writers' Resources on the Web

http://www.interlog.com/~ohi/www/writesource.html
http://www.interlog.com/~ohi/www/vl-feedback.html

All kinds of resources for writers, including conferences, publishers, booksellers, etc. If your business or site fits one of these categories, be sure to get listed here. Figure 8.3 shows how the site is arranged from the top level.

The WWW Virtual Library

http://www.w3.org/hypertext/DataSources/bySubject/Overview.html

The WWW Virtual Library project was started at CERN in 1991 by Tim Berners-Lee to keep track of the development of the World Wide Web that he had just created. The site contains lists of meta-indexes listed by subject, as shown in Figure 8.4. It's a distributed system where individuals volunteer to become part of the library and maintain a meta-index on a specific subject. Use this site to locate a meta-index that pertains to the subject matter of your

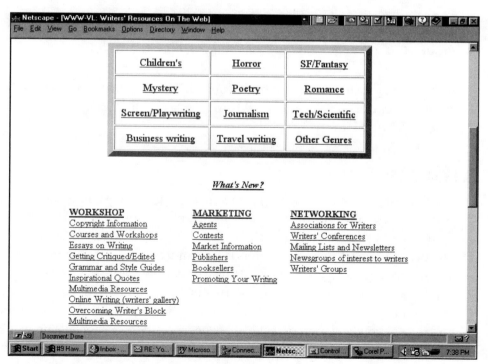

Figure 8.3 *Writers' Resources on the Web.*

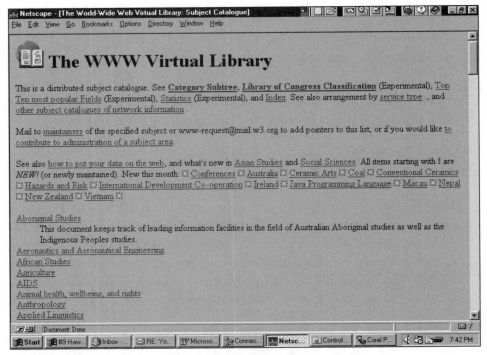

Figure 8.4   The "granddaddy" of Internet meta-indexes.

site. Then visit the site and submit your URL for inclusion in the list (if it's appropriate, of course). Since 1993, Arthur Secret has been maintaining the WWW Virtual Library.

Affinity Promotion

The best way to describe *affinity promotion* is to give an example. Let's say that your business offers tours of a certain area of the country. You can team up with other Web sites that offer a complementary service to your customers or prospects. Perhaps there is a hotel or bed-and-breakfast that is in your town and it happens to have a Web site (this is becoming more likely every day). If you are aware of the site, you can ask them to put a link on their page to yours. In exchange, you can do the same for them. Since you are not in competing businesses, you will not only be offering customers a service but will also attract traffic from the other site that probably would have never known about your site. The variations on this theme are endless. Who says opposites attract?

The FlowerStop (http://www.flowerstop.com) teamed up with Zima (http://www.zima.com) and some others during one Valentine's Day. The event was the common theme that linked all the different Web sites that cooperated in a giveaway. Links were placed on an appropriate page on each participant's site that pointed visitors in the direction of the others' sites.

All it takes is an idea and a few similar sites out there. Email them with your idea. Contests and giveaways work well. If you own a hotel, you can offer a few night's stay for the winners. Then proceed to hook up with a restaurant that's in your area, an airline, etc. Get each party to give away something. Then announce the giveaway on all the participating Web sites. Simply require people to fill out an entry form that requests each person's contact information and asks that they answer a few questions. These questions can be things like "how often do you travel, what airline do you like to fly, where do you like to travel, etc." This valuable demographic and contact information can be shared among the sponsors and provides you all with a valuable set of leads. If you do something like this, though, be sure to let people know what you will and will not do with their information. And be sure to name the winner on your sites.

This cooperative approach to promoting complementary Web sites can be very effective in driving new traffic to your site. People who visit some of the other sites may have never known about yours and vice versa.

The key to capitalizing on this chapter is to do your research, contact the appropriate meta-indexes, get listed, and see if you can work a deal for sponsoring their sites. In addition, keep an eye out for possible affinity promotion partners. In the next chapter, I'll discuss how you can promote your site for a lot less than you think at some cybermalls. Of course, cybermalls may not be an appropriate place for your Web site to be listed. If this is the case, you can simply move on. Even if you are a government agency or nonprofit organization, some malls will give you a free listing in an appropriate area on their site. You can never have enough links out there!

Promote 'til You Drop with Cybermalls

CHAPTER 9 TOPICS

FEATURES OF CYBERMALLS

CYBERMALLS WHERE YOU CAN PURCHASE A LINK TO YOUR SITE

WHERE TO FIND OTHER CYBERMALLS WHERE YOU CAN PROMOTE YOUR SITE

Promoting your Web site in a cybermall may or may not be appropriate depending upon the content and theme of your site. If your Web site is geared toward selling a consumer-based product, then it may be very appropriate. Flowers, jewelry, gifts, apparel, just about anything you would see in a "real" mall would be appropriate for a cybermall. Even if your organization is a nonprofit or government agency, there are some malls that offer a place for a link. Some even donate a link or space on their server to nonprofit organizations. If your organization is nonprofit, you should be able to get quite a few free links to your site just by asking.

In 1994 when the Web started to get rolling from a business standpoint, the big thing was cybermalls. People thought that if they were associated with the right real estate, lots of people would visit their site. Unfortunately, it takes a lot more than being on just one cybermall to generate the type of traffic most people would like. As time progressed, Internet vendors realized this. During 1995, cybermalls remained rather low key, but as of the beginning of 1996, they were starting to make a bit of a comeback. I think the reason behind it is that people are starting to look to the Net as a place to purchase things, while many malls are starting to offer secure transactions, making consumers feel more comfortable purchasing things online.

Cybermalls offer Web space rental on their servers, as well as Web site creation and consulting services. In most cases, the Web space rental charges are a little higher than you may find elsewhere. If you already have a Web site on a server somewhere, many malls will provide you with a listing for a lot less than you would have to pay to rent space on their servers. The reason for this is that when someone clicks on your listing, they are transported to the Web server where your Web pages are physically located. At that point, the person is using the resources of that server and not the resources of the cybermall that contained the hyperlink to your site. Therefore, many malls charge a small fee to list you. It's usually a matter of 15 minutes work to add you to a mall. Once you're listed and linked, that's all the work there is.

The strategy I recommend for you is to research the various malls out there, find the ones that your site would be appropriate for (see Table 9.1), and contact them regarding the cost to provide a link to your existing Web site. If you are thrifty enough, there's no reason why you can't get listed in a dozen malls for $1,000 or so. The FlowerStop, which is quite successful online, is listed in many malls using this exact same strategy.

Table 9.1 Web Site Categories Found in a Typical CyberMall

Art and collectibles	Health and fitness
Automotive	Housewares
Books and media	Money and finances
Business	Professional services
Computers	Specialty shops
Electronics	Sports and recreation
Food court	Toys and games
Gifts	Travel

Cybermall Features

There are a number of features that a cybermall may offer its tenants, as part of the standard fee (that would cost a lot more if you built them on your own), and its users, to make shopping there all the more convenient. Some of these features include:

- **One-Stop Convenience.** Larger malls contain a wide variety of products and services. People can visit a mall and get most anything they need in one location.

- **"Passerby Promotion."** By being in a mall, you can benefit from the "walk-in traffic" that is generated by the mall's promotion and all its individual vendors' promotions combined. Some malls place a link on each vendor's page that directs users back to the mall home page. This creates a domino effect from all the listings in the mall, which brings users back to where they'll have another opportunity to visit your site (if you are part of the mall).

- **Searching.** As malls have grown, they've begun to offer users the ability to search for what they are looking for using keywords, in addition to a traditional category listing scheme.

- **Shopping Carts.** This is a rather new technology that allows users to visit multiple mall vendors and click on the various products they want. When users are done shopping, they can review the contents of their carts and place an order. Without a shopping cart, users would have to order from each vendor separately. *Access Market Square* is an example of a mall that uses shopping cart technology.

- **Secure Ordering.** Some malls use a secure server to offer secure (encrypted) transactions. Also, there are a few that have credit card merchant status that they offer to vendors who do not currently accept credit cards.

- **Value Added Services.** If you want an Internet mailing list, FTP, Gopher (see next chapter for these), or automatic email responder, these services may be available to you at no extra charge (or a small additional fee). You can leverage the mall's technology for your own use. Why do it all yourself?

Cybermalls Where You Can Purchase a Link to Your Site

There are hundreds of cybermalls out there. In this section, I list sites that I think charge a fairly reasonable price for a link. Your cybermall Web site promotion strategy should be the following:

1. Determine if your site can benefit from being linked in cybermalls.
2. Figure your budget for these links.
3. Contact the malls about getting a link.
4. Try to negotiate a deal with them.

Some malls are flexible about negotiating a deal, and you can often get a link at a lower price than they publish. Others, however, offer a link at such a low price that they won't lower their listed rates. Offer to provide a link back to them (a reciprocal link) for a discount.

Some malls are better than others. I prefer the ones that have been around for more than a year. If they charge more than $100/year, check their visitor statistics before buying a link, and contact a few of their vendors to see what their experiences have been. Additional information for signing up with these malls can be found on their sites.

Access Market Square

http://www.icw.com/mall.html
info@icw.com
(801) 487-0888
Link Charge: $125/month

Access Market Square requires a one-year contract for links (see Figure 9.1).

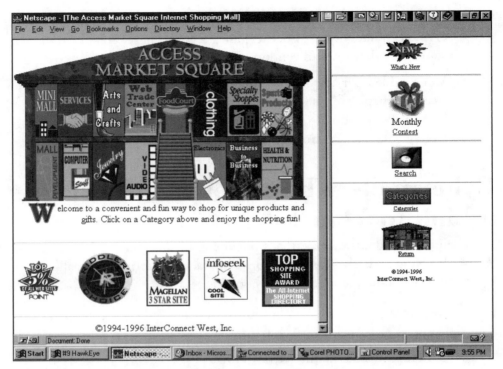

Figure 9.1 Access Market Square's cybermall.

BizCafe Mall

http://www.bizcafe.com
bizcafe@best.com
Link Charge: $14.95/month.

The link gives you their "basic yellow pages listing," which consists of a three-line description with a link to your site under one of BizCafe's categories.

Branch Mall

http://www.branchmall.com
nan@branch.com
(800) 349-1747
Link Charge: $80/month

The Branch Mall (see Figure 9.2) is one of the oldest cybermalls and has been featured on PBS and in the *New York Times,* the *Wall Street Journal, Fortune Magazine, US News and World Report,* and others.

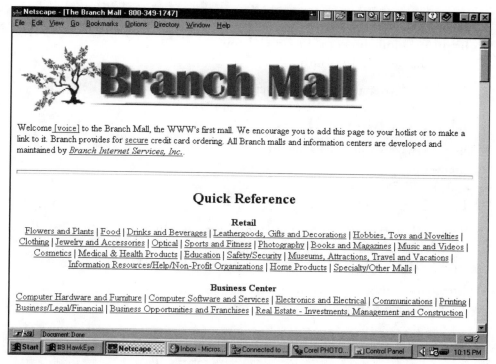

Figure 9.2 The Branch Mall, an oldie but goodie.

Internet Business Connection

http://www.intbc.com
Link Charge: $75/year

Run by Sally Elliott, who also created the Internet Sleuth (which was mentioned in Chapters 3 and 6). Highly recommended.

Majon's Cybermall

http://www.majon.com/majon/
Link Charge: $125/6 months

If you don't have a Web site and just want a quick and dirty presence, Majon has an online Web site creator that you use with your Web browser. Just fill out the form and you'll instantly have a Web page created for you. See site for pricing.

The MegaMall

http://infotique.lm.com/megamall.html
Link Charge: $7.50/month

Contains 49 departments and over 140 stores.

MJA Cybermall

http://www.mja.net/cybermal.htm
mall@mja.net
(305) 427-7888
Link Charge: $99/month

They will host your site for the same charge as a link.

ShopOnLine

http://www.shoponline.com
Link Charge: $50/year

The link is for their "guide" section.

Sparky's Entrepreneur-NET Ads

http://www.cyberzine.org
enet@cyberzine.org
Link Charge: $7.50/month

Links must be purchased quarterly ($22).

TAG Online Mall

http://www.tagonline.com
sales@tagonline.com
(800) TAG-8281 or (201) 783-5583
Link Charge: $240/year

TAG offers additional services such as FTP, mailing lists, mailbots, programming, and more.

The Awesome "Mall of the Internet"

http://malls.com/awesome/
dmw@flinet.com

(407) 434-4247
Link Charge: $25/month

They charge a one-time $10 setup fee to get your link in there. If you pay in advance for 6 months or 12 months, you get a 10 percent to 15 percent discount, respectively.

The Sphere Mall

http://www.thesphere.com
info@thesphere.com
(800) 664-7434 or (408) 369-9105
Link Charge: $50/year

The Sphere has been around for well over a year and therefore meets the criterion I stated earlier. Highly recommended.

Niche and Regional Malls

Some of the more successful malls are those that concentrate on a specific type of product or service category. If your Web site fits in with any of these, you'll probably want to investigate getting a link on them. On average, these sites may be a little more expensive. They often don't bring in a tremendous amount of traffic; however, they do bring in targeted, interested people looking for a specific type of product or service. You can find niche malls other than what I've listed here with the search engines (Chapter 3) and using keywords that relate to the niche you are looking for and the word "mall."

As more and more people begin to use the Internet within various geographical areas, some regions are reaching the critical mass needed to induce smaller businesses and organizations to put up a Web site. The problem is that if I'm looking for resources that are located in my area (South Florida), it's difficult to find them using most search engines. However, region-based virtual spaces make it easier to find information that local organizations make available on the Web. As part of your overall Web site promotion strategy, it may make sense for you to be associated with a few sites that cater to a regional or localized area.

Arizona SuperMall

http://www.browzinternet.com

All things Arizona.

AutoMall USA

http://www.automallusa.net

All aspects of automobile purchasing.

BayNet Real Estate Mall

http://www.baynet.com
webmaster@baynet.com
(415) 424-0994

Contains commercial and residential real estate services of all kinds for the San Francisco Bay area.

Canadian Internet Mall

http://www.bltg.com/cdnmall/default.html
Link Charge: $39.99+GST/6 months.

If your site is in Canada, this may be the mall for you.

EcoMall

http://www.ecomall.com
ecomall@internetmci.com
(212) 289-1234
Link Charge: $500/year

EcoMall contains all kinds of "green" products, services, and organizations. Environmentally friendly stuff is the theme here (see Figure 9.3).

Electronic Newsstand

http://enews.com
modus@enews.com

The first site of its kind, Electronic Newsstand contains more than 300 publications and over 2,000 dedicated exclusively to magazines (print and electronic). Permits users to browse publications at no charge and subscribe for less. The Electronic Newsstand is also sponsorable by sites that aren't publication related.

Florida Internet Real Estate Guide

http://www.floridaguide.com

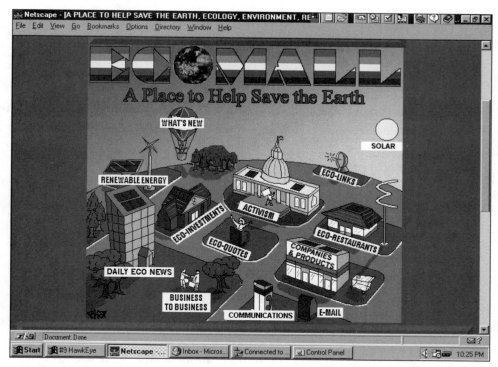

Figure 9.3   EcoMall, where green is king (or queen).

blynn@gate.net
(305) 964-3717

Florida's most comprehensive guide to real estate and relocation sites. Contains Web sites that focus on real estate sales, regional schools, chambers of commerce, moving services, mortgage services, and anything else that is related to relocation and property.

Internet Green Marketplace (The EnviroLink Network)

http://www.envirolink.org
admin@envirolink.org
(412) 683-6400

Another environment-related product/service mall. EnviroLink was one of the first environment-oriented organizations to go online.

TravelWeb

http://www.travelweb.com
travelweb@thisco.com
(214) 528-5656

TravelWeb contains detailed information on 5,163 individual hotels—and you can book reservations at 4,836 of them. Contact them for rates.

Other Malls of Mention

These aren't cheap and most don't offer links, but they are noteworthy.

Downtown Anywhere

http://www.awa.com
downtown@awa.com
Link Charge: $200 to $700/month

Downtown Anywhere is one of the oldest malls, and as you can see, it's one of the most expensive for links. The monthly fee depends on where in Downtown Anywhere your site is. The more prominent, the more it costs.

marketplaceMCI

http://www2.pcy.mci.net/marketplace/index.html

Stores with strong brand names, unique products, large selection, and low prices are the best fit. At least with MCI, you know they are going to be around for a while (see Figure 9.4).

Shopping2000

http://www.shopping2000.com

Lots of big-name companies and products, many catalog companies.

WorldWide Marketplace

http://www.cygnus.nb.ca

Located in Canada, another one of the older malls worth a look.

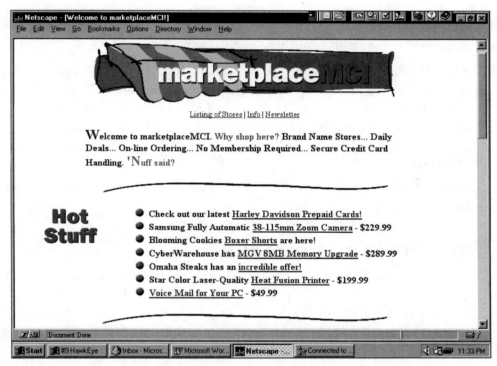

Figure 9.4   Check out marketplaceMCI. Is bigger necessarily better?

Where to Look for Cybermalls

As you've seen previously, at the end of some chapters, I like to point you in the direction of some key resources that contain expanded lists of what I provided you here. Those listed here are essentially meta-indexes for cybermalls and they contain fairly comprehensive lists of cybermalls. It is a rather time-consuming task to visit different malls, see if your site fits in, and get the prices. Some malls don't provide pricing on their Web site and require that you call or email them for more information. The following lists save you some of this effort.

The Hall of Malls

http://nsns.com/MouseTracks/HallofMalls.html

Created by New South Network Services, an Internet presence provider, the Hall of Malls is one of the older lists of cybermalls. I used this list in addition to previous research for this chapter.

The Shopper

http://www.hummsoft.com/hummsoft/shopper.html

Contains lists of malls by categories, such as large cybermalls, regional malls, specialty (niche) malls, international malls, and small malls. Be sure to check out The Shopper's "Top Ten Tips for On-Line Malls and Merchants" page. It contains useful information if you are looking to sell things online.

Yahoo!

There are quite a few sites listed in the **Business and Economy:Companies:Shopping Centers** category.

Concluding Remarks

Cybermalls can be a another good way to attract traffic to your Web site, especially if you are selling a product or service. To recap, seek out malls that you can see your site fitting in with, and negotiate a price. Anything that's under $100/year is a good deal. Keep doing this over and over until you've exhausted your budget for cybermall links.

Try to track your traffic by adding a small set of checkboxes to any order or response forms on your site. Designate each mall (as well as all the other methods mentioned in this book) with its name next to a checkbox. Title the section "How did you find our Web site?" Use this information to see which malls are worthwhile and which ones aren't. Continually adjust your link strategy to what's working, and prune the dead wood. Web site promotion is an ongoing process, so keep vigilant.

Beyond the Web: Promoting Your Site with Usenet Newsgroups, Internet Mailing Lists, Email, FTP, and Gopher

CHAPTER 10 TOPICS

CREATING AN EFFECTIVE "SIGNATURE FILE"

USING USENET NEWSGROUPS TO SPREAD THE WORD

TIPS FOR PROMOTING YOUR SITE WITH NEWSGROUPS

MARKETING WITH INTERNET MAILING LISTS

DON'T FORGET ABOUT EMAIL, FTP, AND GOPHER!

The World Wide Web has practically taken the Internet over. Much of this book has focused on ways to promote your Web site via the Web itself. This chapter will focus on the orphans of the Net: Usenet newsgroups, mailing lists, email, FTP, and Gopher. Granted, these applications are still used extensively. More than 65 percent of all Internet users use email the most. Web usage actually comes in second, with Usenet coming in third. The other utilities and resources are less used but still significant. When you add up all the things you can do with these tools to promote your Web site, there's a significant chunk of traffic that can be generated.

Before we start talking about these tools, I'd like to introduce some terms that relate to our conversation in this chapter. You may be familiar with some of them, but for the sake of completeness, I'll state them anyway.

Netiquette—Netiquette is simply the "rules" of conduct for the online world. As you may have guessed, the word is a combination of Net and etiquette. Just as there are a set of rules for table etiquette in the real world, there are various things that you should and should not do in the virtual world. A good example is: DO NOT TYPE MESSAGES IN ALL CAPITALS BECAUSE THIS IS CONSIDERED SHOUTING. If you ignore netiquette, you and your organization will likely suffer. A good resource on this is Arlene Rinaldi's *The Net: User Guidelines and Netiquette* which can be found at **http://www.fau.edu/rinaldi/netiquette.html**.

Lurking—Lurking is the act of reading Usenet newsgroups, consumer online service forums, or Internet mailing lists without posting. A lurker is more of an observer, watching what everyone else is doing. Before you "barge in" and post a message, it's a very good idea to lurk for a while. Watch what other people are posting, what they are saying, and perhaps most importantly, how others are reacting to postings. After you've lurked for a while, you'll have a better understanding of what's appropriate to say when you're ready to post.

Signature files—A signature file (also called a *sig*) is a short message that is attached to an email message, Usenet newsgroup (or online service forum) posting, or Internet mailing list message. It can have many purposes, from making a particular statement, saying what you do for a living, telling who you work for, advertising a subtle message for a product or service, or promoting your Web site address. One reason people use them is to save time. They create a file to contain something they often say in their messages and include the contents of that file automatically in each message they create. This way, you don't have to re-type the same things over and over again each time a message is created and you want your signature included.

Signatures are completely optional—many people don't even use them. They are typically four to eight lines in length. Anything longer than eight lines may be considered obnoxious by most Internet users. Figure 10.1 shows examples of signature files from my friend David Citron and me. They should give you an idea of what people do with them. It's easy to create a signature file. Once you know what you want it to say, create it in a word processor. I use Windows Notepad myself. Then save it as an ASCII text file. You can configure your email software to automatically include the few lines of text in the file into each message you send out. The same goes for your Usenet newsreader software.

```
Vince Gelormine                    Director of Business Development
vince@linkstar.com                 LinkStar Communications Corp.
Search the Net; Add Your Site FREE http://www.linkstar.com
```

```
Legion Publishing Corp.            The Internet Marketing BlackBook
8084 W. McNab Road, Suite 430      ISBN: 0-9643834-0-3 (317 pp.)
N. Lauderdale, FL  33068-4255      URL: http://www.legion.com/books/

Order Line: (305) 978-3444
Order Fax : (305) 426-1350         E-mail: editor@legion.com
```

```
 *  David H. Citron  *  Tech Writer/Journalist/Copywriter/Web Author  *
          * a/k/a the CyberCurmudgeon syndicated columnist *
                   * e-mail: dcitron@univox.com *
    The CyberCurmudgeon Column Archives: http://www.univox.com/writer/
```

```
"It is one of our most important laws that none of us may interfere
in the affairs of others."
     ... Captain Kirk (in Bread and Circuses episode of Star Trek),
     stardate 4040.7 ... quoted from _Star_Trek_Speaks_, by Susan
     Sackett, Fred Goldstein, and Stan Goldstein (Pocket Books, 1979)
```

```
"Live long and prosper - without government interference!"
     Mr. Spock, before the NBC censors got to him, stardate 1966
David H. Citron * Tech Writer/Journalist/Copywriter * dcitron@univox.com
```

Figure 10.1 *Some signature file examples.*

The nice thing about signature files is that they are universally accepted online. You can be posting a message in the knitting forum on Prodigy, contributing to an Internet mailing list on Internet marketing, writing an email message to an old friend, or posting to the *alt.politics* Usenet newsgroup and use a signature that promotes your Web site that focuses on tennis for all of these. The more you interact with the online community, the more people see that small little *tag line* at the end of your messages inviting them to visit.

You may want to use different signature files for different occasions. One reason you might want to do this is because of the limited space an appropriate signature file provides. Other reasons include using a business oriented signature for business correspondence and something a little more relaxed for personal correspondence, and using different signatures to promote different sites, products, or services. In this case, you will need to decide which signature file you want to use in each message and then tell the software program you are using which file you want to include. It's a couple more mouse clicks, but it sure beats typing in your signature each time.

The key to a good signature (aside from keeping it short) is to provide a compelling line or two of text that will cause the reader to visit your Web site (if that is the purpose of your signature, of course). If your site contains lots of coin collecting resources and information, then you would want to say that in your signature. This way, people who are interested in that stuff will know that your site matches their interest, and it increases the chance that they will visit. Of course, make sure your URL is listed, and double-check your copy for spelling and typos!

You can also create a signature file even if you are using one of the consumer online services:

- **America Online:** For newsgroup postings enter the keyword *newsgroups* and then choose *Set Preferences*. Type the text of your message in the Signature box. If you want to include your signature in a message posting, simply click the Use Signature box which is located at the bottom of the post message window.

- **CompuServe:** Click on the "Special" button and choose *Preferences* then click on *General*. You'll see a button labeled *Set Function Keys*. Click on that, and enter the name of your signature file in the *Key Label* field and then type your signature text in the Key Definitions box, and then click

OK. Your signature will be associated with an ALT key combination, most likely ALT+1. The next time you are sending an email message or in a forum writing a message press the ALT key and then 1 simultaneously. Do this at the end of your message, and the text of your signature will be inserted at that location.

- **Prodigy:** Click on the *Edit* pull-down menu button and choose *ScratchPad.* Simply type your message, and save it with a *.mac* extension (for macro). The next time you want to post a message to a Prodigy Bulletin Board, choose *Play Macro* from the *Goodies* menu. Your signature will then be included in your message.

Usenet Newsgroups

Usenet is not really a part of the Internet but, rather, it is comprised of many computers that run network news server software. The software is primarily used to send messages from computer to computer. Over 75,000 Internet sites participate in exchanging Usenet messages. The potential Usenet audience is estimated to be over 7 million people. I use the word messages instead of news because the word "newsgroups" is a bit of a misnomer. Usenet newsgroups are actually subject groups. The groups are arranged by subject in a hierarchical structure. The number of Usenet newsgroups is always increasing, with current estimates of over 15,000 individual topic groups.

In case you have not seen them elsewhere, here are some popular Usenet top-level categories:

alt	Alternative discussions ranging from the useful to the inane to the absolutely ridiculous.
biz	Business discussions. One of the few places where advertising is likely to be tolerated.
comp	Computer related discussions. As you may guess, this is one of the largest categories.
misc	Miscellaneous discussions that don't really fit anywhere else.
news	Usenet news and administration-related discussions.
rec	Recreational discussions.
sci	Science-related discussions.
soc	Social issues and discussions.
talk	Conversational discussions.

If you are new to Usenet, check out the *news.announce.newusers* and *news.newusers.questions* groups as well as the Usenet Info Center Launch Pad at **http://sunsite.unc.edu/usenet-b/home.html.** In addition to these online resources, a couple of good books about Usenet are:

The Usenet Handbook by Mark Harrison, O'Reilly & Associates, Inc., ISBN 1-56592-101-1.

The Usenet Book by Bryan Pfaffenberger, Addison-Wesley, $26.95, ISBN 0-201-40978-X.

Posting to a particular group or set of groups is the means by which Usenet can be used to promote and market your Web site. Keep in mind that when you post to a newsgroup, there's the potential of hundreds, thousands, or even tens of thousands of people seeing your message. If you've never posted to Usenet, you may want to try posting a test message to the group *misc.test* first.

Tips for posting to Usenet newsgroups

- **Find the right newsgroup for your posting.**

  Posting a message about cars in a newsgroup that covers artistic paintings is obviously inappropriate. Unless of course, your message is about a painting that has a car in it! Use DejaNews and/or the search feature within your newsreader software to find places that relate to the theme of your Web site and its intended user audience. I did this when I published my first book. I searched for books and found a number of newsgroups that focused on books. Only some of them were appropriate because the topic of my book was Internet marketing. It would have been a very bad idea to post a message about this new book in a group that dealt with poetry. After lurking in each group, it became apparent which ones were appropriate. When I saw another book like mine mentioned in a particular book-related group, that made it easy for me. My point is, look for postings similar to what you would post. If they are there and people don't respond negatively, then it's probably appropriate to post a message there.

- **Research what's acceptable to post and where.**

  This relates to the previous tip. Find a copy of the FAQ (Frequently Asked Questions list) if there is one, and read it thoroughly. The FAQ may also be called the "posting guidelines." These documents are commonly posted to each newsgroup once a month. Scroll through the group's messages to see if you can find it. Between reading the FAQ and lurking, you should have a good handle on what you should and should not discuss within a particular group.

- **Choose a meaningful subject line.**

People choose to read your message based primarily on its subject line. When someone browses a newsgroup message base, they look through pages of message subjects. Many newsreaders chop the subject line after 30-40 characters. Create a subject line that is brief, that will catch the attention of your intended audience, and that will compel them to read your message. Which message in Figure 10.3 would you read?

- **Avoid inane messages.**

Posting a one-word or one-line response doesn't help you establish yourself as an expert or gain you much respect with the other readers. When posting to a newsgroup, try to say something informative and constructive. I encourage you to post messages that are nonpromotional and of interest to the group's readers. Your signature file can do the rest.

- **Avoid posting duplicate messages.**

It can take several hours to several days before your message gets posted to a particular newsgroup. Don't assume that your message was not posted because it did not appear immediately. It takes time for your message to propagate out to all the computers that get the "feed."

- **Never spam the Net.**

Keep your postings to a few relevant newsgroups. Don't post messages to irrelevant newsgroups. *Spam* or *spamming* is defined as posting identical or nearly-identical messages to many irrelevant individual newsgroups. Nothing is as despised on Usenet as spamming.

If everyone ignored the individual newsgroup topics and wantonly posted whatever messages they wanted to, everywhere they wanted to, the entire system would become useless. Like the Internet, no single entity governs and controls Usenet. The only way the system can continue to be useful to the masses is by the users themselves revolting against any messages that are posted off-topic. Therefore, if you post a message that's off-topic, expect to receive several flames. A *flame* is a derogatory or angrily directed message toward another Internet user. Trust me, you don't want to get any. If you do spam or send unsolicited email, be prepared to be placed on the "Blacklist of Internet Advertisers" which can be found at **http://math-www.uni-paderborn.de/~axel/BL/blacklist.html**

- **Be careful when cross-posting.**

When you post a message to a particular discussion group, you have the option of posting that same message to other groups at the same time. For example, if you write a message about computer security, you may post it to the *comp.security.misc* newsgroup and then cross-post it to *comp.risks* and *alt.security* as well because they also discuss computer security. This saves you time since you don't have to individually post to each group. The problem with this approach is if you cross-post to too many groups, it can be construed as a *spam*. You'll want to avoid cross-posting to groups that have a lot of the same readership. People may not mind seeing your message once, but multiple times can be annoying.

Places to mention your Web site

Aside from finding related groups, the #1 place where you can post your new Web site announcement is the *comp.infosystems.www.announce* newsgroup, which is moderated by M. L. Grant. Figure 10.2 shows a typical announcement. Before you post your announcement, read the *How comp.infosystems.www.announce Works FAQ*, which can be found at **http://boutell.com/%7Egrant/charter.html.**

The purpose of *comp.infosystems.www.announce* is to announce Web sites and events related to the Web. The following list was taken verbatim from the FAQ document and details what you should and should not submit to the newsgroup.

This group *does* post the following documents:

a. New World Wide Web resources and sites

b. Changes to URLs of existing Web resources and sites

c. New World Wide Web resources and server, client, and supporting software

d. New releases/versions of existing Web resources and server, client, and supporting software.

e. Short summaries of monthly (or less frequent) changes to Web-based magazines or journals.

This group does NOT post the following types of announcements:

a.   Blatant advertising other than the announcement of the availability of more information about a product or service via a Web page

b.   "Make Money Fast" or any other chain-letter-like message

c.   Announcements of resources not accessible on the World-Wide Web

d.   Posts about Web-accessible resources of only local interest (world-wide relevance is an expected aspect of postings to internationally-distributed newsgroups)

As of February 1996, this newsgroup stopped accepting posts of commercial Web sites. If your site is commercial yet provides a genuine (free) service to the Internet community, it may be appropriate to announce this resource via the newsgroup. Figure 10.3 shows a listing of subjects at *comp.infosystems.www.announce*

Announcements to *comp.infosystems.www.announce* should use one of the following capitalized "ID words" in the subject line of your message:

ARCHIVE	ENTERTAINMENT	MAGAZINE	SCIENCE
ART	ENVIRONMENT	MISC	SERVER
BOOK	FAQ	MUSIC	SOFTWARE
BROWSER	GAMES	NEWS	SPORTS
COLLECTION	HEALTH	PERSONAL	TRANSPORTATION
ECONOMY	HUMANITIES	POLITICS	
EDUCATION	INFO	REFERENCE	
EMPLOYMENT	LAW	RELIGION	

Keep your announcement as short as possible (fewer than 75 lines). Avoid using a signature, or keep it to four lines or fewer. URLs should be included using the following syntax:

```
<URL:protocol://site[:PORT]/path/to/file/or/directory/>
```

For example:

```
<URL: http://www.lod.com/services.html>
```

```
From: Steve Fowler <steve@pdnis.is.paradyne.com>
Newsgroups: comp.infosystems.www.announce
Subject: PERSONAL: The Wonderful World of Steve Fowler
Followup-To: comp.infosystems.www.misc
Date: 17 Feb 1996 03:01:56 GMT
Organization: AT&T Paradyne
Lines: 23
Approved: www-announce@boutell.com
Message-ID: <4g3gf4$ch7@Holly.aa.net>
Reply-To: stevef@ddi.digital.net
NNTP-Posting-Host: boutell.com
Originator: announce@Linux

Steve Fowler is proud to announce the availability of his home page on the
Internet.

Steve has many interests, including baseball cards, Washington Redskins,
aquariums, etc.

However, Steve has started putting together a Clown page.  This page
contains pictures and links to other clown-related sites around the Internet.

Stop by and say Hi!! and visit Steve's Clowns, Clowns, Clowns.

<URL:http://ddi.digital.net/~stevef>


_
Steve Fowler       |URL:    http://ddi.digital.net/~stevef |"MMmmmm, Beeerr!"
AT&T Paradyne      |EMAIL: stevef@ddi.digital.net          | - Homer Simpson
P.O. Box 2826      |LAND:   (813)530-2186                  |
Largo, FL 34649-2826 |ICBM:  27 53 30 N / 82 45 30 W       |
_

 . . . . . . . . . . . . . . . . . . . . . . . . . . . . . . . . . . . . . .
 . .
Charter FAQ of comp.infosystems.www.announce (moderated) is posted twice weekly
and is on the Web: <URL:http://boutell.com/%7Egrant/charter.html>.  Hey!  See
the Best o' c.i.w.announce: <URL:http://www.boutell.com/announce/index.html>!
```

Figure 10.2   An announcement of a personal Web site made to
comp.infosystems.www.announce.

You can post your announcement or send it via email to www-announce@boutell.com. If you have questions about posting, send them to the group's moderator, M. L. Grant, at www-announce-request@boutell.com.

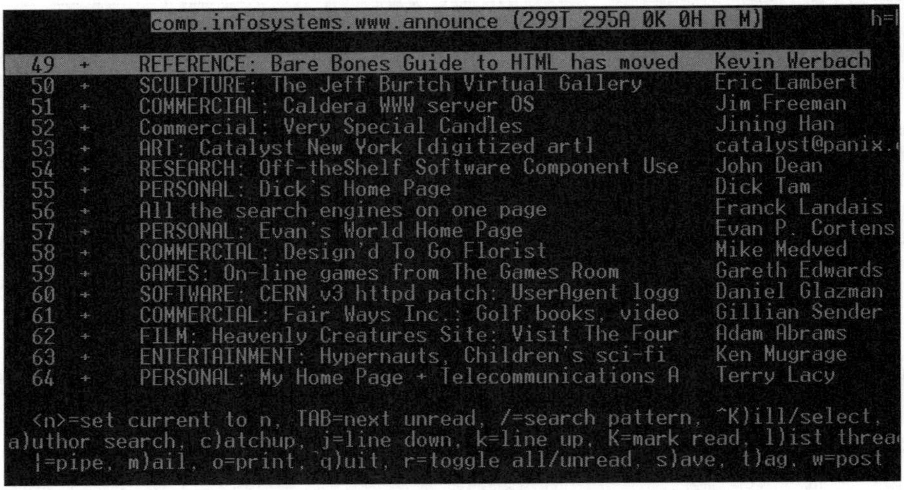

```
comp.infosystems.www.announce (299T 295A 0K 0H R M)        h=l
49  +  REFERENCE: Bare Bones Guide to HTML has moved  Kevin Werbach
50  +  SCULPTURE: The Jeff Burtch Virtual Gallery      Eric Lambert
51  +  COMMERCIAL: Caldera WWW server OS               Jim Freeman
52  +  Commercial: Very Special Candles                Jining Han
53  +  ART: Catalyst New York [digitized art]          catalyst@panix.
54  +  RESEARCH: Off-theShelf Software Component Use    John Dean
55  +  PERSONAL: Dick's Home Page                      Dick Tam
56  +  All the search engines on one page              Franck Landais
57  +  PERSONAL: Evan's World Home Page                Evan P. Cortens
58  +  COMMERCIAL: Design'd To Go Florist              Mike Medved
59  +  GAMES: On-line games from The Games Room        Gareth Edwards
60  +  SOFTWARE: CERN v3 httpd patch: UserAgent logg   Daniel Glazman
61  +  COMMERCIAL: Fair Ways Inc.: Golf books, video   Gillian Sender
62  +  FILM: Heavenly Creatures Site: Visit The Four   Adam Abrams
63  +  ENTERTAINMENT: Hypernauts, Children's sci-fi    Ken Mugrage
64  +  PERSONAL: My Home Page + Telecommunications A   Terry Lacy
<n>=set current to n, TAB=next unread, /=search pattern, ^K)ill/select,
a)uthor search, c)atchup, j)line down, k=line up, K=mark read, l)ist threa
|=pipe, m)ail, o=print, q)uit, r=toggle all/unread, s)ave, t)ag, w=post
```

Figure 10.3   A listing of message subjects for comp.infosystems.www.announce.

NEW PRODUCT ANNOUNCEMENTS

If and only if you would like to announce a new computer-related product, you can post a message to *comp.newprod* (moderated by Chip Rosenthal). Avoid using any hype in your message. Keep it short and point people to your Web site for more information. New products of a more general nature can be posted to *misc.announce.newprod*.

THE BIZ.* HIERARCHY

This set of groups exists primarily for business posts and announcements of various kinds. The quality of messages to some of these groups can be rather poor (like in *biz.americast*), but they can still be useful places to promote your site. The following list contains some of the more relevant ones that may be applicable to you, with the exception of a few that are company specific (which I provide to illustrate how some companies can create an entire newsgroup for their own announcements and promotion purposes).

biz.americast	"AmeriCast" announcements. This is a free-for-all posting environment with lots of ads.
biz.americast.samples	Samples of AmeriCast. (Moderated)
biz.books.technical	Technical book announcements, reviews and discussions.
biz.comp.accounting	A group specific to the accounting software industry.

biz.comp.hardware	Generic commercial hardware postings.
biz.comp.services	Generic commercial service postings.
biz.comp.software	Generic commercial software postings.
biz.general	General business operations discussions & offerings.
biz.jobs.offered	Job position announcements.
biz.misc	Miscellaneous postings of a commercial nature.
biz.next.newprod	New product announcements for the NeXT computer platform.
biz.oreilly.announce	New product announcements from O'Reilly & Assoc. (Moderated)
biz.stolen	Postings about stolen merchandise.
biz.test	Biz newsgroup test messages.

LOCAL ANNOUNCEMENTS

More and more areas around the world now have a set of newsgroups that have been created to be limited to that particular geographical area. These are referred to as a "local hierarchy of newsgroups." These regional (such as *fl* for Florida and *ca* for California) and local hierarchies (such as *ba* for the San Francisco Bay Area) contain numerous subcategories such as *.forsale*, *.marketplace*, and *.announce*. The *.announce* newsgroups such as *fl.announce* can be very useful. These are where announcements of new Web sites and events can be made, but only if they relate to or take place in the geographical area of the newsgroup. I've often used *.announce* groups to promote a new Web site or announce a new Web site feature, and you should, too.

FORSALE GROUPS

Some *forsale groups* permit commercial organizations to post merchandise that's for sale, while others restrict postings to person-to-person selling. This is a fairly comprehensive list of the types of groups that you can post to. The next time you have something you want to get rid of (or buy), check these out. If it's appropriate, you can direct people to your Web site for more information or simply use a signature file if it's not directly related.

misc.forsale	General items for sale
misc.forsale.computers.d	Discussion of misc.forsale.computers.
misc.forsale.computers.discussion	Discussions only about items for sale.
misc.forsale.computers.mac	Apple Macintosh related computer items.

misc.forsale.computers.mac-specific.cards.misc
Macintosh expansion cards.

misc.forsale.computers.mac-specific.cards.video
Macintosh video cards.

misc.forsale.computers.mac-specific.misc
Other Macintosh equipment.

misc.forsale.computers.mac-specific.portables
Portable Macintosh systems.

misc.forsale.computers.mac-specific.software
Macintosh software.

misc.forsale.computers.mac-specific.systems
Complete Macintosh systems.

misc.forsale.computers.memory
Memory chips and modules for sale and wanted.

misc.forsale.computers.modems
Modems for sale and wanted.

misc.forsale.computers.monitors
Monitors and displays for sale and wanted.

misc.forsale.computers.net-hardware
Networking hardware for sale and wanted.

misc.forsale.computers.other
Selling miscellaneous computer stuff.

misc.forsale.computers.other.misc
Miscellaneous other equipment.

misc.forsale.computers.other.software
Software for other systems.

misc.forsale.computers.other.systems
Complete other types of systems.

misc.forsale.computers.pc-clone
IBM PC-related computer items.

misc.forsale.computers.pc-specific.audio
PC audio equipment.

misc.forsale.computers.pc-specific.cards.misc
PC expansion cards.

misc.forsale.computers.pc-specific.cards.video
PC video cards.

misc.forsale.computers.pc-specific.misc
Other PC-specific equipment.

misc.forsale.computers.pc-specific.motherboards
PC motherboards.

misc.forsale.computers.pc-specific.portables
Portable PC systems.

misc.forsale.computers.pc-specific.software
PC software.

misc.forsale.computers.pc-specific.systems
Complete PC systems.

misc.forsale.computers.printers
Printers and plotters for sale and wanted.

misc.forsale.computers.storage
Disk, CD-ROM, tape drives for sale and wanted.

misc.forsale.computers.workstation
Workstation related computer items.

misc.forsale.non-computer
Non-computer items for sale and wanted.

The *marketplace* set of groups is pretty much the same as the *.forsale* set. A few examples include:

comp.sys.ibm.pc.games.marketplace
rec.arts.books.marketplace
rec.arts.comics.marketplace
rec.games.board.marketplace
rec.games.video.marketplace
rec.music.makers.marketplace
rec.photo.marketplace
rec.travel.marketplace

Internet Mailing Lists

An Internet *mailing list* is a quick and easy way to distribute information to a large number of people interested in a particular topic. If the theme or content of your Web site is in sync with the topic of certain Internet mailing lists, then it *might* be appropriate to post a message to the subscribers of the group announcing your Web address and inviting them to visit.

There are thousands of Internet mailing lists. Finding the ones that are applicable to your business, product, service, organization, or Web site is your first step. As you learned in Chapter 3, probably the easiest way to find them is by using Scott Southwick's *The Liszt* (**http://www.liszt.com**) and Stephanie da Silva's *List of Publicly Accessible Mailing Lists (PAML)* (**http://www.neosoft.com/ internet/paml/**). In addition to these resources, you can try the *news.lists* Usenet newsgroup. The consumer online services (America Online, CompuServe, etc.) have their own areas where you can search for lists as well.

When a message is posted to an Internet mailing list, it is electronically duplicated and sent to everyone who has subscribed to that list (subscribing to a list will be explained in a minute). The message will be sent to each subscriber's email box.

For example, if you type up a message that you want to post to a mailing list consisting of two thousand participants, you will send it off to a single email address. This is a special address called the *submission* or *posting address*. This address is provided after you subscribe to the mailing list. The message will be received by the computer at the submission address and be processed by a person or by a computer program. Assuming all is well, your message will then be sent out to each of the two thousand individual subscriber email boxes. You don't need to know the two thousand addresses to send them your message since the mailing list program knows them. The software that manages and distributes mailing lists is commonly referred to as *list servers*. Several popular software programs exist such as listserv, majordomo, and listproc.

By the same token, when someone posts to a list that you have subscribed to, you will receive a message in your email box. In either case, the message will sit there until the recipient accesses it. From there, the recipient may read it, ignore it, delete it, save it, download it, print it, reply to it, or forward it to someone else on the Internet. The last thing you probably want to get is a series of irrelevant messages clogging up your email box—as do the other list subscribers. Keep this in mind before you send out a message announcing your Web site as your message may not be acceptable.

Once you've found a set of list addresses that seem to fit your interests (or those of your Web site users), you need to determine what really goes on within the list. This will help you determine what types of messages are acceptable and whether you want to get involved with the list on an ongoing basis. Your best strategy is to see what types of messages people post on each list. In some cases, there are archives available of the messages that have been posted to the list. The archived messages may be available on a Web site, on an FTP site, or compiled into a large set of files that can be requested by email. If the list is not archived, you should subscribe to the list(s) in question.

The reason I recommend that you check the archives is because some mailing lists have a rather high volume of messages. Imagine getting twenty, fifty, or a hundred email messages *each day*. If you don't check your messages often, you'll probably feel a bit overwhelmed by a few hundred messages to go through. By checking out the list via an archive of its messages, you can sample the list without actually subscribing.

There are three types of Internet mailing lists:

- **Moderated:** These lists are maintained by a moderator who filters out unwanted or inappropriate messages. Therefore, a moderated list usually has a higher quality of messages and less of a *signal-to-noise ratio* (a term used on the Internet to indicate the ratio of useful-to-useless messages that are posted). If you try to post an advertisement to a moderated list where ads are not permitted, your message will never make it out to the list subscribers. The moderator will discard it and may or may not notify you of your goof.

  Most Internet mailing lists are operated by someone who has a keen interest in the particular subject of the list. These maintainers usually offer the list as a free service and aren't compensated for their efforts. Because of this and the fact that the moderator needs to personally read and review each message that is submitted, messages can take a little while before actually being posted to the list.

- **Unmoderated:** The majority of Internet mailing lists are operated without any centralized control or censorship. That is, all messages are automatically forwarded to subscribers. When you submit a message, it gets posted and the subscribers will receive it. This can be bad if you make an error because there is no one to stop you from falling (i.e., if you post an advertisement on a list that prohibits ads, the message will still be posted; the onslaught of negative email you may receive can be a harsh wake-up call to be more cautious and to do your homework before posting to just any list, especially a large one). The turnaround time of your submitted message is obviously much quicker than that of a moderated list. A message posted to an automated unmoderated list can be received by the subscribers within minutes. Since there isn't a moderator to keep an eye on the messages, you are more likely to receive irrelevant and poorly constructed messages than if you were on a moderated list.

- **Digest:** This is simply a compilation of many individual messages sent to each subscriber as one (or several) larger messages. Many digests contain a table of contents of what's inside. The good thing about a digest is you don't receive as many separate emails and so your email box doesn't get all clogged up with messages.

Subscribing to an Internet mailing list is as easy as sending a message to the subscription address. Some lists require certain text to be placed in the subject line while others want you to leave the subject line blank and place text (like subscribe youremail@address.com) in the body of the message. If you have successfully subscribed, you'll get back an email message explaining more about the list, including what address to send postings to.

Announcing your Web site

Here are a few mailing lists where your Web site announcement may be appropriate:

Net-Happenings
http://www.mid.net/NET
http://www.mid.net:80/NET/holinput.html

Net-Happenings is the premier Web site announcement mailing list. It is a service of InterNIC Directory & Database Services and is moderated by Gleason Sackman of North Dakota's SENDIT Network for K-12 educators. Figures 10.4 and 10.5 show submission examples.

Submissions are filtered by Gleason and then distributed to the subscriber list. Commercial Web sites and ads should be posted to the Net-Ads mailing list (shown after this one). Messages are archived and available on the Web site as well as in the *comp.internet.net-happenings* newsgroup.

If you would like to subscribe to Net-Happenings (not necessary to submit your announcement), send email to listserv@lists.internic.net with the following in the body of your message:

subscribe net-happenings YourFirstName YourLastName

As with the *comp.infosystems.www.announce* newsgroup, Net-Happenings also requests that you use a category identifier in the subject of your message:

BOOK	Internet books
CONF-NA-	Conferences taking place in North America
CONF-	Conferences taking place outside North America
CORRECT	Correction to a previous posting
EJOUR	Electronic journals (e-journals)
EMAG	Electronic magazines
FAQ	Frequently Asked Question resources
FEDGOVT	Federal government
FTP	Anonymous FTP sites
GOPHER	Resources available via Gopher
HUNT	Internet Hunt questions/answers
JEWEL	Postings from Gopher Jewels
LISTS	Listserv(s), email lists, etc.
MISC	For everything else
NETLINK	Netlink Server additions
NII	National Information Infrastructure
NEWSLTR	Newsletters [Edupage, etc.]
NYSED	What's New on the OTPAD/ACT gopher
SCOUT	The scout report
SEM	Seminars
SOFT	New software [WWW, etc.]
SYMP	Symposiums
TELCONF	Teleconferences
TRAIN	Training [both commerical and non-commerical]
UPDATED	Update of previous posting(s)
WAIS	WAIS indexed databases, etc.
WRKSHOP	Workshops
WWW	Web resources

```
WWW> Dental Implant Home Page

*** From Net-Happenings Moderator ***

Date: Sat, 10 Feb 1996 18:17:54 -0600
From: srobert@netrus.net

http://www.dental-implants.com

The Dental Implant Home Page is a total resource for patients and dentists.
The major portion of this site features actual patient treatment situations.
Photography and documentation are excellent and almost every type of Dental
Implant restoration is shown. There is no better place on the web to learn
about dental implants and what they can do for you.
```

Figure 10.4 A Web resource submitted to the Net-Happenings mailing list.

```
WWW> www.iguide.com

*** From Net-Happenings Moderator ***

Date: Wed, 14 Feb 1996 12:32:22 -0500
To: online-news@marketplace.com
From: Evan Rudowski <evanrud@newscorp.com>
Subject: www.iguide.com

Thought you'd all be interested to know that the iGuide service from News
Corp. Internet Ventures is now available to the public at www.iguide.com.

The venture's hard-working editorial staff just uncorked the champagne in
the newsroom to celebrate. It's been a well-documented and tumultuous year
here, but on the editorial side there have been some very talented people
creating some great content, and it is now out there for everyone to see and
enjoy. It has always been a primary goal of the venture to create the first
Web site featuring extensive, original content built just for the Internet.
As of today, that's been accomplished.
=====================================
Evan Rudowski
News Corp. Internet Ventures
evanrud@newscorp.com
(212) 462-5077

=====================================
```

Figure 10.5 An announcement of a new Web site to the Net-Happenings
mailing list.

Net-Ads

http://www.mid.net/NET-ADS/
http://www.mid.net:80/NET-ADS/newsubmit.html

Net-ads is in digest format only and should be used for commercial announcements not appropriate for Net-Happenings. Use the same ID words and procedures as mentioned above to submit your announcement.

To subscribe to net-ads, send email to **majordomo@mid.net**, leave the subject blank, and in the body of your message, type "subscribe net-ads" and you will receive the latest information about submitting your site.

The Scout Report

http://rs.internic.net/scout_report-index.html
scout@internic.net

Scout Report is a weekly publication of Net Scout Services and is provided as a fast, convenient way to stay informed about valuable resources on the Internet.

```
Fort Lauderdale Real Estate and Relocation Guide

Date: Thu, 1 Feb 1996 08:55:21 -0600
From: james@introweb.com

http://www.introweb.com/fortlauderdale/property.htm

This site is the best place to visit when considering a move to the Greater
Fort Lauderdale area. There is a special emphasis on luxurious South Florida
living, and waterfront residences are the standard.
```

Figure 10.6 An ad posted to the Net-Ads mailing list.

```
RCS Financial Services, Ltd

Date: Thu, 1 Feb 1996 00:01:04 -0600
From: samlaw12@caribsurf.com

http://www.caribsurf.com/rcs/aboutrcs.html

Offshore financial services which include: company formation, trusts, global
mutual funds & offshore banking. Offices located in the British Virgin
Islands with affiliated offices located throughout the world.
```

Figure 10.7 A commercial organization promoting its Web site on Net-Ads.

Its purpose is to combine in one place new and newly discovered Internet resources and network tools, especially those of interest to our primary audience—researchers and educators. The service is designed for *Internauts* who want their Internet announcements selectively filtered and summarized once each week.

The mailing list version is sent to over 20,000 subscribers. The Scout Report is also available on the Web, FTP, and Gopher. To subscribe, send email to listserv@lists.internic.net and in the body of the message, type the following:

```
subscribe scout-report yourfirstname yourlastname
```

New Product News
rbakerpc@delphi.com

This is a daily newswire available on America Online and Delphi that can include Web site announcements. Send a message to Robert Baker for details and guidelines for submission.

Creating your own mailing list

Many organizations create their own Internet mailing lists to keep their clients and prospects informed of company happenings, such as product announcements and press releases. Having your own mailing lists is also a great marketing tool.

Most Internet access and presence providers offer mailing list management capability for under $100/month and a small (less than $100) setup fee. I've seen many services for $25–$50 setup and $35/month. If you run your own server, you can get majordomo from **ftp://ftp.greatcircle.com/pub/major-domo/** and listserv from **ftp://cs-ftp.bu.edu/pub/listserv/**. Install the one you want to use on your server and configure it.

TIPS TO STARTING YOUR OWN INTERNET MAILING LIST:

- **Name your list.** Check Liszt and PAML (Stephanie da Silva's list) to make sure your list name isn't already used by someone else.

- **Write a FAQ or Charter.** It should state the purpose of the list, whether it is moderated or not, and what types of messages are appropriate.

- **Make your list worth reading.** Try to limit useless messages and keep junk email from killing your list.

- **Advertise your list.** Submit it to PAML, Liszt, and other Internet mailing lists providers.

Email

There is no way to send an email message to every Internet user, nor should you want to. Unsolicited email advertising is not widely accepted on the Internet. There has been an ongoing debate for the past couple of years as to whether it will ever become accepted. So far, I'd say that it's still very much taboo. At this point, you may be thinking, "What's unsolicited mean, exactly?" Anytime that you send a message to someone with whom you do not already have a relationship, it is considered unsolicited. How you define relationship is another thing. Some people feel that if they subscribe to the same Internet mailing list, they have a relationship with all the subscribers. If nothing else, everyone has at least one thing in common. That common thread is often used as a lead-in to an unsolicited message. You really have to be careful about who you send what messages, and under what pretenses.

What you send out can make a difference, however. Sending out some useful information to people you've never corresponded with before may be forgivable, but sending a blatant advertisement may not. It really depends on whom you send the message to and how you present yourself. I've received numerous unsolicited messages from people who saw my post on Usenet or visited my Web site. Their message would usually begin with a reference to the post or Web site and then proceed with whatever's on their mind. I appreciated some of these messages, and others I did not.

Sending unsolicited email, no matter what your lead-in, is a bit like Russian roulette. The safe bet is to not send out unsolicited messages, especially if there is something you want from the recipient. If you offer something to the recipient (information, free link on your site, whatever), an unsolicited message will likely be accepted by most people. No matter what you do, there's always at least one person who is going to take offense. The best thing you can do, in that case, is apologize and avoid contacting that person in the future.

Email sponsorship opportunities

One advantage email has over the Web is that 99.9 percent of all Internet users have an email account while the number of Internet users who surf the Web is much lower. In Chapter 6, you were introduced to Web site sponsorship opportunities. Similar opportunities exist in the email world as well. The nice thing about an email-based sponsorship is that you don't need to create a graphical banner. Simply create the text (which should include your URL!)

that the particular opportunity requires, and pay them some money. There are a lot more sponsorable email opportunities than I list here. They aren't all that easy to find, but my goal here is to make you aware that these exist and that they are usually offered at a very low cost. Keep an eye out for other opportunities, as more continue to pop up every day. Many Internet mailing lists are sponsorable as well, and I list those here, too.

FlashBack

http://www.flashback.com
http://www.flashback.com/www/april.1995/flashback/9050.sponsor.info.html

John J. McLaughlin (**flash@FlashBack.com**) is the publisher and editor of this mailing list and Web site that caters primarily to Sun Microsystems users. Informative articles, product reviews, and announcements are distributed to the subscriber list. FlashBack has over 150,000 subscribers and reaches more than 50 percent of the installed base of Sun Microsystems computers. There are varying levels of sponsorship with the minimum being $500. This gives you the ability to submit two full-length (up to several pages) articles about your Web site, product, and/or service available to the subscriber base (additional articles are $750 each). Additional rates for special offers are available on the FlashBack Web site. A one-paragraph summary of your article will be distributed to the bulk of subscribers. Those interested can request the full article via return email or the Web site. Your articles should be submitted in ASCII text, they will be converted to HTML for the Web version.

Internet Marketing Discussion List

http://www.i-m.com
http://www.i-m.com/sponsor.html

Rates are $500/week ($1,500 for four weeks) which provides you with a one-line (70 characters) message and your URL to be displayed on its single-message mailing list, one line at the top and four at the bottom of each digest message, and a logo (475×40 pixels) plus hyperlink in the archives Web page. You can get an exclusive sponsorship for $1,000 per week ($3,500 for four weeks) as well. Additional information can also be obtained by sending the moderator a message at glenn@popco.com.

This list, shown in Figure 10.8, has been covered in *New York Newsday, Internet World Magazine,* and *Wired.* It has over 5,600 daily subscribers and thousands more who visit the Web site. Subscribers are primarily involved in the field of

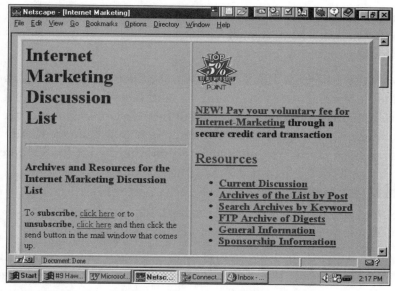

Figure 10.8 *This mailing list is definitely worth your time—be sure to check it out.*

marketing on and to the Internet, including representatives of virtually every company in the field, advertising agencies, journalists, and academics.

LinkStar Search Engine
http://www.linkstar.com
sales@linkstar.com

When users submit their Web sites to LinkStar's Internet Directory, they receive an email message confirming inclusion in the database. These and other routine messages are sponsorable with a description (of one to three lines) for a fraction of a penny each. Contact LinkStar for the latest rates.

NetSurfer Digest
http://www.netsurf.com/nsd/index.html
http://www.netsurf.com/nsm/adhowto.html

NetSurfer Digest is published bimonthly and focuses on things to do on the Web. Rates are $700 for up to 8 lines of text (single insertion rate) on up to $3,500 for other types of exposure. Direct email circulation is over 50,000, and it has an estimated Web readership of over 45,000.

Rosalind Resnick's CyberBiz
http://www.netcreations.com/cyberbiz/
rosalind@netcreations.com

CyberBiz is a list that Rosalind sends out of her periodic columns on doing business online. It's free to subscribe to, and users are informed that they may periodically receive "announcements of new developments and free information we think our readers may be interested in." Contact Rosalind for the latest rates; as of this writing, you could sponsor the list for $350/year.

URL-minder

http://www.netmind.com/URL-minder/URL-minder.html
http://www.netmind.com/URL-minder/sponsor-info.html

The URL-minder tracks World Wide Web pages and will automatically send you an email message any time that page is changed. This is very useful if you want to know the next time a specific Web page is updated with new information. Rather than you having to visit the site repeatedly to check for anything new, you can sign up for the free URL-minder service, enter in the URLs of the Web pages you want to keep track of, and provide your email address. Any time any of those pages changes, you'll get an email message informing you of the change.

URL-minder is free to use because it is sponsor supported. You can have your message (which certainly can include your Web site address) included in the thousands of messages that URL-minder sends to its users each day. URL-minder has over 300,000 unique users tracking over 40,000 unique URLs. Ten thousand to fifty thousand messages go out daily.

The sponsorship fee is a very reasonable $50/month, which gets you access to five percent of the users each day. Over the course of a typical three-month sponsorship, your message (consisting of a maximum of 4 lines of 55 characters each) is likely to be seen by nearly all the URL-minder subscribers.

Other Resources

There are also a couple of new services that provide free email services to the masses. These are just becoming available as I write this. They offer free email addresses, software and/or service to anyone who wants it. A benefit to this is that if you move around a lot, you won't have to keep reprinting business cards and such as your email address can remain the same indefinitely, no matter where you move. These services make money from advertisers who sponsor the service and can place logos and ads within the software screens. Two such services are *FreeMark Mail* (**http://www.freemark.com**) and *JUNO* (**http://www.juno.com**). These services may provide you with additional Web site promotion avenues.

FTP

FTP (File Transfer Protocol) is the principal method of transferring computer files (text, graphics, programs, etc.) over the Internet. With FTP, you can transfer data from "FTP sites" located anywhere in the world, to your PC. In simpler terms, an FTP site is an Internet-connected computer that makes part of its hard disk available to the Internet community.

Computer programs are the most typical files that are stored on an FTP site. You can store text files as well. These files may be articles, special reports, or whatever you want to place on your own site. Within these files can be references to your Web site. If your organization is selling software (or giving it away), you'll probably make it available via FTP on your site.

Your server administrator should know what's involved in creating an anonymous FTP area on your server (it's probably already there). Once you have set up your FTP server, you'll want to begin publicizing it in order to make your files findable by the Internet community. As you learned in Chapter 3, ARCHIE is the tool people use to find files on FTP sites. Submit your site address to ARCHIE by sending an email to **info-archie@bunyip.com**. Remember that people searching FTPspace with ARCHIE will type in keywords or program names. Name your files appropriately.

Gopher

Before the Web, there was Gopher. As you recall from Chapter 3, Gopher is a hierarchical, text-based, menu-organized system of information. You can create text files to be placed on your Gopher server which can direct people to your Web site. Some Internet service and presence providers will setup a Gopher server for a small fee. Then all you do is provide them with the files you want placed online.

The filenames for your Gopher files should contain keywords that your intended users would enter while searching for you in Veronica or Jughead. You should promote your Gopher site in Gopher Jewels (gopher://cwis.usc.edu). Choose *Other Gopher and Information Resources,* then *Gopher-Jewels,* and then *GOPHER JEWELS Information and Help* to get more information. You can submit your announcement to **gopherjewels-comment@einet.net** or your service provider can do this for you.

Concluding Remarks

In addition to all the things I mentioned here, you can create other types of your own electronic documents (newsletters, special reports, etc.) and make them available to the Internet community or on the consumer online services. These articles and documents can be a promotional vehicle for your organization and Web site. In addition, there are plenty of classified ad Web sites out there. Some of them have appropriate areas for listing your site. A good starting point for these can be found on Yahoo! in the *Business and Economy:Classifieds* category.

If there are several people in your organization, you'll want to make sure they all have signature files that have your Web site address in them and that they have a grasp of Netiquette. While they are "out there" interacting with the Internet community on mailing lists, newsgroups, email, and online service forums (discussed in the next chapter), they can be subtly announcing your Web site in those short signature tag lines.

CHAPTER **11**

The Consumer Online
Services

CHAPTER 11 TOPICS

WHY PROMOTE USING THE CONSUMER ONLINE SERVICES?

AMERICA ONLINE (AOL)

COMPUSERVE

DELPHI

GENIE

MICROSOFT NETWORK

PRODIGY

The consumer online services such as America Online, CompuServe, Delphi, GEnie, Microsoft Network, and Prodigy are probably the most overlooked resources and one of the more effective for promoting and marketing your Web site. Each service has numerous ways for you to let people know about your site—anything from inexpensive classified ads (grouped by subject) to outright advertising to posting in forum and bulletin board areas.

Most options are very inexpensive but do take a fair amount of time to implement. For example, consider the various forum areas that are of interest to your potential Web site visitors. Making consistent postings to these areas requires time to read through existing messages, to find things to post about, and to create your messages. Investigating the right classified areas to post your message on also requires time for research. The good news is that once you have created a strategy of places within each service where it is appropriate and effective to get your message out, the hard part is done.

Many organizations assign the task of continual online promotion to one or two people. From time to time or on a regular basis, they will log on to each service and:

- Check and respond to email
- Review the responses posted to their previous messages
- Find something new to post about
- Keep spreading the word
- Continue contributing to the online community of each service

Eventually, users will begin to recognize you and, hopefully, respect what's being said. When users see a reference to your Web site, they may visit. If they like it, they may tell others. With tens of thousands of people likely to see your messages on each service, a small percentage is likely to take action. Over time, this can add up to significant traffic.

Online service users are often hungry for places to go on the Web, especially if the site focuses on their interests. Reach them where they hang out, and let them know there are sites online that you think they may be interested in visiting. List yours as well as others. Be helpful rather than overly self-promoting.

Since mid-1995, the consumer online service industry has been quite chaotic, primarily due to increased competition and the popularity of the World Wide Web. This has lead to all kinds of changes for these services. Prodigy is changing its interface to look and act more like the Web, and it is changing its internal resources from its proprietary format to HTML format. Most online services are working on changing their internal structures to be indistinguishable from the Internet/WWW. Users will be able to seamlessly move to and from the service and the wide-open Internet. In addition, their advertising structures are changing as well. Therefore, even though I list rates in this chapter, you should check with each service to make sure that the rates haven't changed.

Who is using these services, and are they different from Internet users? Each online service has its own demographic profile. However, most surveys have shown that the average consumer online service user has more money and more education than the average Internet user.

Yankelovich Partners, Inc. (YPI) conducted a comprehensive survey in mid-1995 to see who uses the online services and how they use them. It found that about half of those surveyed had yearly incomes of more than $50,000, 57 percent were male, and 71 percent were Caucasian. The full survey results comprise 135 pages and can be obtained from YPI at (203) 845-0100.

America Online

No doubt, you've probably received several America Online (AOL) diskettes in the mail and through magazines you've purchased. If nothing else, AOL knows how to market itself. It is growing fast, with more than five million members currently. AOL (see Figure 11.1) isn't as oriented toward business as CompuServe is but, rather, is more focused on building a virtual community. Within AOL, you'll find several areas where you can promote and market your Web site, as you'll see in this section.

Subscription options

AOL's membership pricing is very simple: $9.95/month for 5 hours of online time and $2.95/hour thereafter. AOL offers 10 free hours to first-time members. AOL can be contacted at:

Figure 11.1 AOL's welcome screen.

America Online
8619 Westwood Center Drive
Vienna, VA 22182-2285
(800) 827-6364
http://www.aol.com

Classified ads

Like the other online services, AOL offers classified advertising but with one difference: it's free (see Figure 11.2). Now this may sound great to you at first, but the problem with the service being free is that anyone can post a message. Popular categories receive many ads each day. If you post a message in the morning, it will likely be way down on the list by the evening. Therefore, the usefulness of the service is diminished somewhat. But still, if you've got a minute, post an ad about your site in the appropriate place from time to time. It can't hurt.

Downtown AOL

Downtown AOL was launched in August of 1995 and is geared toward small- and medium-sized businesses. Instead of being placed within AOL itself,

Figure 11.2 AOL's classified ads are free.

Downtown AOL is situated on the World Wide Web (see Figure 11.2). Advertisers' sites can be seen by AOL members by using the keyword "downtown" as well as by Internet users who visit **http://downtown.web.aol.com.**

If your business doesn't already have a Web site, Downtown AOL is a good way to get an entry-level presence with some limited promotion. If you do have a site, you can get a link to your site from your Downtown AOL listing.

Downtown AOL is organized into more than 37 product and service categories. Users choose which category to look at and browse the listings. If users are interested in a listing, they simply click on it to see either a site created by Downtown AOL or an external Web site. The latest pricing can be found by calling (800) 615-4127 and requesting rate information, which includes all the details. I'll provide a summary for you here (note that all prices are for 6 months):

- A single page (includes 250 words or 1,500 characters of text, a 3"×5" or smaller graphic, and email link) is $495.

- Additional pages are $275 and additional graphics are $250 each.

- A link from your ad to an external Web site is $750.

- If you already have a site and don't want an ad, you can get a listing for $1,000 with a link to your site. Depending on what type of site you have,

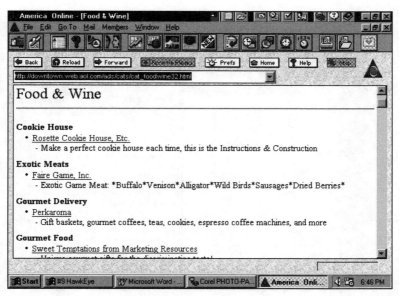

Figure 11.3   A few vendors in Downtown AOL, as shown with AOL's Web browser.

this may be worth it or may not. I'm not sure how much traffic Downtown AOL is receiving nor how many people would actually visit your site.

Marketplace

The Marketplace is essentially AOL's cybermall (see Figures 11.4 and 11.5). It's restricted to large companies by the price required to participate. AOL is also very restrictive as to who they involve. If you are interested, you can try to call (703) 448-8700 and ask for the advertising department. Be forewarned, however, that if you don't get a live person and you decide to leave a message, it's highly doubtful that your call will be returned. In fact, while researching this book *and* my previous book, I never talked to someone live and *never* had a phone call returned from AOL's advertising department. In contrast, the best services were CompuServe and Prodigy who delivered everything they said they would very quickly.

If you have a big budget and require good customer service from your advertising partner (and actually require speaking with a live person!), call CompuServe or Prodigy. With my personal experience with AOL's advertising department (or lack thereof), I would be remiss to recommend AOL. That is not to say other AOL areas aren't good, because they are. When I requested

Figure 11.4 AOL's shopping area.

Figure 11.5 A look at the 800-FLOWERS virtual storefront in AOL's Marketplace.

information about Downtown AOL, I left my mailing information on their voice mail and I actually received it in the mail within a week!

Message boards

Within the various AOL areas, message boards allow members to interact with each other and post messages. There is no charge to read or post, other than the regular online time charges. Although ads are not permitted in these areas, you can use your signature file showing your URL with every message you post. Also, you can promote your Web site within the *World Wide Web Message Board* in "Members' Favorite Web Sites." I've used this to promote sites. Lurk for a while and see what everyone else is doing. You'll see that posting a message about your site or someone else's is just fine. In addition, if you have a personal Web page you want to promote, do it in the "Cool Personal Home Pages" message board. Before you post in other areas, be sure to read the guidelines for the particular message board.

CompuServe

CompuServe is the oldest consumer online service (see Figure 11.6). CompuServe Information Systems began in 1969 as a supplier of computer and network services. In 1979, its online service was launched. Since 1980, it has been a subsidiary of H&R Block. The March 1996 issue of *Internet World Magazine* rated the online services, and CompuServe took the top honor for best service. CompuServe has over 4.6 million members worldwide in 147 countries.

Figure 11.6 CompuServe's welcome screen.

Subscription options

Standard Plan: $9.95/month for your first 5 hours of online time, $2.95/hour thereafter.

Super Value Plan: $24.95/month for your first 20 hours of online time, $1.95/hour thereafter.

CompuServe can be contacted at

CompuServe
5000 Arlington Centre Blvd.
P.O. Box 20212
Columbus, OH 43220
(800) 848-8990
http://www.compuserve.com

User demographics and statistics

- 57% are men, 43% are women

- 64% are married

- 43% have children

- 86% are age 18-49

- Average household income (HHI) is $90,340

- 95% had some college

- Median age is 38

Classified ads

The cost of an ad in CompuServe's classifieds area depends upon the length of time the message stays up and how many lines your message is (see Figure 11.7).

There is a two-line minimum for all ads. One line can contain up to 65 characters, and a maximum of 25 lines are permitted per ad. The subject of your ad may be as many as 40 characters.

Ad Duration	Cost per Line
7 days (1 week)	$1.00
14 days (2 weeks)	$1.50
56 days (8 weeks)	$5.20
182 days (26 weeks)	$14.30

Figure 11.7 CompuServe's Classified Ad area.

CompuServe reserves the right to reject any ads placed in unrelated subject categories. You can submit your ad by selecting "Submit an Ad" within the Classifieds area (which is found by clicking on Shopping at the welcome screen). Simply select the appropriate category and subcategory. You are restricted to placing ads for the length of time shown. CompuServe reviews all ads for appropriateness. To get your ad placed near the top (which is desirable), try to post it in the early morning hours (7am to 9am). This is when CompuServe removes expired ads and replaces those slots with newly posted ones.

Electronic Mall

In 1985, CompuServe's Electronic Mall became the first cybermall of the online services (see Figure 11.8). Now in its eleventh year, the mall has over 150 catalogers, direct marketers, and retailers. CompuServe was also the first service to offer high-resolution product images for its mall vendors.

Aside from providing your graphical catalogs online, you can offer downloadable catalogs and software as well as conduct online market research with surveys through your storefront. Rates are two percent of sales plus $50,000 or $120,000 per year depending upon the size of your mall and additional extras. These fees include a number of benefits, such as marquee ads (prominently displayed

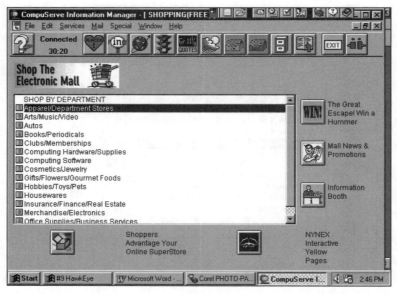

Figure 11.8 CompuServe's Electronic Mall was the first cybermall.

ads visable to people who first enter the mall) and an advertising credit for *CompuServe Magazine.* If you are interested in the Mall, contact Scott Tillett at (614) 538-3437.

File library areas

Many forum areas have associated file download areas. It is possible to use these areas to promote and market your Web site and organization, albeit not blatantly. You can submit text files containing information that would be of value to other CompuServe users, such as useful tips, special reports, etc. Within these files or at the end in a byline, you would make a reference to your Web site and address. Each forum has a moderator who reviews file library submissions (and who will delete any files that are inappropriate). You can, of course, upload free software (see Chapter 13 for a couple of good ideas) that users can download and use.

Forum areas

Also known as SIGs (Special Interest Groups), forum areas are places segmented by topic (just like Usenet newsgroups are on the Net). Many forums have additional costs associated with accessing them, based on how long users stay within them. There are over 700 forum areas on CompuServe. There are a number of opportunities to mention your site in its Internet forum areas. As usual, check the guidelines, and lurk a while before posting.

World Wide Web

The WWW is a new area of advertising for CompuServe (see Figure 11.8). It has introductory pricing that is valid up until June 30, 1996, after which time it may change. Contact CompuServe's Interactive Marketing Group at (614) 457-8600 for the latest pricing. The introductory pricing for placing your ad in several major subject areas is $5,000/month. CompuServe will supply you with the number of ad views and click throughs that your ad gets.

Rates are based on where your ad appears within the site. Its Web site's major traffic areas are the subject areas. The further down in the menu hierarchy your ad is placed, the lower the rate will be. All pricing is done on a monthly basis.

Delphi

Delphi is a menu-driven, ASCII-text based service that was the first online service to offer access to the World Wide Web (albeit in text form). The subscriber base is estimated to be approximately 100,000 (which is quite small for an online service). Delphi had plans to update its service and add a

Figure 11.9 CompuServe NOW, CompuServe's Web site.

graphical user interface, but apparently those plans have been scrapped. A Delphi spokesperson I interviewed said that the service will remain the same and that they are not aggressively promoting it. Basically, it's there for the loyal subscribers at this point. It will be interesting to see how long Delphi will remain.

Subscription options

Delphi offers two membership plans:

- *The 10-4 Plan:* $10/month, which includes the first 4 hours of usage each month. Additional hours are billed at $4/hour.

- *The 20-20 Plan:* $20/month, which includes the first 20 hours of usage each month. Additional hours are billed at $1.80/hour. There is a $19 setup fee for this plan.

If you want full Internet access with your account, there is a $3/month fee.

If you access Delphi directly or via Telnet (from another Internet site), there are no additional connect charges other than the usual long distance or Internet access provider charges. If you access Delphi through BT's Tymnet or SprintNet, there is an additional $9/hour fee during the time period from 6 am to 6 pm, your local time. For general inquiries, contact Delphi at:

Delphi Internet Services Corporation
1030 Massachusetts Avenue
Cambridge, MA 02138
(800) 695-4005 or (617) 491-3342
email: info@delphi.com

Custom forums

Delphi's custom forums are very inexpensive and permit you to set up your own bulletin board within the service. Delphi has over 100 custom forums, many of which are operated by business people who use them to promote their companies and to interact with their clients and potential clients.

The setup fee is just $29.95, and the monthly maintenance fee is $5.00. Delphi users who visit your forum are billed the usual Delphi membership and online time fees.

You have control over the content and over who may access your forum. To obtain an online application and more information, type GO CUSTOM within Delphi.

If you don't want to set up your own forum, you certainly can get involved with other ones by posting messages. Use the same common sense you would with posting to Usenet newsgroups. Signature files are fine here as well.

Classified ads

The Delphi Flea Market provides a place where users can promote their Web sites as well as their organization, product, or service. There is no charge to post a message.

GEnie

GEnie was created by General Electric Information Services in 1989 and was sold to Youvelle Renaissance Corporation in the beginning of 1996. Since this change-over occurred during the writing of this section, I expect many changes to take place. GEnie has a mall area that has been floundering for the past one to two years. Perhaps the new ownership will renovate it. Stay tuned, and if you have an interest in GEnie, contact them for the latest scoop.

Subscription options

For GEnie, $23.95/month includes up to 9 hours of online time. Additional hours are $2.75/hour. Depending upon how and when you log on, there may be additional telecommunications surcharges. GEnie has additional premium services, which vary in price. Its graphical interface software is free for the down-

Figure 11.10 GEnie's Web site contains subscription details and its free software.

loading via its Web site (see Figure 11.10). You can request it on diskette by calling GEnie. Contact GEnie or visit its Web site for additional information.

GEnie Online Services
P.O. Box 6403
Rockville, MD 20849-6403
(800) 638-9636
http://www.genie.com

Classified ads

GEnie has the most individually distinct ad categories of all the online services, with 19 major categories containing over 200 individual subcategories. This is beneficial to you since people looking for something in particular can find it easily. In addition, there are fewer ads per category than AOL, for example, thus increasing the chances of your ad being noticed and read. The fees for classifieds are minimal.

When you place an ad, you can choose up to three keywords. These are useful when users are searching for something. Choose the keywords that best describe what you are offering or are most likely to be typed by your prospective site visitors.

Forums

On GEnie, forums are called *RoundTables*. There are lots of them, and they operate the same way as they would on the other services. GEnie also has a file library area that contains over 200,000 files.

Microsoft Network (MSN)

If you've got Windows95, it's pretty easy to sign up to MSN (see Figure 11.11). Wedding an online service with an operating system was a good idea on Microsoft's part and has helped MSN generate over 850,000 subscribers in a very short time. Many of the things you can do on MSN can be done on the other online services; the primary difference is that there are more steps required with the other services. However, I found MSN to be more difficult to navigate around in if you don't know what you're looking for.

Subscription options

MSN's entry-level pricing appears attractive at $4.95/month but is comparable with the other services when you see that the fee covers just the first 3 hours of usage. Additional hours are $2.50 each. There is a frequent-user plan

Figure 11.11 Microsoft Network's welcome screen.

that is $19.95/month for 20 hours of online time and $2.00/hour thereafter. MSN can be contacted at

The Microsoft Network
Microsoft Corporation
One Microsoft Way
Redmond, WA 98052-6399
(800) 386-5550
http://www.msn.com

Content providers

MSN has less content than the "big 3" (America Online, CompuServe, and Prodigy) with over 200 companies sponsoring its online areas (see Figure 11.12). Some of these include Charles Schwab & Co., FEDEX, Equifax, *Success Maga-zine,* United Airlines, and *USA Today.* As I write this, MSN has suspended taking on new content providers until it determines its strategy with respect to the Internet and World Wide Web. You can still obtain information and guide-lines about being a content partner by calling (800) 643-2220.

World Wide Web

MSN offers advertising on Microsoft's Web site from $2,000 to $35,000 per month depending on location. The advertising comes in the common banner

Figure 11.12   An advertisement on MSN for Kellogg's (lower right).

ad format, as discussed in Chapter 6. At press time, they were in the process of creating a rate sheet. You can reach their advertising sales department for the latest at (206) 703-7777.

Prodigy

Prodigy is probably the most commercially oriented of the consumer online services (see Figure 11.13). Prodigy takes online marketing very seriously and has numerous options available to you for general marketing and Web site promotion. It was the first online service to offer a graphical Web browser but is now dumping it and has agreed to license Netscape's Navigator, due to be implemented in 1996.

Prodigy was conceived in 1984 through a partnership of IBM and SEARS and went online in 1988. As I write this, Prodigy is considered to be the number three online service in the United States, and both IBM and SEARS are deciding whether they will sell off their 50 percent stakes in the service.

At the beginning of 1995, the service was considered to be the number one service with over 2.7 million users. A year later, it was down to around 1.9 million members and dropped to the number three service.

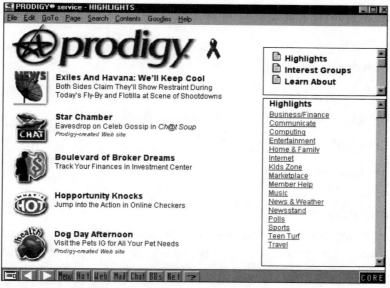

Figure 11.13 Prodigy's welcome screen.

Subscription options

Prodigy charges $9.95/month for 5 hours of online time and $2.95/hour thereafter. You can opt for its heavy-user plan, which is $29.95/month for 30 hours of online time and $2.95/hour thereafter. Prodigy can be contacted at:

Prodigy
445 Hamilton Ave.
White Plains, NY 10601
(800) PRODIGY, (800) 776-3449
http://www.prodigy.com

You can have up to six username/mailboxes per account. This is helpful if you have multiple Web sites you wish to promote or multiple businesses or products/services. You can create different usernames that identify with different purposes.

User demographics and statistics

The primary source of this data is from Mediamark Research's 1995 study. The information is available from TeleRep, which handle's Prodigy's advertising under the name Team Prodigy at (212) 759-8059.

- 57% are men, 43% are women

- 64% are married

- 54% have children

- 86% are age 18-49

- 42% have an average household income (HHI) of $75,000 or more

- 84% had some college

- Median age is 38

Awareness ads

Since Prodigy is restructuring the "guts" of its service, portions of it are considered part of the "new" Prodigy while other parts are referred to as the "old" Prodigy. The old Prodigy uses rotating banners placed at the bottom of each screen. When users click on the ad, they are taken to a screen such as the one shown in Figure 11.19. These screens may have several buttons leading to other ad screens.

The new Prodigy does away with the large amount of screen real estate that an awareness ad takes up and uses a small 2"×1" clickable button. An example of this type of ad is shown in the lower right of Figure 11.14, labeled "Online Brokerage."

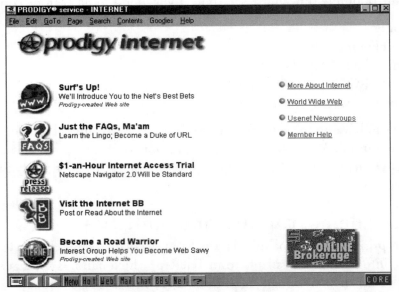

Figure 11.14 An ad for Online Brokerage (lower right) appears on the Internet interest area.

When users click on an awareness ad, which may be a banner or button that rotates throughout Prodigy and reaches the entire Prodigy audience (at a price of $45,000/month!), they can be taken to a Web site or to an ad site located within Prodigy.

Bulletin boards (BBs)

There is no charge to use or post on Prodigy's subject-oriented bulletin boards except for standard online time charges. Like Usenet newsgroups, Prodigy bulletin boards are an inexpensive way to reach people. Users are required to adhere to guidelines when posting. This information is available when you enter the BB area. For example, you cannot post blatant advertisements in these areas. The correct thing to do is to interact with the community, post helpful and interesting messages, and, of course, make sure your signature file contains your URL.

If your Web site contains information that a user is looking for (which was determined by you reading their plea for help), then by all means, post a message stating that your site contains information that could help. Otherwise, keep your URL and site announcement to your signature file. There is a special BB called "Announce URLs" in the Internet BB section where you can announce your site or post about others. You should take advantage of this as soon as you can.

Figure 11.15 Prodigy's Bulletin Board area welcome screen.

Classified ads

If you don't have the budget for awareness ads and premium positions, you can still reach Prodigy users, although not as aggressively, with classified ads (see Figure 11.16). The classified ad section can be found by using *Jump To* (first entry after you click on the Go To menu button) *classifieds*. It is managed by TPI Tele-Publishing, Inc. of Boston (617) 536-7977, which reviews all ads. It takes up to one day for your ad to appear, and you must pay by credit card. There are over 25 ad categories, most of which are shown in Table 11.1. Classified Ad rates (for the first page, consisting of about 240 characters, with additional pages at $1/each) are as follows:

Ad Duration	Cost
30 days	$10
60 days	$20
90 days	$30

Marketplace

Prodigy's CyberMall (Marketplace) contains dozens of places to shop (see Figure 11.18). It's not cheap to set up shop here though. Contact Prodigy at (914) 448-8176 if you want to create a virtual storefront within Prodigy.

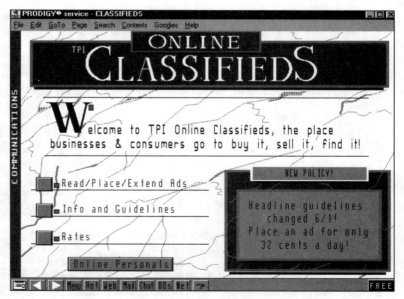

Figure 11.16　Prodigy's Online Classifieds section (Jump To: classifieds).

Table 11.1   Many of Prodigy's Online Classified Ad Categories

Help wanted	Work at home
Money makers	Career services
Real estate	Business opportunities
Travel tours	Business services
Phone services	Adult services
Audio/visual	Computer technology
Disks/games/toys	Books/magazines
Autos/boats/cycles	Household items
Food and recipes	Appliance/electronic
Arts/gifts/crafts	Sporting goods/memorabilia
Health/fitness	Miscellaneous

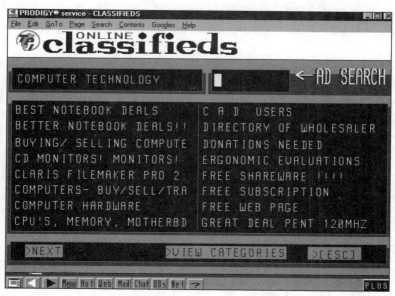

Figure 11.17   Some classified ad titles in the computer technology section of Prodigy.

Premium positions

These are ads placed in specific subject-oriented, high traffic areas within Prodigy. Prices range from $4,000/week for placement in the "People News" area to $20,000/week for placement in the "Headline News" area. The esti-

Figure 11.18   Prodigy's Marketplace contains dozens of virtual storefronts.

Figure 11.19   A full-screen ad on "old" Prodigy for Chase's credit card.

mated audience for these and the other premium position areas (Business News, Chat, Market Watch, and Sports News) ranges from 100,000 to 400,000 people each week.

Prodigy Direct E-mail (PDE)

Prodigy Direct E-mail allows your message to be sent directly to selected Prodigy users' electronic mailboxes. This is essentially "junk email." Unlike Internet users who will react strongly to unsolicited electronic mail advertisements, Prodigy users are accustomed to finding ads in their email boxes. I wouldn't say that everyone welcomes them, but they are at least tolerated without protest. Of course, there are many people who welcome them as well. Those who hate them have the opportunity to block unsolicited messages.

You can target your market according to age, gender, geography (ADIs, states and zip codes), and interests (sports, travel, cars, etc.), among other criteria. Your message will be automatically deleted after a week. If you want your message to remain in the mailboxes of your recipients for another week, there is an additional 25 percent surcharge. This is desirable since many users don't access the system once each week, and you will reach more people by extending the lifetime of your message. Table 11.2 shows the PDE fees.

World Wide Web pages

Prodigy has essentially two types of ads: graphical banners and text, called Banner Ads and Marketplace Ads respectively. A Banner Ad is displayed just under the page header that it's placed on. It is a clickable logo (much smaller than the typical banner size of 468×60 pixels) with three short lines of text whereby the first line is clickable and says "sponsored by: advertisers name." Figure 11.20 shows a Banner Ad for Fidelity Investments placed on Prodigy's home page (**http://antares.prodigy.com**). Marketplace Ads may be as many as 180 characters in which the advertiser's name is included and clickable. These ads appear lower on the page. The page shown in Figure 11.20 has a Marketplace Ad for PC Flowers & Gifts located near the bottom (not shown). These ads are quite a bit cheaper because they are less prominent than a banner. Table 11.3 shows pricing for ads placed on Prodigy Web pages. Note that each ad can be linked to your Web site and is designed to drive traffic your way.

Table 11.2   Costs for Prodigy Direct E-mail

Quantity	Cost per Thousand (CPM)
20,000-149,999	$350 (35 cents/send)
150,000-249,999	$300 (30 cents/send)
250,000+	$250 (25 cents/send)

Figure 11.20 Prodigy's Web site using its Web browser. Notice Fidelity's banner ad.

How to contact TeleRep

There are over 150 interest group pages. You can get a list online or from TeleRep.

Table 11.3 Prices for Advertising on Prodigy's Web Site

Page	Price/month	Ad type	Est. impressions
Home page	$25,000	Banner	2,100,000
Home page	$10,000	Marketplace	2,100,000
Search Tools	$10,000	Banner	650,000
Interest Group home page	$3,000	Banner	150,000
Business & Finance Site	$1,000	Banner	25,000
Internet Group	$1,000	Banner	Varies
Internet Group	$400	Marketplace	Varies
Shopping home page	$250	Marketplace	17,000

"Guerrilla PR"— Announcing Your Web Site with Press Releases

CHAPTER 12 TOPICS

ANATOMY OF A PRESS RELEASE

ESSAY: HOW TO PUBLICIZE YOUR WEB SITE

EXAMPLE OF WEB SITE ANNOUNCEMENT PRESS RELEASES

WHERE TO RELEASE YOUR RELEASE

You don't have to spend lots of money to let the world know about your Web site. This chapter will help you get the word out faster than you can say "high-priced PR firm!" Rather than provide traditional contact methods for various writers and publications, this chapter provides a list of email addresses to send your release to. As you know, there is no guarantee that any publication or writer will give your press release the time of day. The more interesting, compelling and unique it is to them and more importantly *their readers*, the more likely you'll get a mention.

Unfortunately, today it's a lot harder to get into the press just because you have a Web site. In 1994 it was much easier. Take Grant's Florist, widely believed to be the first flower shop on the Web. Grant's received untold amounts of play in the press, which ultimately resulted in extra sales—on and off the Net. Today, nearly every type of company from every type of industry has a Web presence. Being first counted for a lot in 1994, but the odds are that whatever you are doing now has already been done. That's not to say that certain aspects of your Web site aren't newsworthy. Leave some room when designing or re-designing your site to account for the publicity factor.

Perhaps have a brainstorming session to generate ideas for a wacky or playful site feature that may get some press play. Even if your site isn't all that exciting, you may still be mentioned in a few places. Some publications print lists of Web sites they have compiled and share them with their readers. If your Web site has lots of information about a specific niche business or industry, your chances of being mentioned as a resource for their readers is increased. But you must "be in it to win it" and create and distribute your press release.

Anatomy of a Press Release

An engaging press release can garner plenty of off-line promotion for your Web site. Unfortunately, even the best-written press release may not be enough. Certain topics are "hotter" than others, certain products or services just aren't very interesting to many people. However, you don't know what response you'll get unless you try. Keep your release short since editors don't like to sift through a lot of material, and be sure to followup. Following up can make the difference between getting noticed and being lost in the shuffle. Here's what your release should look like:

- *Grabber headline.* Crucial to getting people's attention. Basically, you should condense your entire press release into a dozen or fewer words. Sell the sizzle, not the steak.

- *Opening paragraph.* Second in importance to the grabber headline. Explain why people should care about your site, get them to read more.

- *Press release body.* Typically contains a quote or two from a company representative (often the CEO or President) and/or a third party testimonial in addition to the "steak."

- *Closing paragraph(s).* Should contain general information about your firm and additional contact information such as URL, contact person, phone number, email address, etc. Some press releases also include a trademark disclaimer.

I asked one of the top high-technology PR firms in the country—Parker, Nichols & Company, Inc.—to share some tips for creating your press release and what to do with it after you create it.

How To Publicize Your World Wide Web Site
by Steven H. Parker
Parker, Nichols & Company, Inc.

Having a site on the World Wide Web won't guarantee that potential customers will click a path to your home page. First they need to know that you're out there—and why they should visit your site. Registering with the major search engines, like Open Text, LinkStar, Yahoo!, Infoseek, Lycos and AltaVista will make it much easier for people who are actively seeking you to find you on the Web. But that's not enough. You must market and promote your site both on-line and off-line, through traditional public relations methods, so more people will seek you out. How? The first and most basic step is to write a press release announcing your site.

Here are a few tips that should help you develop a more effective press release to announce your Web presence:

1. WHAT'S THE NEWS? Think about what, if anything, is most "newsworthy" about your site. What value does this information you're offering have, and who is your target audience? Your release must explicitly explain the benefits of visiting "yoursite.com" to just those people whom you're trying to attract.

2. WRITE A STRONG LEAD. Every press release has a "lead," or first paragraph. You must try to capture the essence of your site in that lead paragraph. How an editor reacts to that one paragraph largely determines whether he or she will read on and become interested enough in your news to consider using it.

3. DON'T EXAGGERATE! Avoid overhyping your Web site—it usually backfires. Don't make claims that you cannot substantiate to an editor. If your Web site offers some technical information that auto mechanics might find useful, don't claim that by visiting your site, they can throw away all of their parts manuals! For content to be king, it must be real.

4. DESCRIBE A VIEWPOINT. In writing your release, make sure the reader can understand for whom you've developed your site—exactly who is the target audience. That way, the editor can decide quickly if his or her publication reaches that audience and therefore if covering your site would be appropriate.

5. LIST YOUR URL ADDRESS prominently in the release.

6. GIVE SITE SAMPLES. If possible, include some listings and descriptions of the kind of information available at your site. This can be included as part of the press release, if it's short, or added as a second document for background.

6. MAKE A LIST. Make a list of those members of the press whom you wish to contact. Don't forget to include local and regional media, business publications and those trade journals serving your industry. Keep records of your contacts with them in a database, such as a contact manager like Act! or GoldMine.

7. DISTRIBUTE YOUR NEWS. Once you're satisfied with your release, proactively send it to those editors on your list. Use both "snail" mail (postal) and email for those editors whose email addresses you know. Do NOT send unsolicited faxes. Keep your cover message on the release for emails very brief—no more than four or five lines.

8. GET ON THE PHONE. After enough time has elapsed that you're sure the editors have received your release, give them a call. Do NOT call and ask, "Did you get my release? Are you going to publish it?" Instead, explain the gist of the release over the phone, assuming they don't remember it, and try to sell your ideas verbally. If you're successful, then they will find it in their pile of mail or ask for another one.

9. MAKE IT EASY TO REACH YOU. Don't forget to list contact information prominently somewhere in the release. If an editor shows interest, chances are at least 50/50 he or she will want to contact you. Make it easy for them: list your phone, fax, email addresses, voice mail, even home phone number if appropriate.

10. FOLLOW UP. If editors express mild interest, but put you off, or if they don't return your phone call, then be sure and try again. (Remember, they have real deadlines, and sometimes can't talk no matter how good your story is!) Be persistent without being a pest. If an editor fails to return three calls or messages, they're usually not interested and you should move on.

Steven H. Parker is Chairman and Co-Founder of Parker, Nichols & Company, Inc., Concord, Massachusetts, an on-line marketing and public relations firm that specializes in serving the Internet industry and other clients with on-line marketing and PR requirements. He can be reached via email at sparker@parker-nichols.com.

Examples of Web Site Announcement Press Releases

Here are some examples (taken verbatim) of press releases:

Kellogg Company
"It's Fun To Put Snap!® Crackle!® Pop!® Into Your Web Page; Kellog's® Famous Rice Krispies® Trio Hosts Home Page On The World Wide Web"

BATTLE CREEK, Michigan., Oct. 25. PRNewswire.—In a move that could set a new trend for the intensely competitive breakfast foods market, Kellogg Company has announced the launch of its first home page—and a first for the cereal category—on the Internet's World Wide Web. The site was developed by Magnet Interactive Communications, a leading interactive media development agency and key Kellogg interactive technology partner. Site content was provided by Leo Burnett and J. Walter Thompson, Kellogg's global advertising agencies. The Kellogg site will be hosted by the company's popular Rice Krispies® cereal brand spokescharacters, Snap!® Crackle!® Pop!®.

"We always look for new opportunities to communicate with our customers about Kellogg products and the importance of a good breakfast," said Dave Vroom, assistant to the Chairman, Worldwide Marketing, Kellogg Company. "By creating a colorful and fun home page on the World Wide Web, we'll be offering our consumers a way of interacting with the company in an exciting new format. Additionally, the Web site will allow us to easily integrate new interactive venues with our traditional advertising and packaging promotions."

Users will log onto the site at **http://www.kelloggs.com** and begin their adventure at the Kellogg Clubhouse™. From the foyer, Snap! Crackle! and Pop! direct users to the rec room, lounge and kitchen where each character hosts a different room. Bold colors and graphics invite the users to visit the rec room for downloadable commercials and audio clips, and a Snap! Crackle! and Pop! screen saver; the lounge for games, coloring activities and images of spokescharacter promotional items from the past 30 years; and the kitchen for recipes, nutritional information and a look at Kellogg's® cereal boxes from around the world. Visitors to the Kellogg Clubhouse™ can also access updated information on new products.

Kellogg and Magnet are committed to creating an entire Kellogg community on the World Wide Web. In the near future, adults can attend Kellogg's

Nutrition University™ and learn about what makes a better breakfast. Recipes and nutritional information will also be available at Nutrition University™. Children will enjoy their favorite Kellogg's cereal brands including Tony the Tiger® and Toucan Sam®, in the Clubhouse. Additionally, Web site visitors from the investment community will find information in a special section on the Keogh corporation, including investor updates and stock value/returns. The entire site will continually evolve and be refreshed seasonally with new themes.

"Magnet is excited to facilitate Kellogg's foray into electronic commerce," said Basel Dalloul, chairman and CEO, Magnet Interactive Group. "We share their commitment to create an informative and fun Web site that will promote one-on-one relationships between Kellogg and their consumers."

Kellogg Company, the world's leading breakfast cereal manufacturer, is headquartered in Battle Creek, MI.

Magnet Interactive Communications is a full service interactive marketing, entertainment and online communications agency. A subsidiary of Magnet Interactive Group, Inc., Magnet Interactive Communications is located in Washington, DC. **http://www.magnet.com**

CONTACT: Karen Macleod of Kellogg USA, (616) 961-3989 or Meredith Clements of Magnet Interactive (202) 625-1111 or email: meredith@magnet.com.

PageNet

"PageNet Launches World Wide Web Sites, World's Largest Paging Company Offers Paging From Web Site; Links Hard-Wired Internet To Wireless Paging World"

DALLAS, Sept. 21. PRNewswire.—PageNet, the world's largest and fastest-growing wireless messaging company, launched two Internet World Wide Web sites today with alphanumeric paging capability. Anyone with Web access now can send alphanumeric pages to PageNet's nationwide customers.

One Web site is an on-line magazine-style source of information about digital paging and wireless technology called "Wireless Source;" the other is PageNet's corporate site, devoted to the practical aspects of selecting and using wireless digital paging services as well as company information.

The "Wireless Source" site, at **http://www.wireless-source.com**, contains information on rapidly advancing paging technologies, downloadable animations, a glossary of wireless technology terms, a tongue-in-cheek wireless "Top 10 List," a rundown of the newest and coolest gadgets available today and in the future, and other material.

PageNet's Corporate Web site, at **http://www.pagenet.com**, includes a utility to page PageNet nationwide customers. It also features a variety of downloadable animated art and information about PageNet, its service offerings and its nationwide digital wireless network; advice on how to choose a pager; and a slot for e-mail inquiries on obtaining local paging service throughout the United States.

The PageNet Web site employs an image of an alphanumeric pager as the navigation device. Clicking on the buttons of the pager triggers different responses, and on occasion, the pager will deliver a "message" to the site visitor.

Douglas R. Ritter, PageNet's vice president for new business development, said, "The World Wide Web is a great forum for educating the public about PageNet and about wireless communications generally. Our Web site also provides added value for our nationwide alphanumeric customers, who will be able to receive messages from anyone with Internet access. We are currently exploring additional ways to use the Internet to serve our customers and the public."

Ritter said that PageNet is employing two Web sites in order to separate PageNet specific information from the industry wide scope of the "Wireless Source" site.

Dallas-based Paging Network, Inc. (Nasdaq-NNM: PAGE), or PageNet, is the world's largest and fastest-growing wireless messaging company, and is recognized as a leader in the broader wireless communications industry. Founded in 1981, the company provides local, regional and nationwide digital transmission network services to more than 6 million subscribers across the United States.

Inquiries to PageNet may also be sent via e-mail to julie_sullivan@pagenet.com.

CONTACT: Scott Baradell, (800) 943-0497, or Julie Sullivan, (214) 985-6258, both of PageNet.

Excerpts of Articles Written from Press Releases

The following are excerpts from articles that were written from press releases. It will give you an idea of how information from a press release is reworked into an article.

Alamo Rent A Car
Source: Written by Dale K. DuPont, Business Writer for the *Miami Herald*.

Alamo Offers Online Route
Service provides immediate bookings

Travelers on the information superhighway can now rent a car directly from Alamo. The Fort Lauderdale company is the first auto rental firm to provide real-time, online reservations.

Alamo's new system hooks directly into its mainframe reservation system, and customers get confirmation numbers as soon as the booking is made. Internet users can book travel now, but may wait 24 hours for a confirmation response through email.

Freeways also provides a variety of other services like kids games and weather reports as well as a forum for travelers to exchange tips on restaurants and scenic drives.

And for consumers squeamish about giving a credit card, Alamo says you don't need one for the booking.

Southwest Airlines
Source: John Maines, Staff Writer for the *Sun-Sentinel* (Ft. Lauderdale)

You Can Fly Through Cyberspace
Southwest to sell tickets on Internet

When Southwest Airlines begins service in South Florida early next year (1996), travelers should be able to make flight and hotel reservations over their computer throughout the Internet.

"For all intents and purposes, it will be a free service," said Beth Harbin, spokeswoman for the Dallas-based airline. "People will be able to book reservations from their home, their office, anywhere."

Anyone can already look at Southwest's "home page" on the Internet's World Wide Web. Although reservation service won't be possible until the end of the year, fares and flight times are easily viewed by clicking on graphics-oriented instructions.

The Internet address is **http://www.iflyswa.com**

Southwest's home page also includes mild entertainment, including images of the cockpit of a Boeing 737-200, some of the company's most off-beat advertisements over the years, and photographs of its uniquely painted aircraft, including three "Shamus," the killer whales.

Where to Release Your Release

Now that you've written your press release announcing your Web site or some additional features of your site, it's time to get it out there! The following resources and lists will help your site get the exposure it deserves.

Via the Internet

gina—global internet news agency
http://www.gina.com
Contact: Michael Shuler (mshuler@gina.com)
(310) 577-9346 or (800) 414-gina (4462)

This is a great low-cost way for you to do guerrilla PR. In addition to a press release discussing your Web site, gina accepts press releases of all kinds. For just $250, the "gina News Distribution Service" will distribute your press release to over 2,000 high technology reporters via email, and your release will stay on gina's site for three months (see Figure 12.1). Simply email your release in ASCII text and indicate when you would like the release to go out. Provide your contact/billing information, and they will invoice you (net 15 day cycle). No prepayment is required as of this writing.

In addition to this service, gina provides a number of others including the "gina Experts and Speakers Bureau" via which, if you are a consultant or expert in your field, you can have your biographical information sent to thousands of reporters and trade show representatives. Your photo and bio will be available on gina's site for one year. The price for this service is $250 a year.

There are third-party companies that will post your Web site description and URL to many (if not all) Internet directories listed in Chapter 5 and some of these companies also will submit a press release to various publications. The PostMaster is one such company. See Chapter 14, "Third-Party Web Site Promotion Services" for more.

Via email and the Web

I've listed email addresses and a few Web addresses for various publications and media for you to submit your press release and site update information to. Since these addresses are subject to change, and people move from one position to another, you should first ask if it's appropriate to submit a press release to the address before actually sending it. Your email software should have an "address book" feature that will enable you to send one message to multiple email addresses. This cuts down on the time required to send out your mes-

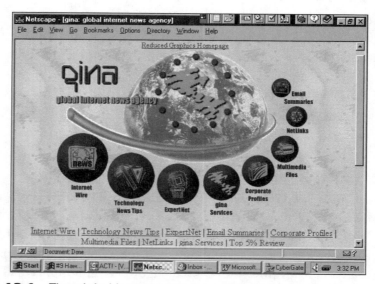

Figure 12.1 The global internet news agency (gina), a great way to get the word out cheaply.

sage. Be sure to use the BCC (Blind Carbon Copy) feature so each recipient does not see who else you're sending the message to. Some people disregard automated or mass mailings. In some cases, it may be better to send your message individually. The last thing many publications want to do is publish the same thing as everyone else.

PRINT PUBLICATIONS

"off-line"

Advertising Age
Submission Address: 75301.70@compuserve.com
Let Jeff Zbar, a contributing writer to *Ad Age* and other publications, know about your site.

BoardWatch Magazine
http://www.boardwatch.com
Submission Address: dave.hakala@boardwatch.com
Monthly magazine available at over 12,000 newsstands; covers the Internet, online services, and the communications industry.

Bradenton Herald (Florida)
Submission Address: savage@gate.net
Sean Savage, business reporter and frequent Internet writer.

Cyberspace Today
http://www.cybertoday.com/cybertoday/
Submission Address: vern@cybertoday.com
A monthly free newspaper based in California; covers news and happenings in the online arena.

Dave Peyton, Internet and Technology Writer
Submission Address: 74777.462@compuserve.com

InfoBahn
"The Magazine of Internet Culture"
Submission Address: publicity@postmodern.com

Internet Underground
http://www.nuke.com/underground.html
Submission Address: IU@mcs.net
"Covering the cool side of the Internet."

Internet Week
http://www.phillips.com/iw/
Submission Address: mcaesar@phillips.com
Internet Week is an eight-page newsletter concentrating on business issues of the Internet.

Internet World Magazine
Submission Address: ak@iw.com
Andrew Kantor

Ft. Lauderdale Sun-Sentinel
Submission Address: lorek@sunsent.com
Laura Lorek, technology reporter

Miami Herald's New Web Sites List
Submission Address: dtkeats@ibm.net
Dan Keating's list of new Web sites and CyberGuide column.

Net Traveler, The Internet Directory
http://www.primenet.com/~ntravel/
Submission Address: ntravel@biznetusa.com
Print and Online publication focusing around the Boise, Idaho area.

Newsweek's CyberScope
Submission Address: cscope@newsweek.com
Weekly column about cyberspace and interesting Internet sites.

Orlando Sentinel
Submission Address: barrycoop@aol.com or 74777.1550@compuserve.com
Barry Cooper, computer writer for the *Orlando* (Florida) *Sentinel*

PC Guide's NetSurfing Guide
Submission Address: kenny@gil.net
Monthly NetSurfing feature in *PC Guide,* a south Florida-based computer magazine.

Roadside Attractions
Submission Address: roadside@cris.com
Periodic column by Dave Farrell in the *Ft. Lauderdale Sun-Sentinel* newspaper.

the net
"The High-Intensity Internet Magazine"
http://www.thenet-usa.com

Submission Address: blue@thenet-usa.com (for The Blue Pages Internet Directory)
Covers general Internet topics with a lot of emphasis on the Web.

Web500

http://www.web500.com
Submission Address: info@web500.com
The *Web500* is a new publication dedicated to the World Wide Web. In addition to Web-related articles, top Web sites are ranked.

WebTrack's InterAd Monthly Newsletter

Submission Address: interad@webtrack.com
"Actionable Intelligence For Net Marketers"
Make the subject line of your message: "new site"

Web Week

http://pubs.iworld.com/ww-online/index.html
Editorial Calendar Page: http://pubs.iworld.com/ww-online/calendar.html

XSO's Lost In CyberSpace

Weekly column by Wendy Aron which helps new users navigate the Net. *XSO* (South Florida's News, Arts and Entertainment Weekly) is a sister publication to the *Ft. Lauderdale Sun-Sentinel.*
Submission Address: aron@xso.com

ELECTRONIC/ONLINE PUBLICATIONS

CLiCK! Interactive Magazine

http://click.com.au
Submission Address: editor@click.com.au
Australian-based online publication focusing on interactive multimedia production, design, and writing.

CyberWire Dispatch

http://cyberwerks.com:70/1/cyberwire
Submission Address: brock@well.com
Written by Brock N. Meeks. A free Internet service started in January of 1994 that concentrates on issues relevant to cyberspace.

Digital Highway Report

http://www.dhrpt.com
Submission Address: dhrpt@japanmedia.com

"The first WWW-based Japanese language newsletter devoted to reporting on computer and telecommunications industries in the United States as well as digital culture."

GNN's Web Review
http://www.gnn.com/wr/
Submission Address: wr-info@ora.com

infoHIGHWAY
http://www.infohighway.co.uk/infohighway/
Submission Address: http://www.infohighway.co.uk/infohighway/getstory.html
UK-based publication. "The new way to get IT information from the Internet."

Internet Marketing Digest
http://www.informatiebank.nl/digest/indexgb.htm
Biweekly electronic magazine based in the Netherlands, with articles on marketing and communication via Internet.

WEBster—The Cyberspace Surfer
http://www.tgc.com
Submission Address: sos@webster.tgc.com (automated general info via email)
Provides text-on-demand news and information about the Web. It was a runner up for Best Online Publication at the 1994 Computer Press Association Awards.
Submission Address: dianna@webster.tgc.com

Weird Online World
http://www.dorsai.org/~tristan/MAG/mag.html
Submission Address: tristan@dorsai.org

Where It's @
http://www.mistral.co.uk/wia/
Submission Address: whereits@mistral.co.uk
"UK's favourite publication on and about the WWW."

Radio Shows

clnet Radio
http://www.cnet.com
Submission Address: bcooley@cnet.com
Hosted by radio veteran Brian Cooley, clnet radio is a few-minutes-long Internet

news feature available via Real Audio on clnet's Web site. A new show is put online every weekday, Monday through Friday.

Craig Crossman's Computer America
Submission Address: 1 Herald Plaza, Miami, FL, 33132.

The Internet Show
http://www.internet-broadcasting.com
Submission Address: cfoster@internet-broadcasting.com
Hosted by Carl Foster, this nationally syndicated show airs every Sunday at 11 am. Carl's always looking for new, interesting Web sites to share with his listeners. Past shows are available on the Web site via Real Audio.

net.radio
Submission Address: scott@netradio.net

"Networks" Radio
Submission Address: notlih@top.monad.net

13

Offline Web Site Promotion

CHAPTER 13 TOPICS

PROMOTING BEYOND THE INTERNET

PLACES AND THINGS TO PLACE YOUR URL

PRINT ADVERTISING OPPORTUNITIES TO FURTHER YOUR
PROMOTION EFFORTS

One of the key things you can do to promote your Internet presence is to put your Web address on *everything*. Obvious things like placing your URL on your business card help, but there are a lot of creative things you can do as well. If you've read Chapter 12, you have a good start with public relations. I hope that at least a few of the ideas I present in this chapter will get your wheels turning in the direction of *even more* creative and effective ways to let the world know you, indeed, have a Web site and, more importantly, how browsers can get to it.

A number of World Wide Web yellow page directories have come out in print and CD-ROM. Nearly all of them accept free submissions and will include your site at no charge. A good example is New Rider's *WWW Yellow Pages*. Many offer paid advertising opportunities to make your listing more prominent.

The benefits to cross-promoting your Web site with your traditional media and print materials include

- Your Web site can answer a lot of questions and provide more information than you can fit on paper.

- Your site can be kept more up to date.

- If you allow them, people can request more information or order right there on your site via an online form.

- You leverage your existing resources to promote your site at essentially no additional cost. A good example of this is *Disaster Recovery Journal*, a quarterly magazine I receive. Right there on the lower right-hand side cover reads "Internet Address www.drj.com." It didn't cost them anything extra to promote their site there!

Creative Ways to Promote Your Site

Now that you've seen the benefits, here are some specific ideas for promoting your site. See Table 13.1 for some examples.

Bank Checks—In addition to your other contact information, put your email and URL on your checks as well.

Billboards—Do it only if your URL is simple.

Table 13.1 Places to Put Your Internet Address

Business Cards	Letterhead
Stationery	Brochures
Catalogs	Fax Cover Sheets
Giveaway Items	Advertisements
Press Releases	Newsletters
Forehead (tatoo!)	Side of Car/Building

Bookmarks (physical ones)—These are inexpensive to print and useful to people you give them to. Open Text Corporation printed on both sides, as shown in Figure 13.1. The company gave bookmarks to people who stopped by their booth at a DCI Web World conference and exposition I went to in Toronto, Canada. You can even make your own bookmarks with a laser printer if you are on a budget.

Building Signage—Plaster your URL on your building. Place it on the entrance, on the side, even the roof (for those airplanes and helicopters that fly overhead)! SportsLine USA had to put up a fight to get **http://www.sportsline.com** on the entrance to its offices, but they persevered as you can see in Figure 13.2.

Bumper Stickers—"Take a ride on the Information SuperHighway, http://www.blahblah.com."

Figure 13.1   Open Text Corporation's URL on a bookmark.

Figure 13.2 *SportsLine USA's URL as part of its building signage.*

Business Cards—For a while, it was the cool thing to do; today it's the minimum you should do. Try to cram your URL on your card. If there's no room, print it on the back of the card.

Buttons—A good trade show item as people are likely to wear them (and they are rather inexpensive). Figure 13.3 shows a good example of what the Project Management Institute did to promote its Web site.

Calendars—I've seen a lot of customized company calendars. Why not put a dozen screen shots of your site with URL into a calendar. If you have any special events planned on your site throughout the year, mention those prominently on the corresponding days.

Catalogs—The first catalog that I saw a Web address on was Hello Direct, the company that sells telephone products. They promoted their Web site URL and CompuServe address. Put a blurb in your catalog that directs people to your site to get a "special gift if you order online" or something to give them a reason to visit.

Figure 13.3 *The Project Management Institute put its URL on a button.*

Chocolate Bars—Yum! Doing this is certainly a novel idea that gets people's attention. The only problem is they eat the promotion! Who thought your Web address could be so tasty? Wimsey Information Services, an Internet provider located in British Columbia, Canada had hundreds of regular, white and dark chocolate bars made with its URL (**http://www.wimsey.com**) on it by Rocky Mountain Chocolate Factory of Vancouver and distributed them to people who visited the Wimsey booth at a trade show I attended.

Envelopes—LinkStar places its URL on standard envelopes as you can see in Figure 13.4.

Figure 13.4 *LinkStar promotes its search engine address on its envelopes.*

Figure 13.5   DCI placed its URL on a greeting card I received.

Fax Cover Sheets—How many faxes do you send out a month? Why not promote your site with your URL prominently displayed on every fax you send?

Forehead—Just joking. Tatooing your URL on your body is probably a bit extreme.

Greeting Cards—I received a card wishing me a good holiday season from Digital Consulting, Inc. (DCI), which placed its contact information on the back of the card, including its Web address, as shown in Figure 13.5.

Key Chains—You can say something witty like, "Unlock our door with http://www.blahblah.com/."

Letter Openers—Of all the giveaways I've received, these are probably the things I keep the longest and use the most. Perhaps the appropriate wording on a letter opener would be, "Open your browser to http://www.blahblah.com."

Magnets—Well, maybe just give these out to people whom you don't like! I'm not sure how good an idea these would be. Just think of all the complaints about data on the recipients' diskettes being corrupted because they set your magnet down near their computer before putting it on their refrigerator! You may want to create magnetic signs that can be placed on the side of your organization's vehicles. Lots of people see your vehicle in a day's worth of driving. Why not take advantage of it?

Pens—These can be very inexpensive and can be obtained at any specialty advertising business (as can many other things I mention in this chapter). Hopefully, your URL isn't too long, otherwise it may not fit on a pen!

Post-It Notes—Wouldn't it be nice to have people with small pieces of paper with your URL on them stuck all over their computer screens? You can order custom printed paper pads with that glue on the back that kind of sticks to things from most printers.

Rulers—Print something like "Come see how our Web site measures up, http://www.blahblah.com."

Software—People love free software. For just $89.95 plus $2.50 S&H (one-time fee) you can purchase Personal Assistant software from Piper Software (**http://www.pipersoft.com**) that gives you unlimited free distribution of the software. It can contain your company name and URL (up to 70 characters total), and this information is displayed on the entrance screen. Another good idea is to create a screen saver with your URL on it. Make it available for free download from your Web site as well as put it on a diskette and distribute it.

Sunglasses—You can get some plastic "el cheapo" ones for about a buck. "Our Web site is so hot, you gotta wear shades."

T-Shirts—Wear your Web site! Or better yet, have other people wear it. This is another good premium incentive item to give out at trade shows, since people are likely to put them on right there. I found a place on the Net that specializes in putting your site on a shirt (see Figure 13.6), Mackey Special Tees (**http://www.pe.net/~spcltees**).

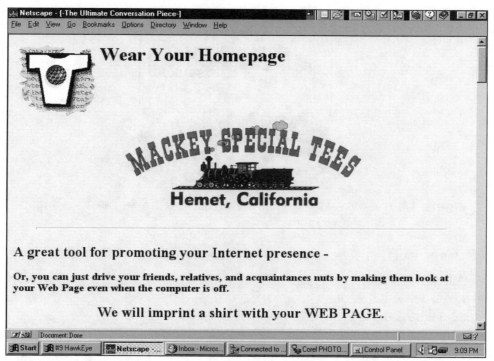

Figure 13.6 Put your site on a shirt.

Watches—These are more costly than many other specialty advertising options (minimum of $5/piece depending upon quantity). It is a gift that is likely to be used, however. "Isn't it *time* you visit http://www.blahblah.com?"

Advertising Opportunities

More and more organizations are purchasing print advertising specifically to promote and market their Web site. Organizations who regularly purchase advertising are adding their URL to the ad as well (see Figure 13.7), which is practically a zero-cost way to promote a site (because they're paying for the ad anyway). In this section, I just wanted to introduce you to some of your options and what the costs are likely to be. There's no shortage of publications and media to purchase advertising from. Choosing the right resources at the right price is the key. Do your research first, compare your options, and then

Figure 13.7 An ad placed in the FT. LAUDERDALE SUN-SENTINEL for a radio station's site.

take action.

Aldea's NetPages
http://www.aldea.com
ads@aldea.com
(619) 929-1100
Probably the oldest Internet white and yellow page directory with a circulation of over 100,000. A basic listing is just $9 for two lines (company name and electronic address). Display advertising starts at $240 for a black-and-white quarter page up to $1,600 for a full-page color ad. Aldea will design your ad at no additional charge. Rates are for 6 months. Your first basic listing is free; simply fill out the form on their Web site at **http://www.aldea.com/cgi-bin/add2netpages**. In addition to the print version, they have an Adobe Acrobat and also a Web version. Your listing and advertising is placed in all versions.

The Globe and Mail's Web Site Guide
(416) 585-5413
"Canada's National Newspaper" periodically includes its Web Site Guide special section. Contact them for rates.

MultiMedia Source Book
http://www.mmsource.com/multimedia/
(212) 293-3900
Contains listings of manufacturers, services, resources, and more for the multimedia industry. Text and graphical listings are available. Rates are quite

Figure 13.8 Online Access' Web flash page.

reasonable; contact them for the latest rate sheet.

Online Access' Webflash
(800) MODEM-01

Features a screen shot of your site, its URL, and up to a four-line description for $695 (one-time insertion rate). Take a look at Figure 13.8 for the page.

Wall Street Journal's Internet Directory
http://www.wsj.com

(800) 648-4778 or fax (212) 597-5956

With a global audience of over 4.5 million people, this can really help launch your site. You can advertise in the *Internet Directory* for $2,647.05 and up, depending upon the size. The rate I just stated was for a 2 9/32×21/2 inch ad. The *Internet Directory* is a monthly feature and you get a free listing with URL and email address in the online version called *adfinder.wsj* located at **http://adfinder.wsj.com.** For $400 more, you can get a 50-word description added to your one-line entry in the adfinder.wsj directory. Obviously discounts apply if you purchase multiple insertions.

Concluding Remarks

WARNING: Printers and typesetters are notorious for messing up Internet addresses!

No matter where you put your Internet address, be sure to get a proof copy of what the printer or vendor is going to produce *before* you go to production. If there are errors, correct them, and then ask for a proof yet another time! Trust me, if there was an error and you think it's corrected, there's still a chance that there will be an error with the correction. I've seen this happen all too many times. Remember, your printer may not know what a proper Internet address

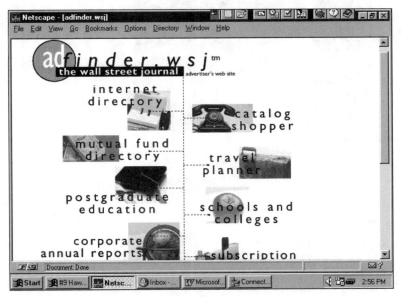

Figure 13.9   The Wall Street Journal's online version (adfinder.wsj) of its Internet directory.

Figure 13.10 An ad I saw in BARTER AGE MAGAZINE. Notice the typo (;) in the URL.

looks like. People make mistakes. I put my email address on my publishing company's checks, and they put in spaces where there aren't any and left out the "dot" in legion.com. Figure 13.10 is just one of many examples of the typo's that occur when promoting Web sites in print.

Third Party Web Site Promotion Services

CHAPTER 14 TOPICS

DO YOU REALLY WANT TO DO IT YOURSELF?

MULTIPLE SITE REGISTRATION SERVICES

COMPANIES YOU CAN HIRE TO PROMOTE YOUR SITE

If all this talk about do-it-yourself Web site promotion has overwhelmed you, don't fret. There are third-party vendors and automated posting systems that can do some things, but not everything, for you. This chapter starts with the automated, multiple-site registration services (such as Submit-It! and The PostMaster). The second half lists some of the companies that will promote your Web site for a fee.

As you've seen in this book, there are many different vehicles you can use to get the word out about your Web site's existence. Most third-party Web promotion services will register you with the various Internet directories and search engines (Chapter 5) and post some announcements to key Usenet newsgroups and Internet mailing lists (Chapter 10). A few companies will also help you with online media buying (Chapter 6). Unfortunately, there aren't many companies that can do a *competent* job of all these things *plus* promotion in traditional media.

So far, traditional PR firms that get involved with the online medium are using their existing employees and throwing them into the fire, so to speak, to learn about Internet/online promotion. I think they need to hire someone who's already familiar with the online aspect, someone who has been doing it for *years* and not *months*. Those firms that recruit specialized talent will have the edge. Eventually, traditional firms will also learn the ropes of online promotion enough to be effective. But for now, they are behind the eight ball. I guess what I'm driving at is that I don't recommend that you use your traditional PR firm to do nontraditional PR. The companies listed in this chapter focus on Internet promotion and know the tricks to making people aware of your site without ticking them off in the process.

You may now be asking, doesn't my Internet Presence Provider (IPP) promote my site after they create it? The answer is that some do, some say they do but don't do a very good job of it, and some don't. There are a few things that I recommend you ask your provider about what they do to promote you:

1. Where *exactly* do you announce my site?

   I've found that just one in ten IPPs will readily have a list of the sites and actual places where they announce you. That's right, only ten percent! And I mean a complete typed list, not a couple of paragraphs saying they'll post you all over creation. Don't let them pull the wool over your eyes. Promotion is important. Ask for exactly what they are going to do, *in writing!*

2. How long will the process take?

   Try to pin them down as to when promotion will start and when it will finish. Once the campaign is completed, it should still take about one month before the more backlogged Web sites and cool sites lists integrate your listing into their sites, directories and databases.

3. What happens if my site isn't listed with the places where you said you would list it?

   Some services will resubmit your site at no additional charge, while others will not. Either way, you really need to visit the sites that your provider says they post to. A few provide you with a confirmation printout of where you've been submitted to or actually listed. Perform some searches to see if you have been added. If not, you'll either need to list your site yourself, or ask that your provider try again. There are some Internet sites that are selective as to who they will add. Yahoo!, for example, is under no obligation whatsoever to list your Web site. Don't expect your provider to work miracles for you. Sometimes you'll need to follow up yourself.

4. Do you promote my site yourself, or do you hire a third party to do it?

   Some IPPs hire an outside firm to perform the promotion of the Web sites they create, while others do it in-house. The good thing about them doing it internally is that you aren't paying extra (a markup) for the service. The downside is that they may not be as good and dedicated to it as a firm that does nothing but promotion.

5. Do you use any multiple-site submission services like The PostMaster?

   There's nothing wrong with your IPP using these shortcut methods, but realize that these services only do so much. There's still a need for manually submitting to some places as well as posting to newsgroups and the like. Also, as great as Submit-It! is, it only posts to a fraction of the sites that take submissions and you're limited to a briefer announcement (25 words or less) than some sites allow. This restricts the number of keywords that you may use to be found by.

The bottom line is that an IPP simply isn't going to admit that it's not very good at promoting Web sites. Most IPPs concentrate on creating Web sites and placing them on a server. Many IPPs say they'll get your site listed "everywhere," but few fully deliver. Get it in writing or, if you're so inclined, do it yourself (after all, you did buy this book didn't you?). Some providers build-in the price of promotion with their creation price while some providers sell promotion separately. Find out how and how much. A lot of the questions I listed above apply to the promotion services companies listed later. Don't be afraid to ask them.

Multiple-Site Registration Services

As you've seen in Chapter 5, posting to Internet directories and search engines can be a lot of work. It's a very time-consuming process. If you've ever seen those Miller Lite beer commercials that start out saying "Wouldn't it be great if...," you're probably thinking "Wouldn't it be great if I could fill out one form, click a few buttons and *voilà*, my Web site would be listed and announced all over the place." Well, with a multiple-site registration service, you can! I must caution you, however, that none of them will do everything for you, they won't get you everywhere, and sometimes there are errors and complications that cause some listings to fail (in which you'll have to resubmit your announcement manually with whatever sites your automated posting failed). Even Internet Presence Providers use these services to save time in promoting the sites they create for their clients.

These services aren't magic. The information you type into their forms is sent directly to each individual site that the service posts to. For some sites, the information is directly transferred, while for others, the information is placed into an email message and submitted. It just depends on how the site on the other end accepts submissions.

Submit-It!
http://www.submit-it.com
At the end of 1994, Scott Banister, a student studying computer science at the University of Illinois (where Mosaic was born) decided to create a tool that made it easier to register a new Web site with some popular Internet directories and search engines. The first version of what's become known as Submit-It! went online in February of 1995 (see Figure 14.1). It was really just a collection of a half dozen or so directories. As time went on, Scott added more sites and rewrote the programming to allow for a more automated process of submitting announcements and Web site descriptions.

Submit-It! quickly became known as *the* shortcut to posting your Web site announcement. No longer did Internet users seeking more hits to their sites need to go from site to site wearing out their keyboards entering the same information over and over again. And perhaps the best thing about Submit-It! aside from saving hours of work is that it's free! When I last checked, Submit-It! was receiving an average of 5,000 visitors and 1,500 submissions each *day*. You can find hyperlinks to Submit-It! on many Web sites, including WebCrawler and Yahoo!.

Submit-It! posts to over 15 different sites including Yahoo!, LinkStar, Open Text, Starting Point, Infoseek, WebCrawler, What's New Too!, Lycos, EINET Galaxy, GNN's Whole Internet Catalog, Apollo, Harvest, New Rider's WWW Yellow Pages, Nerd World Media, and Digital's Alta Vista.

The PostMaster
http://www.netcreations.com/postmaster/
The PostMaster was created by Ryan Scott of NetCreations, an Internet Presence Provider and programming company based in Brooklyn, New York. NetCreations was started by Ryan and Rosalind Resnick, author of *The Internet Business Guide* (SAMS Publishing). It's not as widely known as Submit-It! but

Figure 14.1 Submit-It! was the Internet's first automated multiple-site submission service.

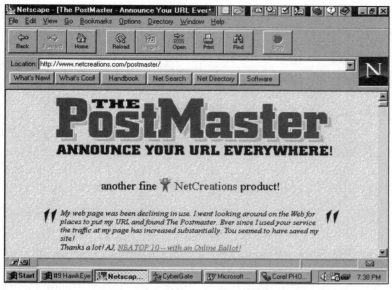

Figure 14.2   NetCreation's PostMaster offers a free and a fee-based automated promotion service.

is rapidly gaining. The PostMaster has two versions, a free version that submits to more sites than Submit-It! and a fee-based version (see Figure 14.2).

The fee-based version of the PostMaster is essentially Submit It! on steroids. It submits your URL and associated site information to over 100 popular directories, search engines, and cool sites pages. In addition, it sends your Web site announcement to several hundred key editors and journalists of print, radio, and TV media via email. To use the expanded version (called the Registered List), you need to purchase a "key" from NetCreations. You can purchase a key online via their Web-based form or you may call NetCreations by telephone. A single key is $500. If you have multiple Web sites to promote or plan on announcing your site several times in the future, you can purchase four keys for $1,000 ($250 each). NetCreations is constantly adding sites to, and refining the Registered List version. I highly recommend this service, as it can save you a lot of time and even gets your announcement out to the media. You can reach Ryan Scott at **rscott@netcreations.com** and can also reach him by phone at (718) 522-1531.

SME's WebPost
http://www.sme.com/webpost/
A newcomer to the automated posting business, WebPost is free and submits to over 25 popular sites. An enhanced version of the service called WebPost

Pro was free at the time of this writing, but SME (Sales & Marketing Exchange) stated that there will be a one-time fee to use it.

Tips for Posting to the Multiple Submission Services

• The forms used to submit your Web site are rather long. Some Web browsers may choke on them (Netscape doesn't). The more RAM your machine has (8+ MB) the less chance there will be a problem.

• Type your site URL, title, and description into an ASCII text file, and cut and paste it into the appropriate place within the form. This protects you from typo's (assuming everything was spell checked and verified originally) and from errors (if the submission returns an error, you'll just try again later and cut and paste rather than retype everything again.)

• Proofread your submission (especially for The PostMaster's Registered List). Once your submission goes out, they cannot undo it. The accuracy of each listing is your responsibility.

• Be sure to have all the information you need for the form before starting. You may want to print out the form and fill that in by hand first. Some require that you know which subject categories you want to be listed under. In these cases, you will need to visit the particular site (Yahoo! and the World Wide Yellow Pages are good examples), and see what categories apply to you.

Purveyors of Promotion

If you don't like doing dishes, hire a maid to do 'em! By the same token, if you would like to avoid the tediousness of some aspects of promotion, there are firms who'll gladly do it for you—for a fee. By listing these companies, I am not endorsing them in any way. You'll have to evaluate and compare them yourself. I simply want to present some additional resources that may be able to help you get additional traffic. The companies are listed in alphabetical order. Please note that as of this writing, there are surprisingly few companies that concentrate on Web site promotion. This list is most of what I could find online! Even as new ones pop up, these are the "old timers" who are likely to have more experience.

A word of caution: When hiring a third party to promote your Web site, you are essentially putting your reputation and image into their hands. If they promote you inappropriately, your online reputation can suffer irreparable damage. Be sure the firm you hire intimately understands *netiquette.* I list contact information and pricing (if available) which was valid as of the time of writing. Keep in mind that prices may change.

A1 WWW Web Page Promotion and Advertising Services
http://www.a1co.com/promo.html
a1support@a1co.com

Services:
Individually and manually submits your URL and associated information to the top 50 sites for $89.95 and to the top 100 sites for $159.95 (see Figure 14.3).

AAA Internet Promotions
2052B Elise Way
Santa Barbara, CA 93109

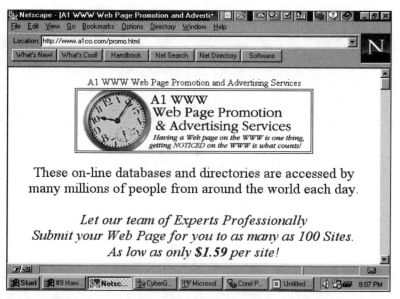

Figure 14.3 A1 WWW Web Page Promotion and Advertising Services.

(805) 962-9625
http://www.websitepromote.com
info@websitepromote.com

Services:

AAA Internet Promotions offers two plans. Plan (A) will list you in the top 50 Internet directories for $89.95. Plan (B) will list you in 50 more directories and search engines for $89.95. AAA offers a discount if you combine Plan (A) and Plan (B), which lists you in the top 100 directories for $159.95. The Web site lists the sites AAA submits to. To hire the company, all you have to do is fill out an online form with information about your site and your payment information (credit cards are accepted). You can also call, of course. There is an informative FAQ about the service and some tips and an article on promoting your Web site. (See Figure 14.4.)

CyberAd, Inc.
6261 NW 6th Ways
Suite 207
Ft. Lauderdale, FL 33309
(954) 772-1595
http://www.cyberad.com
cyberad@interpoint.net

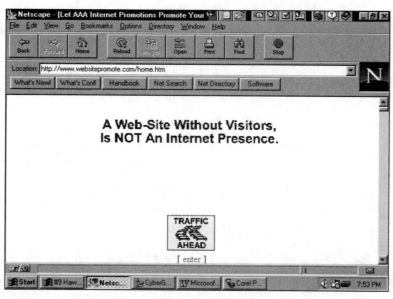

Figure 14.4 AAA Internet Promotion's home page.

Services:

Complete online marketing programs, including listing in directories and search engines, submission of press releases online, Usenet and mailing list postings, online media buying of banner space, cybermall listing and link negotiating, meta-index research and submission, and so on. CyberAd caters to clients who are serious about promoting their Web sites. Customized online promotion programs are created on a quote basis.

gina NetCoverage

Michael Shuler
(800) 414-gina
http://www.gina.com/ginaserv.html
mshuler@gina.com

Services:

With service beginning at $600, gina (global internet news agency) will list your new or existing Web site in dozens of popular directories, search engines, news groups, and frequently traveled links. It also can manage your hyperlink marketing campaign.

NetPOST™ Internet Press Services

Eric Ward
4034 Taliluna Avenue
Knoxville, TN 37919
(423) 637-2438
netpost@netpost.com

Services:

NetPOST claims to be the first company performing personalized, comprehensive Internet media awareness campaigns for company Web sites. NetPOST was one of the few companies selected as the 1995 Tenagra Awards for Internet Marketing Excellence (other sites that have won this award include Yahoo!, Federal Express Corp., Ragú, Software.Net, and Virtual Vineyards).

PROMOPHOBIA

346 Starling Road
Mill Valley, CA 94941
Tel: (415) 380-8244
Fax: (415) 383-8676
http://www.interbiznet.com/ibn/promophop.html
promophobia@interbiznet.com

Services:

All of PROMOPHOBIA's services are offered through retainer contracts. Rates vary from $500/month for 8 hours of Web site promotion to $1,500/month for 20 hours of Web site promotion.

WebConnect
(A division of WorlData, Inc.)
5200 Town Center Circle
Boca Raton, FL 33486
Tel: (800) 331-8102
Fax: (407) 368-8345
http://www.woldata.com/webcon.htm
webconnect@worldata.com

Services:

WebConnect is different from the other firms listed in this chapter. WebConnect is specifically a "link placement service." WebConnect has established a relationship with over 500 key Web sites that offer links or banners. For a one-time setup of $50 per link and a $750 minimum monthly link charge, you can select niche or general interest sites to provide a link to your site. Each site has a different rate. The $750 can apply to many different links. WebConnect can be used in addition to the other services listed in this chapter or to supplement your existing Web site promotion activities.

WebStep Traffic & Impact Building
(A division of Multimedia Marketing Group)
John Audette
333 South State Street, #183
Lake Oswego, OR 97034
(503) 635-7506
http://www.mmgco.com/webstep.html
ja@mmgco.com

Services:

Provides all types of Web site promotion services, including a press release service. WebStep offers five levels of service from a one-time fee of $35 for "do-it yourselfers" to $595 + $500/month for the "Blitz + Saturation Campaign." See Figure 14.5.

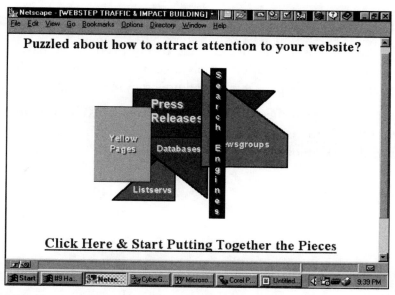

Figure 14.5 Are you putting the pieces together?

WebPromote

(A division of Superhighway Consulting, Inc.)
Chicago, IL
(312) 248-6116
http://www.webpromote.com
manager@webpromote.com

Services:

WebPromote offers three tiers to its service, Bronze ($250/month for 4 hours of promotional service), Silver ($675/month for 12 hours), and Gold ($1,200/month for 24 hours). WebPromote is a division of the same company that provides the Starting Point, a popular Internet navigational service.

You can find additional companies that will do the work for you in Yahoo! under the following category: Business and Economy:Companies:Internet Services:Web Presence Providers:Announcement Services

Conclusion

Well, you're almost to the final chapter. By now, you should have a substantial arsenal of Web site promotional tools at your disposal. You've built it (Chapter 2), promoted it (Chapters 4-15), and now they're coming! That's great!

Do you know what the number one challenge to Web marketers is, besides getting people to visit the site itself? Getting them to *return!* Turn the page and we'll work on overcoming this challenge.

How to Keep 'Em Coming Back

CHAPTER 15 TOPICS

KEYS TO KEEPING VISITORS: USABILITY AND SPEED

A RECIPE FOR SITE SUCCESS

FEATURES TO ATTRACT A LOYAL USERBASE

CASE STUDIES

Y ou've finally reached the last chapter! By now you know how to get visitors to your Web site and from the things you learned in Chapter 2, make sure your site is useful to them as well. Now that you have built it and they have come, will they come again?

There are two important and perhaps obvious things that bear repeating in order to ensure a loyal user base. These things are

- Usability—Your Web site should be very usable, including a site map or index, intuitive navigation, and a pleasing look.

- Speed—If your site is slow, so will be the growth of your user base.

The speed of your site is a function of four variables:

1. *Your users' computers and Internet connections.* You don't have much control over this factor, so assume they are using a 386 PC with a 9600 bps modem (pretty much the least common denominator these days) even though most people have faster setups. Design for slowness, and your site will be fast.

2. *Your Web site's computer and Internet connection.* Regardless of whether you are renting space on another server or have your own, the speed at which your pages are served out to visitors depends upon the speed of the computer and its memory (RAM) as well as the type of leased-line Internet connection. Keep an eye on these things to foresee when it's time to upgrade or expand your capacity.

3. *Size of the elements within your Web site.* If your Web pages use lots of large graphics, it will take longer for your users to view your pages. Sound and video files are huge and can take minutes to download even with a 28.8 Kbps connection. Offering large files is fine if you give the users the option of using a slimmed down version.

4. *The amount of traffic your site attracts.* With the techniques you've learned in this book, I hope that too much traffic is your biggest problem! The more visitors you have, the more time it takes for the packets of data to be served to them. Don't be tricked into ordering more capacity until you are sure that you can sustain the traffic. Many sites see a spike due to being listed somewhere strategic or mentioned prominently in the press and then fretfully watch the traffic subside.

Speed up your site by making the appropriate adjustments in variables 2 and 3 (above). The faster your users can receive, view, and interact with your Web server, the more likely they will return. That being said, let's move on to some less obvious site design strategies to keep them coming back.

The "CRIDO" Web Site Approach

I know, CREDO is the correct spelling of the word, but this is the best I could come up with! This approach is my recipe for site success:

C—Content: Interesting content draws people in. "The content's the thing," or "content is king" some people say. No one turns on his or her TV to watch commercials (except perhaps, advertising professionals!). If your site is just an online brochure, you simply will not have much success getting people to return. I'm not saying an online brochure won't get you sales, but if you want customers and prospects to return over and over, you'll need more.

R—Resource: Become a resource for specific information. One way that sites attempt to become a resource is by linking to other sites that they think their users are interested in. This is a good start, but if you *really* want to be a *true* resource, you will invest some time finding *every* possible site out there that is appropriate. That is, if your site has to do with selling gardening supplies, you want to become THE place to go on the Internet for gardening tips, tricks, information, etc. Some of this can be content, and some can be in the way of scouring the Net for gardening resources. Make your site the "Launch Pad for Gardeners on the Internet," but be sure to keep it up-to-date!

I—Interactive: People like to participate, not just observe. Unfortunately, most people will pay more (or spend more time) to be entertained than they ever will to be educated. If you can entertain them while they are within your site, they are more likely to return. Things like trivia, contests, and games keep visitors interested.

D—Dynamic: Avoid "dead look." Keep your Web site new and fresh. Stale sites don't taste very good! If people want static information, they will request your print material. Site maintenance is one of the most overlooked expenses that organizations make when placing a site on the Web. The most popular sites on the Net (Time's Pathfinder, HotWired, ESPNet's SportZone, SportsLine USA, etc.) update their content regularly.

O—Originality: Be original with your graphics and layout. Your site really needs to be different. It's getting really noisy out there! Thousands of new sites go up each week. Competition for mindshare is heating up, and being a stand-out site (even if you are a small one) can help you attract and retain users.

Attractive Web Site Features

Adding some of the following Web site features can help you attract loyal users.

Online chat sessions

You may have already heard about the chat sessions that some of the consumer online services, like Prodigy and America Online, have produced (featuring famous athletes and celebrities). The technology now exists to hold chat sessions from your very own Web site:

- **ChatPlus** is one such product available from Interactive Marketing Services, Inc.—the same company that's involved with the Virtual Yellow Pages (**http://www.vyp.com**). For more information about ChatPlus, email **lmahoney@imsworld.com**.

- **Global Chat** software from Prospero Systems Research, Inc. of San Francisco, California. More information is available at Prospero's Web site **http://www.prospero.com/globalchat/**

[handwritten: invite scientist to conduct an online chat]

If you are in the coin collecting business, perhaps there is a famous or well-respected authority on the subject that your users would instantly know. Invite that person to conduct an online seminar or question-and-answer session with your users for an hour or two. You can even promote your session in some of the print publications mentioned in Chapter 12. For example, Catherine McNamara writes a monthly column for *Online Access Magazine* called "Online Events: Catch what's going on online." Because of their production schedules, if you plan to promote your event in a magazine, be sure to let them know about it two to three months in advance. Additional events can be found at http://www.redflash.com. Some listings I saw in the January 1996 issue of *Online Access* included:

- **Art Talk on America Online.** "Join host Gabrielle Loperfido, the curator of Rogue's Gallery, to discuss the works of artists Ephraim Rubenstein, Dave Lindamood, David Dodge Lewis, and Duane Keiser."

- **Comics Talk on Microsoft Network.** "HERO Interactive will host a discussion with Hank Kanalz, line editor for Malibu Comics, in the HERO Chat Forum. Kanalz will discuss *The Phoenix Resurrection* comic book series and upcoming Malibu comic book projects."

If your event hosts a very prominent personality, you can even issue a full-blown press release about it. CMP Publications did this. The title of the release was "CMP's CommunicationsWeek Hosts Netscape's James H. Clark in a Live Web Chat Session about Business on the Internet." The release proceeded to give the day and time and content of the chat. I found it a bit humorous to read that "Doors to the live Web session will open 15 minutes before show time," and "...seating is limited to 1,000."

Bookmark/hotlist reminders

You may have seen Web sites that say "add us to your hotlist!" Encourage visitors to add you to their bookmark list. This way, all they will need to do is click on the name of your Web site from the bookmark list in their Web browser, rather than having to remember your URL. If you don't ask them to add your site, they almost certainly won't do it. It's simply the power of suggestion that works here.

Bulletin boards

Software is now available that you can purchase and easily integrate into your existing Web site to permit visitors to interact with *each other*. This is new to the Web but not new to the modem world. Bulletin boards were the cradle of cyberspace. I ran my own BBS (bulletin board system) in 1984 on an Apple 2+ that had 64 KB RAM, two 150 KB disk drives, and a 300-baud (later upgraded to 1200 bps!) modem. It was very satisfying to see people call in from all over the country just to interact with each other. If you offer a few message areas that concentrate on a specific theme, users will interact. But beware, you'll have to keep an eye on the messages and may even have to play referee from time to time. And with the vagueness in the laws of who's responsible for what content is placed on their computer, you'll want to be extra careful before you implement this idea. But if you do it successfully, your site will take on a life of its own.

Contests and competitions

There's no question about it, people like to win FREE $tuff! By offering a contest or competition, you'll not only keep people coming back but will attract new visitors as well. Figure 15.1 shows some listings from *The Thread Treader's WWW Contest Guide,* which is located at **http://www.4cyte.com/ThreadTreader/**. This is a place where you can post your contest at no charge (yet another way to promote your site). Internet users interested in contests check in often to see which sites they should visit.

Contests are so popular on the Net that an entire company was based on it. Riddler.com (**http://www.riddler.com**) boasts over 4 million "hits" a week and estimates that it receives 50,000 to 100,000 (or more) visitors each week. Users have to visit various Web sites to find "clues" that Riddler leaves on their pages. You can request that a clue be left on your site by sending email to **quibbler@riddler.com**. Be sure to place "Hide a Clue on My Page" in the subject line and provide your name, email address, URL, and what keywords people use to find you in the various search engines in the message. This is free and worth a shot. If they think your site is neat, it will be selected. Of course, if a clue is left, you need to add some HTML code (that Riddler will provide

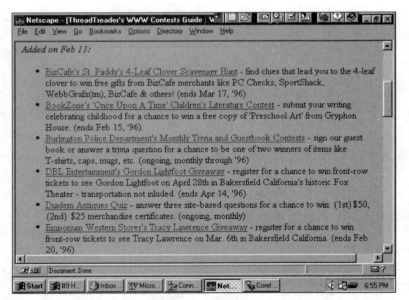

Figure 15.1   Web site contest examples from The Thread Treader's WWW Contest Guide.

to you) to the page that the clue is to be left on. Additional information is available from the Riddler site.

The Bank of America created a contest called Build Your Own Bank (see Figure 15.2) which offered $5,000 to visitors of its Web site.

What's New page

If your site is dynamic, you'll want to add a page that updates your users with the latest additions and features. It is extremely important to list the date when the page was last modified, even if you change it every day. This way users who drop in for a quick look will see if your site was updated since their last visit. (See Figure 15.3.)

Calendar of events

Post a calendar of events so visitors will know when to come back for new features. This is akin to the What's New page idea but gives the user advance notice of things to come. You don't have to restrict this to online events. If you exhibit at trade shows, you may want to provide a listing of those with your booth number at each. Invite your users to visit.

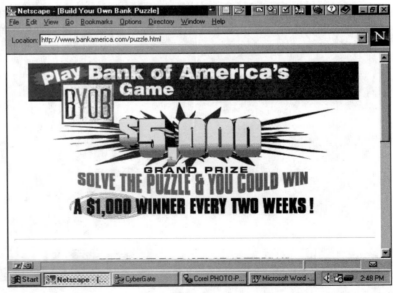

Figure 15.2   Bank of America's Build Your Own Bank (BYOB) $5,000 contest.

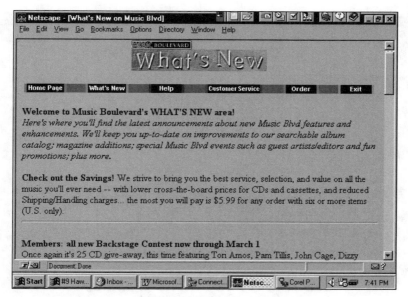

Figure 15.3 Part of Music Boulevard's What's New page.

Trade shows

Before your next trade show, you can pull from your database of Web site users and physically mail them the complimentary admission tickets exhibitors get. This way, they can visit your booth and interact on a physical rather than virtual level. This helps you build a more tangible relationship with your users.

Cartoons

LinkStar hooked up with Randy Glasbergen to provide the "LinkStar 'toon of the Day" feature (see Figure 15.4). LinkStar's president, Stewart Padveen, found Randy's work elsewhere on the Net and thought it would be neat to provide the entertaining cartoons on his site as well. This is a good example of keeping a site dynamic and evidence that you don't necessarily have to create all the content and features yourself.

Jokes

With all the stress in our lives, a little humor can make a big difference. Rodney Dangerfield's Web site (http://www.rodney.com), shown in Figure 15.5, has a "Joke of the Day" page. He says it's the most popular feature of his site and keeps users coming back regularly. Rodney was the first entertainer to

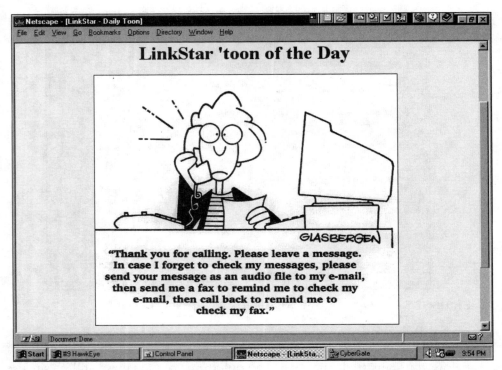

Figure 15.4   LinkStar's 'toon of the Day, courtesy of cartoonist Randy Glasbergen.

have his own personal site, owned by an individual rather than a movie studio or public relations firm. The site was launched in early 1995 and has been constantly evolving ever since. The Weekender Online (http://www.microserve.net/weekender/) voted Rodney's site number one of the Top 10 Humor Sites on the Web. In addition to jokes, he's got letters, movie clips, sound clips, a feedback mechanism, what's new page, contest, and more. His site is a great example of creating interesting and entertaining content along with some sales and promotion. (He offers various items including a "Rodney Mousepad.")

Trivia

People seem to like trivia. Look at how many copies of the board game Trivial Pursuit were sold. Tens of thousands of people sat around for hours trying to answer quirky questions. There are lots of sources for trivia that you could draw from and provide to your visitors. Again, be sure to keep it up-to-date. The best way to do this is to hire a programmer to write a simple perl CGI script (a computer program written in the perl language) to display a new

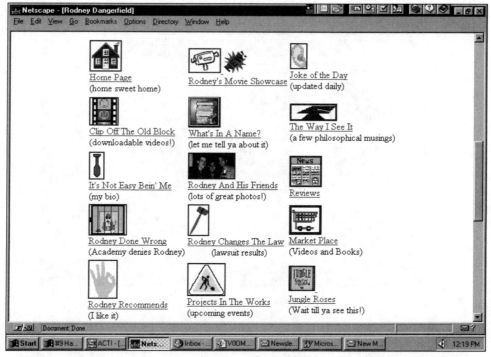

Figure 15.5   Rodney Dangerfield's www.rodney.com Web site. Notice the many features available.

question each day on your trivia page. The questions are kept in a data file. Just fill the file up with lots of questions, and let the program do the rest. BBN Planet, a provider of dedicated Internet server hosting facilities, offers "BBN's online trivia challenge" (shown in Figure 15.6).

Employment opportunities

People looking for a job or interested in moving to a different company will revisit your site from time to time to check out your list of available positions. Many companies leverage their Web site investment by listing job openings. Fill a position, *and* get people to come back to your site. Such a deal!

Reminder services

These are great. Reminder services were first conceived by florists to remind forgetful Internet users about important dates. Not only can you remind people of something that they want to be reminded of, your email message in and of itself reminds people of your site as well.

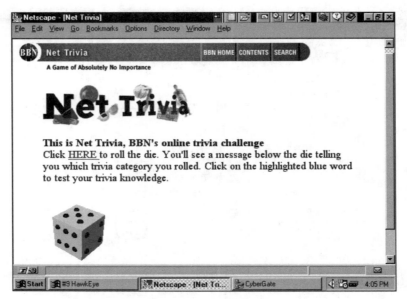

Figure 15.6   BBN Planet offers its users a dose of trivia.

User contact information

One of the biggest assets of any organization is its database of customers and prospects. The mailing list industry is huge. Although I don't recommend gathering contact information for the sake of selling it, I do feel that it's important for you to invite users to provide their names, addresses, phone and fax numbers, email addresses, and perhaps even their Web addresses. Users typically won't just give you their contact information without a reason. Many companies offer a free product catalog or a free report or newsletter to users who fill out their online form. You may want to do the same. If you plan to keep private the information that people provide to you, be sure to say so on your Web page. Most people value their privacy, and if there is any doubt that you will be free with their information, they won't give it to you.

Surveys

Surveys in and of themselves won't get hardly anyone to return because people don't like to fill in blanks for no apparent reason. That is, unless you do the following with your survey:

- Use the results to give users a chance to offer their opinions of what they want to see you offer on your Web site (in general).

- Use the results to give users a chance to offer their opinions of what to offer in the way of products or services (if you are a business).

- Actually *make use of* the results to have the effect of improving your site and increasing the likelihood of all of your users returning.

I placed a survey on the Web site for my first book. My goal wasn't to improve the site but rather to find out what types of people were using my site. In order to entice them to fill out the survey, I offered to give away a copy of the book each month. I received hundreds of responses and learned things like the average age of my visitors, where they came from, what type of Web browser they used, and much more. This information can be useful to you in determining what types of people are most likely to use your site, and then you can make the appropriate adjustments to cater to that type of audience.

Case Studies

Learning through example is sometimes the best way to learn. In this section, I want to share with you several interesting case studies of how some organizations promoted their Web sites, launched them, and have kept them going.

Flower Stop
http://www.flowerstop.com/fstop/
Chuck Haley is one of online marketing's true pioneers. He first set up an electronic shop on CompuServe years ago and also has stores on Delphi and GEnie. In October 1994, the Flower Stop Web site went online. Since then, he estimates that over 500 other Web sites link to his (determined by using the Alta Vista search engine with his URL as the search criteria). In addition to being listed in directories and search engines, the site is also linked in nearly 100 cybermalls, of which he's paying for 30 to 40 of them. The others have simply put him in their malls because they like his Web site.

The Flower Stop has been mentioned quite a bit offline as well. The Flower Stop's home page is prominently displayed on *The Internet Marketing BlackBook*'s cover, listed in Jaclyn Easton's *Shopping on the Internet and Beyond*, listed in *New Rider's Top 1,000 Web Sites* and mentioned in numerous magazines like *NetGuide, Computer World, PC Magazine* and the *Internet Business Journal*. The Flower Stop site has even been featured on a couple of TV shows.

The Flower Stop has been selected by several "cool sites pages" such as the Point survey of the top 5 percent of all Web sites and as a Magellen cool site among others. It is also listed on the Farm Direct Marketplace, a meta-index/ cybermall type of site, and it participated with the Riddler.Com games site.

Overall, the Flower Stop has found that the Internet is becoming a greater percentage of its business. As the 1996 Valentine's day approached, Flower Stop had to shut down its site on CompuServe and the Web placing a "sold out" sign on them. It was overwhelmed with orders and had to stop taking them to ensure that all flower orders were delivered on time. It is currently working on a "smart" order form that will let users know that if they order after a certain date and time, their order may be delivered late. Another challenge is in accurately tracking what promotion efforts brought in which visitors. It is working on better measurement. Once done, experimentation with some banner advertising is planned.

The combination of techniques mentioned in previous chapters has been employed by the Flower Stop to produce results. Chuck tells me that sales just keep on increasing as time goes on. With every new mention, every new link, a few more people visit, and some of those become customers. Over time, it all adds up—kind of like a snowball rolling down a hill. The Flower Stop is an excellent example of balanced, ongoing Web site promotion and marketing.

Music Boulevard
http://www.musicblvd.com

This is more of an example of how to get users to return. Music Boulevard keeps people visiting regularly by providing news, contests, talks, and a 30-second sampling of songs. It's got the content (over 145,000 album titles available for sale, thousands of cover art and audio samples, current Billboard® charts, Daily Music Wire(sm) News, Reviews, and Interviews and access to various publications like *Spin, Dirty Linen, Fanfare, Blues Revue, @Country*, and others, and thousands of biographies of artists, performers, and composers). Music Boulevard offers frequent contests and CD giveaways. If users want to order something, they must establish an account. This yields contact information that Music Boulevard can use for reminders and promotions. As you saw in Figure 15.3, a What's New page keeps users abreast of the latest happenings on the site. Overall, this site is practically a how-to on creating "boomerang Web site users."

Valvoline

http://www.valvoline.com

Valvoline decided to conduct a two-phased launch of its site. The first phase was a site that was oriented around its strength: car racing. The second phase was a site that has a corporate focus. The site's first-phase launch was scheduled to coincide with the Indy 500. The site was announced at the Indianapolis Motor Speedway on May 11, 1995. During the race, Valvoline's URL was shown on its TV commercials, which aired on ESPN and ABC. What I think is one of the neatest Web site promotion strategies done by any major company is that the Web site address was prominently displayed in front of the in-car cameras for the various drivers. In addition, race updates were constantly made to the Web site during the race. Needless to say, the site received thousands of visitors during the race. In just one day, Valvoline made millions of people aware of its Web presence—all without much additional cost. It just made use of its existing advertising, PR, and marketing infrastructure.

Concluding Remarks

When I first proposed the idea of this book to my publisher, Keith Weiskamp and the Coriolis Group, there was some skepticism as to whether an entire book was required to talk about promoting a Web site. After all, there were several Internet business and Internet marketing books out there that touched on the subject. All it took was a detailed outline and Coriolis' knowledge of their own Web site and its place on the Net to convince them that there's a lot more than registering your site with a few search engines. And I think that after reading this book, you realize this as well.

So many organizations spend resources on creating a site only to let it stagnate and fade into obscurity. Maintaining a successful Web presence takes a lot of work. But it can be fun as well—surfing the net for neat places to associate your site with; placing banners for all to see; working deals; using your creativity to get users to visit and to return; creating a bond with your users, prospects and customers; and learning all the time. I recommend that you budget several times the amount you paid to create the site to promote and maintain it.

Before you set this book down, be sure to turn the page to the appendix and check out the Internet marketing and Web site promotion resources list.

There are many useful publications that can aid you in your efforts and keep you up-to-date with the latest trends.

Your Web site will bring you visitors and customers that you probably won't expect. If you properly promote it, you'll attract all kinds of people from all kinds of locations. This may seem like an odd statement, but the goal of many Web sites should be to get users *off* the Web! Invisibly guide them to contact you, to buy your products, to tell others, and to learn more about you. Satisfy them quickly, and watch them come back for more.

May your site runneth over with visitors!

Internet Marketing and Web Promotion Resources

This short list of selected resources may be useful for your Internet marketing and Web site promotion efforts. I highly recommend these publications and encourage you to check them out.

Books

How to Grow Your Business on the Internet, Vince Emery, Coriolis Group Books, (800) 410-0192, ISBN 1-883577-29-2, 1995.

The Internet Business Guide, 2nd Edition, Dave Taylor and Rosalind Resnick, SAMS, (800) 428-5331, ISBN 1-57521-004-5, 1995.

The Internet Marketing BlackBook, Vince Gelormine, published by Legion Publishing Corp., (305) 978-3444, ISBN 0-9643834-0-3, 1995.

Newsletters and Online Publications

WebTrack's InterAd Monthly (Newsletter)

http://www.webtrack.com
interad@webtrack.com
(212) 627-4584

This is one of the best publications for people interested in Internet advertising opportunities and Web site promotion. It's not cheap, but the information is current and extremely useful. An electronic subscription is $199 per year for eleven online issues and a print subscription is $299 per year for eleven issues, which includes online access.

Web Digest For Marketers (Online Publication)

http://wdfm2.com/wdfm/index.html

This online publication provides various Web marketing resources and gives pointers to more information.

Who's Marketing Online (Online Publication)

http://www.wmo.com

Published by Sayers Publishing, Inc., this free resource online publication has very informative and original articles.

Wilson's Small Business and Effective Web Marketing List

http://www.wilsonweb.com/rfwilson/webmarket/

This site provides links to more than 225 online articles about effective Web marketing. It also gives helpful links to online resources for business. The focus is on small business, though some articles and links reflect applicable lessons from larger firms.

Index

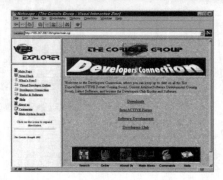
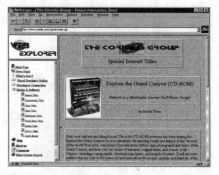
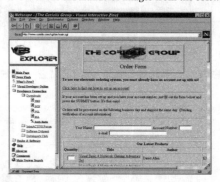